Working With Functional Grammar

Working With Functional Grammar

J. R. Martin

Associate Professor of Linguistics, University of Sydney

Christian M. I. M. Matthiessen

Associate Professor of Linguistics, Macquarie University

Clare Painter

Lecturer in Social Semiotics, University of New South Wales

A member of the Hodder Headline Group
LONDON • NEW YORK • SYDNEY • AUCKLAND

First published in Great Britain in 1997 by
Arnold, a member of the Hodder Headline Group,
338 Euston Road, London NW1 3BH
175 Fifth Avenue, New York, NY 10010

Distributed exclusively in the USA by
St Martin's Press, Inc.
175 Fifth Avenue, New York, NY 10010

British Library Cataloguing in Publication Data
A catalogue record for this book is available from the British Library

Library of Congress Cataloging-in-Publication Data
A catalog record for this book is available from the Library of Congress

ISBN 0 340 65250 0 (Pb)

Typeset by Scribe Design, Gillingham, Kent
Printed and bound in Great Britain by J W Arrowsmith Ltd, Bristol

CONTENTS

Preface   ix

1 Introduction   1

2 Theme – clause as message   21
   1 Orientation   21
   2 Survey of options   22
   3 Troubleshooting   28
      Picking out the units of analysis   28
      Identifying the Theme   28
      Identifying the metafunction   29
      Subject *it* as unmarked topical Theme   31
      There's a ... 'existential clauses'   34
      Recognizing longer Theme units   34
      'Hypotactic' clause as Theme   36
   4 Analysis practice   37
      Phase I: exercises   37
      Phase I: texts   38
      Phase II: exercises   39
      Phase II: texts   43
      Phase III: exercises   47
      Phase III: texts   49
   5 Review and contextualization   53

3 Mood – clause as exchange   57
   1 Orientation   57

	2	Survey of options	61
	3	Troubleshooting	70
		The unit of analysis	70
		Identifying structural elements	71
		Ambiguous mood type	75
		Ambiguous POLARITY	76
		'Will': TENSE or MODALITY	76
	4	Analysis practice	77
		Phase I: exercises	77
		Phase I: texts	81
		Phase II: exercises	83
		Phase II: texts	88
		Phase III: exercises	90
		Phase III: texts	92
	5	Review and contextualization	95
4		Transitivity – clause as representation	100
	1	Orientation	100
	2	Survey of options	102
	3	Troubleshooting	114
		A topology of processes	114
		General probes helpful in analysing for TRANSIVITY	115
		One process or two?	116
		Material clauses	117
		Mental clauses	120
		Relational clauses	122
		Verbal clauses	125
		Behavioural clauses	127
		Discriminating circumstance type	127
		Distinguishing between circumstances and other elements	127
	4	Analysis practice	131
		Phase I: exercises	131
		Phase I: texts	135
		Phase II: exercises	139
		Phase II: texts	146
		Phase III: exercises	149
		Phase III: texts	155
	5	Review and contextualization	157
5		The clause complex – above the clause	165
	1	Orientation	165
	2	Survey of options	167

3 Troubleshooting   173
   Procedure for analysis   173
   Picking out the unit of analysis   174
   Complexing versus embedding (downranked clauses)   179
   Parataxis or hypotaxis   184
   Identifying the logico-semantic relation   184
   How many 'layers' to the clause complex?   187
   Implicit clause complex relations   188
   Projection   188
   'Surfacing' from an embedding   189
4 Analysis practice   190
   Phase I: exercises   190
   Phase I: texts   194
   Phase II: exercises   197
   Phase II: texts   201
   Phase III: exercises   202
   Phase III: texts   204
5 Review and contextualization   206

Key to Chapter 2: Theme   210
   Phase I: exercises   210
   Phase I: texts   211
   Phase II: exercises   213
   Phase II: texts   215
   Phase III: exercises   218
   Phase III: texts   219

Key to Chapter 3: Mood   226
   Phase I: exercises   226
   Phase I: texts   229
   Phase II: exercises   231
   Phase II: texts   235
   Phase III: exercises   245
   Phase III: texts   247

Key to Chapter 4: Transitivity   253
   Phase I: exercises   253
   Phase I: texts   256
   Phase II: exercises   259
   Phase II: texts   265
   Phase III: exercises   272
   Phase III: texts   277

Key to Chapter 5: The clause complex   284
        Phase I: exercises   284
        Phase I: texts   288
        Phase II: exercises   290
        Phase II: texts   293
        Phase III: exercises   297
        Phase III: texts   299

Index   303

PREFACE

This workbook is the culmination of a project initiated in the early 1980s by Jim Martin and Clare Painter, who were joined in the endeavour by Christian Matthiessen in 1988. We three were all concerned to provide support materials for students and colleagues who were learning the analyses proposed in Halliday's *Introduction to Functional Grammar*. In particular we shared the experience of guiding students through familiar kinds of difficulties year after year – and wanted to prepare materials which would help learners through and around these experiences. We also wanted to provide some support for people learning the grammar on their own, or without the dialogue provided by a critical mass of systemic linguists such as we enjoy in the Sydney metropolitan region.

We are of course much indebted to the many colleagues who have discussed aspects of these materials with us (especially Chris Nesbitt); to the many tutors who have dealt first-hand with problems (Arlene Harvey, Petie Sefton and Peter White in particular); and to the now thousands of students who have committed at least a hundred hours of their lives each to learning functional grammar in our undergraduate linguistics and MA applied linguistics programs at the University of Sydney, Macquarie University, the University of Technology, Sydney and the University of New South Wales.

Halliday's presentation of the grammar in IFG was designed for use in text analysis, and this is the main context in which we have taught the material. Our experience of this context is that nothing is more challenging to one's understanding of grammar, and the theory from which it derives, than helping students apply it to texts of their choosing. So much happens that intuitions don't intuit, that argumentation doesn't argue about, that explicitness in computer generation elides! It's certainly driven us crazy over the years and has been just wonderful too. We hope this workbook will help keep you and your students somewhat sane as you explore the wonders of the language people really use.

Finally, to disengage the 'we' of this preface, Christian and Jim would like to thank Clare, who alongside her fair share of writing and editing had to take a set of more rough than ready notes, and a pair of more distracted than reliable colleagues, and re/organize them so that this project could be completed. Scaffolding this joint construction above and beyond the call of duty – as ever. Bravo Clare!

1

Introduction

What is functional grammar?

Functional grammar is a way of looking at grammar in terms of how grammar is used. In the field of linguistics, the main alternative to functional grammar is formal grammar, which is concerned with the ways in which our genes constrain the shape of our grammars, and thus constrain what we can and cannot say. Functional grammar is not genetically oriented to our neurophysiology in this way. Rather, it focuses on the development of grammatical systems as a means for people to interact with each other – functional grammar sees grammar as shaped by, and as playing a significant role in shaping, the way we get on with our lives. Its orientation is social, in other words, rather than biological.

Functional grammars are used for a variety of tasks. First and foremost they are used for describing languages in functional terms. Many of the principles of functional grammar you are studying in Halliday's (1994) *Introduction to Functional Grammar* (henceforward IFG) were initially worked out for Chinese, which was the first language Halliday studied in detail. Subsequently he developed these principles in his work on English grammar. The IFG is a brief synopsis of Halliday's ground-breaking research in this field. Halliday's work has inspired work on a wide range of languages, including French, German, Tagalog, Pitjantjatjara, Akan, Japanese, Chinese and Indonesian to name some of the better known; a wide range of references to work of this kind is provided in the Further Reading section near the end of the IFG. Recently, functional interpretations of languages have inspired work on other semiotic systems as well – in particular, on visual images (Kress and van Leeuwen, 1996; O'Toole, 1994).

Functional grammarians seldom stop at simply describing the grammar of a particular language. They typically go on and do something with what they have found out. The functional grammar you are studying in IFG has been used to develop literacy programmes for primary and secondary school students (e.g. Cope and Kalantzis, 1993), as the basis for automatic text analysis and generation in computational contexts (e.g. Matthiessen and Bateman, 1991), and as the basis for critical discourse analysis (e.g. Fairclough, 1992) including analysis of culturally significant texts (e.g. Thibault, 1991). Recently it has been used for purposes of diagnosis and therapy in speech pathology, for text analysis in forensic settings and for the development of workplace training programmes. The range of applications is growing all the time. One way to get in touch with people using functional grammar in your area of interest would be to make use of e-mail, and write to the bulletin board for systemic functional linguists: sysfling@u.washington.edu. For those not on e-mail, there are plenty of relevant references in the Further Reading section of IFG to follow up.

Why this functional grammar?

There are many possible purposes for writing functional grammars, and different contexts will have somewhat different requirements. For example, a grammar for teachers and school students would not assume the same shared technical under-standings as a grammar for the professional linguist, a grammar for computational contexts would need to be particularly explicit about the relation between system and structure to facilitate automatic text generation and parsing, while a grammar for critical discourse analysis would need to include considerable social contextual information to facilitate informed text deconstruction. Halliday's main purpose in writing the IFG grammar, however, was not to orient the grammar to any single defined area of application, but to provide a general grammar for purposes of text analysis and interpretation. It is therefore a grammar which provides a basic lingua franca for text analysts working in a wide range of differing contexts; and it is very effectively organized as a tool of this kind.

You will find the IFG grammar much richer semantically than either formal or traditional school grammar. This makes the analyses you undertake more insight-ful when it comes to interpreting a text. It will tell you more about a student's writing abilities, and more about what is semantically at stake in text generation, and more about discourse and subjectivity than any other grammar available today. The grammar has also been designed to be relatively easy to apply to texts. We have found that between 26 and 39 hours of lectures[1], plus tutorial support, is enough to give most students in undergraduate or MA programmes a working knowledge of the grammar. This workbook is designed to support introductory programmes of this kind, and to provide some scope for users to work more deeply into the grammar and its application to texts.

Compared with traditional school grammar and formal grammar, you will find that the IFG grammar makes use of class labels like *noun*, *verb* or *adjective*, with which you will have some familiarity. Beyond this, the IFG grammar makes exten-sive use of function labels like Actor, Process, Goal, Theme, Rheme, Deictic, Numerative, Classifier, Thing and so on, many of which will be new to you. The function labels are there to make the grammatical analysis semantically revealing – to show how the clauses, groups and phrases of a text map its meanings. Without the function labels, the grammar would be too shallow to be of much use in text interpretation.

For readers with a background in traditional school grammar we should also say that a functional grammar is not a prescriptive grammar which tells you what you

---

[1]We have found it possible to compress these lectures into a single week of full-time intensive study, or to spread them out over one or two semesters' work.

can and cannot say and provides rules for correcting what are often referred to as grammatical errors. A functional grammar, in other words, is not a grammar of etiquette. Rather, a functional grammar provides you with tools for understanding why a text is the way it is – for understanding precisely in grammatical terms the difference between *I don't have none* and *I don't have any* and thinking about who would say which of these clauses in what kind of situation to whom; or the difference between *to whom* and *who ... to*; or the difference between *it was I* and *it was me*. It presents the difference between these variations as a choice about what is functional in a particular context (not as a question of mistakes, and right or wrong) and shows you why the grammar of English sometimes pulls you in different directions. In this sense, a functional grammar is a grammar that respects speakers' rights to make up their own minds about how they choose to talk; at the same time it makes speakers explicitly aware of the choices they have available, so they can make an informed decision about the options they choose.

Using the workbook

This workbook focuses on those parts of IFG that deal with the clause and it has been organized to reflect the organization of Halliday's IFG. Chapters in *Working with Functional Grammar* support IFG chapters as follows:

Workbook Chapter	IFG Chapter
1 Introduction	Introduction
	1 Constituency
	2 Towards a functional grammar
2 Theme	3 Clause as message
3 Mood	4 Clause as exchange
4 Transitivity	5 Clause as representation
5 The clause complex	7 Above the clause: the clause complex

However, we have written the workbook in such a way that the chapters need not necessarily be used in this order.

Each chapter following the Introduction contains the following sections: Orientation, Survey of options, Troubleshooting, Analysis practice (containing Exercises and Texts for analysis), Review and contextualization and Further Reading. Below, we outline very briefly the nature of each of these sections.

Orientation   We begin each chapter by referencing the relevant sections of the most recent edition of IFG and providing a brief characterization of the aspect of grammar to be covered.

Survey of options   This section provides an outline summary of the principal grammatical options described in detail in IFG. No knowledge of the metalanguage built up in other chapters is assumed in this opening description.

Troubleshooting   In this part we aim to sort out misunderstandings, queries and issues that may arise when you apply the particular analysis being learned. We intend it to be used as a reference that you can access when you have difficulty with any of the exercises or analysis tasks, rather than as preliminary material to read straight through before you start.

Exercises   Exercises provide practice in working with individual clauses before complete texts are attempted, and at various points you are referred to the relevant part of the Troubleshooting section for help. The exercises, like the texts for analysis, are organized into three phases in increasing order of difficulty. Phase I is for getting started; Phase II is designed to get you to the point where you can have a go at analysing a text on your own; Phase III takes you further into some more problematic issues, points that arise less frequently, or tend to occur in more difficult texts.

Texts for analysis   Like the exercises, these are presented in three phases. The Phase I texts can be attempted after Phase I exercises and are quite simple, having been edited where necessary to remove problems. By Phase III the texts are more difficult and have not been adapted in any way.

Review and contextualization   This section provides a summary of the relevant aspect of the grammar, drawing on the metalanguage learned in previous chapters and showing where that part of the grammar fits into the overall picture. This section puts the various aspects of the grammar into relation with one another and is partly designed for those who have some knowledge or experience of the IFG grammar. It can therefore be used as the principal summary for those revising their understanding of IFG or as an extension for those moving through the workbook, taking the chapters in order.

Further reading   At the end of each chapter, we provide a short bibliography of further reading related to the relevant aspect of the grammar.

Key   At the back of the book there is a key to the exercises and text analysis tasks. Where you disagree with an analysis given, it is a good idea to check the Troubleshooting section to see if this resolves your difficulty.

In designing the workbook we have aimed for enough flexibility to serve the needs of a range of readers, whether working alone or as part of a formal programme of study. For example, if you are not a linguist and you are currently undertaking only a brief introductory study in functional grammar, you may go through the workbook doing only Phase I exercises and texts. On the other hand, if you have some experience with grammatical analysis or are involved in a course of study that aims at independent text analysis, you may focus your attention on Phase II exercises and texts. The book also aims to cater for those who are extending or revising their understandings of IFG and who may prefer to begin with the review and contextualization section of each chapter and concentrate on analysing Phase II and Phase III texts. At whatever level you are working, you will find some parts of the Troubleshooting section helpful.

Getting started with text analysis

The first problem you will face when using functional grammar for text analysis is the problem of what to analyse. How do you divide the text into pieces that the IFG analyses can be applied to? Thankfully, most texts offer some help.

If you are dealing with a written text (like this one you are reading), then it will probably have been divided into sentences for you. These units (sentences), beginning with a capital letter and ending with a full stop, are a good starting point. There is a useful description of punctuation in relation to functional grammar in Halliday (1985: 34–39). If you are dealing with a spoken text, then it may involve a number of speakers, who take turns. These units (turns), beginning where one speaker starts talking and ending where they stop, are another good starting point. Of course, neither of these strategies will work for spoken monologue – in which case you could try punctuating the text on your own, dividing it into sentences as you go.

The most important unit for a functional grammar analysis is the clause rather than the sentence, however, and to identify clauses you have to start using what you know about grammar to divide up the text. Basically, there are three ways in.

One way is what Halliday would call **ideational**. This involves looking for the processes in a text – processes name events taking place ('go', 'cook', 'think', 'sleep' and so on) or relationships among things ('is', 'seems', 'has' and so on). Then you divide the text up into processes and whatever 'goes with' them (who did what to whom, where, when, how, why etc.). If you have some idea of what a verb is, you can think of looking for processes as looking for verbs. Some of you may remember from traditional school grammar the notion that verbs are 'action' words. This can be helpful, as long as you keep in mind that lots of verbs (e.g. *be* and *have*) refer to relationships, not actions.

For example, here is part of a report on whales[2], with processes highlighted in bold face:

> There **are** fewer species of the larger baleen whales, that **filter** krill and small fish through their baleen plates. The largest **is** the Blue whale which **is seen** frequently in the Gulf of St Lawrence. It **reaches** a length of 100 feet and a weight of 200 tons. The young **are** 25 feet long at birth and **gain** about 200 lbs a day on their milk diet.

We can divide the text into clauses by grouping each process with its dramatis personae (who's who) and scenery (where, when, how, why etc.):

> There **are** fewer species of the larger baleen whales,
> that **filter** krill and small fish through their baleen plates.
> The largest **is** the Blue whale
> which **is seen** frequently in the Gulf of St Lawrence.
> It **reaches** a length of 100 feet and a weight of 200 tons.
> The young **are** 25 feet long at birth
> and **gain** about 200 lbs a day on their milk diet.

You can see that the punctuation helps – four of the seven clauses end with a full stop and one with a comma, and four of the clauses begin with a capital letter.

Another way in is what Halliday would call **interpersonal**. This involves treating the text as a dialogue (even if it has a silent partner, as with monologue). Basically this means dividing the text into things you can argue with. Here is the whales report again, but with arguing added:

> There are fewer species of the larger baleen whales, [- **Are there?**] that filter krill and small fish through their baleen plates. [- **They do not.**] The largest is the Blue whale [- **Is it?**] which is seen frequently in the Gulf of St Lawrence. [- **It isn't.**] It reaches a length of 100 feet and a weight of 200 tons. [- **Does it?**] The young are 25 feet long at birth [- **They aren't always.**] and gain about 200 lbs a day on their milk diet. [- **Do they?**]

[2](i) As with many of the texts in this volume, we have simplified the text slightly to avoid unnecessary complications at this stage. (ii) Descriptors like 'report' used for texts in this volume are those developed in Iedema 1995, Iedema, Feez and White 1994, Rothery 1994, Rose, McInnes and Korner, 1992.

This approach also works to divide the text into clauses, but this time round with the clause defined as something you can interact with:

There are fewer species of the larger baleen whales,	**[- Are there?]**
that filter krill and small fish through their baleen plates.	**[- They do not.]**
The largest is the Blue whale	**[- Is it?]**
which is seen frequently in the Gulf of St Lawrence.	**[- It isn't.]**
It reaches a length of 100 feet and a weight of 200 tons.	**[- Does it?]**
The young are 25 feet long at birth	**[- They aren't always.]**
and gain about 200 lbs a day on their milk diet.	**[- Do they?]**

A third way in is what Halliday would call **textual**. We'll use another small text to illustrate this – part of a whaling recount:

> For one thousand years, whales have been of commercial interest for meat, oil, meal and whalebone. About 1000 AD, whaling started with the Basques using sailing vessels and row boats. Over the next few centuries, whaling shifted to Humpbacks, Grays, Sperms and Bowheads. By 1500, they were whaling off Greenland; by the 1700s, off Atlantic America; and by the 1800s, in the south Pacific, Antarctic and Bering Sea. Early in this century, whaling shifted to the larger and faster baleen whales.

This approach takes advantage of the fact that texts may tend to return to closely related starting points at the beginning of successive clauses. In the whaling recount, for example, the text keeps coming back to setting in time, in order to move the history of whaling along:

> **For one thousand years**, whales have been of commercial interest for meat, oil, meal and whalebone. **About 1000 AD**, whaling started with the Basques using sailing vessels and row boats. **Over the next few centuries**, whaling shifted to Humpbacks, Grays, Sperms and Bowheads. **By 1500**, they were whaling off Greenland; **by the 1700s**, off Atlantic America; and **by the 1800s**, in the south Pacific, Antarctic and Bering Sea. **Early in this century**, whaling shifted to the larger and faster baleen whales.

These temporal expressions organize the text into units as follows:

> **For one thousand years**, whales have been of commercial interest for meat, oil...
> **About 1000 AD**, whaling started with the Basques using sailing vessels and row boats.
> **Over the next few centuries**, whaling shifted to Humpbacks, Grays, Sperms and...
> **By 1500**, they were whaling off Greenland;
> **by the 1700s**, off Atlantic America;
> and **by the 1800s**, in the south Pacific, Antarctic and Bering Sea.
> **Early in this century**, whaling shifted to the larger and faster Baleen whales.

This way into dividing up a text into clauses is less reliable than the other two, since few texts have such a consistent pattern of starting points. But it can be helpful when a text leaves out processes, as in two of the clauses above – since a text which leaves some processes implicit makes the first two ways in harder to apply.

Ideally, in the best of possible worlds, the results of all three approaches coincide. So, the units you get by looking for processes are the same as the ones you get by arguing and looking for similar beginnings. Procedural (instructional) texts are about as near to this ideal as you can find. Try out the three approaches outlined above on the following instructions from a secondary school science classroom:

> Collect two petri dishes. Place a thin layer of soil in one dish and some cotton wool in the other dish. Label the dish with soil 'soil' and the other dish 'no soil'. Next, place about 20 seeds in each petri dish. Spray each dish with water. Finally, put the dishes in a warm sunny spot in the classroom.

Constituency: functional and class units

Once you have divided your text into clauses, you can begin to analyse each clause as outlined in Chapters 3, 4 and 5 of the IFG. This will involve identifying the functional parts of the clause from each of the three perspectives just outlined: ideational, interpersonal and textual. For example, if we take an ideational approach (clause as representation) to the clause *Quite recently the Norwegians were whaling off Greenland*, we can identify four functional parts, as in Fig. 1.1.

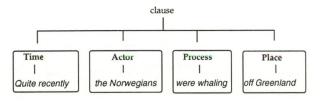

Fig. 1.1 Breaking a clause into functional parts

In Fig. 1.1 the labels in bold print provide functional names for the parts of the clause when viewed as an ideational structure. As you can see, this kind of labelling is semantically oriented, which will prove helpful when you are using grammar to interpret a text.

As Fig. 1.1 illustrates, the functional parts of any clause take the form of phrases or groups of words of various kinds. For example, the Process part takes the form of, or is **realized** by, a verb or a group of verbs (technically, a verbal group), as shown in Fig. 1.2.

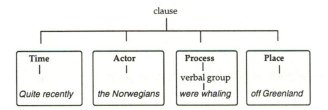

Fig. 1.2 Clause structure picking out a verbal group functioning as Process

A functional role like Actor, on the other hand, telling you who or what is involved in the Process, takes the form of a noun or pronoun or else a group of words (such as articles, adjectives, numerals) which are associated with a noun. As shown in Fig. 1.3, we will call this a nominal group.

Functional roles such as indications of Time and Place are expressed as an adverbial group or a prepositional phrase, as shown in Fig. 1.4. Adverbial groups consist of one or more adverbs while a prepositional phrase consists of a proposition followed by a nominal group[3].

---

[3]In the example, *Greenland* is a nominal group, even though it consists of just one noun; in general groups consist of one or more items; they are still called groups when they consist of a single word.

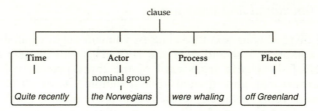

Fig. 1.3 Clause structure picking out a nominal group functioning as Actor

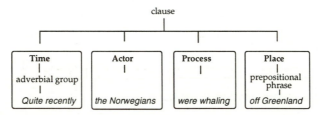

Fig. 1.4 Clause structure – picking out adverbial group and prepositional phrase

Just as a clause can be broken into its functional parts, so groups and phrases can be analysed into their functional parts. For example, the short nominal group *this red flower* has three functional parts as shown in Fig. 1.5. Here the Deictic part functions to pick out and identify, the Epithet describes and the Thing tells you what it is being picked out and described.

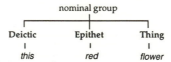

Fig. 1.5 Breaking a nominal group into functional parts

The functional parts of a group or phrase are realized by different classes of word. This is shown in Fig. 1.6 for the nominal group we have been looking at.

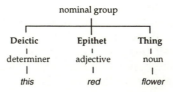

Fig. 1.6 Nominal group structure

Our discussion so far has shown that a clause can be analysed into its constituent parts, which are groups and phrases; and these groups and phrases can be analysed into their constituent parts, which are words. (It would also be possible to analyse words into their constitituent parts – morphemes, but IFG does not take this step.) The scale of units from clause to word (or morpheme) is known as the **rank** scale.

As you can see from the examples, when we analyse a structure at clause rank or at group/phrase rank into its constituent parts, every part can be labelled in two ways: according to the function of the part and according to class of unit performing that function. In Figs 1.1 to 1.6 the functions of each part of the structure have been written in bold. They are also conventionally written with an upper case letter to remind you that they are function labels – labels which tell you what job that unit is doing, what role it is playing, what meaning it has in the structure.

For all the functions we have identified so far, we have also identified the class of unit which **realizes** or expresses it. In Figs 1.1–1.6 the class labels have been written in normal roman type. A class label tells you what kind or category the unit is by virtue of its form, without reference to its role in any particular context.[4] Class labelling may be all that is necessary when analysing clauses using a formal grammar, but if we are interested in analysing and interpreting texts, then functional labelling of the kind provided in IFG will prove a much more useful tool.

In addition, there is important grammatical work for function labels to do. For one thing, they help distinguish ambiguous sequences of classes. We can exemplify this briefly by looking at the nominal group *a running shoe*. This word sequence consists of a determiner, followed by a verb, followed by a noun. But it can mean more than one thing. Probably the first meaning that comes to mind is that of a shoe made specially for running. However, it might mean, say in a children's cartoon context, a shoe that is running (with little legs protruding from the sole). In a functional grammar we can say that on the first reading *running* functions as a Classifier, telling us what type of shoe (Fig. 1.7); on the second reading *running* is an Epithet, describing what the shoe is doing (Fig. 1.8).

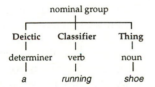

Fig. 1.7 A classifying nominal group

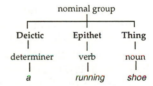

Fig. 1.8 A descriptive nominal group

In a similar way, the structure of the nominal group *this red flower* can be distinguished from that of *this red wine* through the function labelling. Both have the same sequence of word classes, but the adjective *red* does not have the same function in each case. In one case it is an Epithet functioning to describe the flower; in the other it is a Classifier, telling us what type of wine.

If you have followed the discussion this far, you will have a basis for beginning to learn to use a functional grammar to analyse text. One key point we have made in this introduction is that there are three possible angles on analysis – the ideational (clause as representation), the interpersonal (clause as exchange) and the textual

[4]In formal grammars the term 'category' is often used for class and 'relation' for function.

(clause as message) – and that these can ultimately be brought together into a synthesis. We have also discussed the part-whole, or constituency, structure of the clause, showing how it is made up of groups and phrases which in turn are made up of words. In the discussion of constituency we have emphasized that these smaller units have particular functions to play in the larger structure and that analysis using a functional grammar involves identifying these functional parts.

In the following sections of this chapter we will develop these initial points, taking you further in understanding the theoretical orientation of the IFG and exploring some more complex aspects of constituency. Particularly if you have no previous experience of grammatical analysis, you may find that you wish to return to these points later when you have gained some familiarity with the IFG.

Reasoning in a functional grammar

We have discussed the relevance of functional labelling for discriminating potentially ambiguous structures. The other important grammatical work for function labels has to do with reasoning in a functional grammar. This reasoning is concerned with how grammatical items are related to each other. Let us continue with the example *a running shoe*. The point of labelling *running* a Classifier is to show that the nominal group in question is related to other nominal groups which classify shoes: *gym shoes, dress shoes, walking shoes, leather shoes, second-hand shoes* and so on. Labelling *running* an Epithet, on the other hand, shows that the nominal group is related to other nominal groups which describe shoes: *big shoes, black shoes, old shoes, dirty shoes, favourite shoes* and so on.

This in turn affects the way in which the nominal groups can be expanded. For example, with *running* as a Classifier, the group can be expanded through further classification: *the Adidas running shoes*. With *running* as an Epithet, on the other hand, the group can be expanded by grading the description: *the quickly running shoes*. At the same time, our functional description explains why we cannot say *the quickly running shoes* when we are classifying, any more than we can say *the quickly gym shoes*; in English, Classifiers are categorical – we do not intensify them. Similarly, we cannot say *the Adidas running shoes* when we are describing, because in English Epithets always come before, not after, Classifiers. So when we label *running* as Epithet or Classifier according to its function, we are showing what kinds of nominal group the one we are analysing is related to.

Relevant related structures can be refered to as **agnate** structures, and reasoning about an optimum analysis in any instance inolves looking at the patterns of agnation. So, for example, if you were unsure whether *red wine* in a clause like *she likes red wine* was a Classifier+Thing or an Epithet+Thing structure, you would need to consider agnate groups. This would lead you to ask whether *red wine* relates to *white wine, rosé wine* and *sparkling wine* (open to extension as *Hunter red wine* or *Italian sparkling wine*) or to *pale wine* and *red medicine* (open to extension through intensifiers, as in *very pale wine, bright red medicine*). If the former are more plausible in the context, then you will have grounds for a Classifier+Thing analysis.[5] Reasoning about a specific instance therefore involves putting the example into a set of similar examples to find out where it fits.

[5]Can you think of a context in which *red* would be interpretable as an Epithet in the nominal group *the red wine*?

Table 1.1   A paradigm for present tense English *be* (person and number)

	singular	plural
1st person **2nd person** **3rd person**	*I am* *you are* *s/he/it is*	*we are* *you are* *they are*

Ultimately, the purpose of function labels is to show how the items you are analysing arc related to the grammatical choices they embody. Traditionally, the way of focusing on grammatical choices has been through a paradigm (hence the term 'paradigmatic relations'). Representing grammatical choice as a paradigm is often used when learning noun or verb inflexions in a second language. Table 1.1 gives an example for the simple present tense forms of the English verb *be*, plotting choices of person (the rows) against choices of number (the columns).

But paradigms can be used to display relations among units of any size. Table 1.2 shows a simple paradigm for MOOD in the English clause (with just one dimension of alternatives arranged by row).

Table 1.2   A simple paradigm for English MOOD

declarative **interrogative** **imperative**	*He was tickling the baby.* *Was he tickling the baby?* *Tickle the baby!*

The labels in a paradigm are the names of grammatical 'choices' or 'selections' and any choice made will have an implication in grammatical structure. MOOD choices are relevant to the interpersonal structure of the clause, and Halliday's function labels for the parts of the clause – when we look at the clause as an interpersonal structure – will show which MOOD choices have been taken up. For example, if the choice of imperative is taken up, there will typically be no Subject or Finite function in the clause. If the choice of declarative is taken up, the Subject function will precede the function of Finite, whereas if the choice of interrogative is taken up, the Finite will precede the Subject. Figs 1.9 and 1.10 contrast the declarative and interrogative structures.

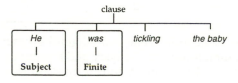

Fig. 1.9 Declarative clause showing Subject and Finite

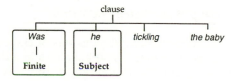

Fig. 1.10 Interrogative clause showing Subject and Finite

The functional labels in Figs 1.9 and 1.10 identify the structures as being declarative or interrogative. In other words, they show where these examples fit into the paradigm – the set of available choices. Every time you analyse a clause as having the function structure of Subject followed by Finite (Subject^Finite), you are analysing it as a declarative clause (and thus different from but related to an interrogative or imperative clause). Thus a particular function structure (such as Subject^Finite) represents an embodiment or realization of a particular choice from the paradigm (such as declarative).

While the simple paradigm in Table 1.2 focuses on just one set of choices, it is more usual for paradigms to focus on two sets of choices at the same time (Halliday uses this kind of display in IFG Chapter 6, on pages 181 and 199 for example). To illustrate this, Table 1.3 adds the option of having a tag or not to the earlier paradigm.

Table 1.3   A simple paradigm for English MOOD and TAGGING

	not tagged	**tagged**
declarative interrogative imperative	*He was tickling the baby.* *Was he tickling the baby?* *Tickle the baby!*	*He was tickling the baby, wasn't he?* *Was he tickling the baby, was he?*[6] *Tickle the baby, won't you?*

In Table 1.4, we have included the relevant function labels for Subject and Finite into the paradigm we have been working with. The analysis suggests that every time you analyse a clause as Finite followed by Subject, with a tag having Finite followed by Subject, you are analysing an example that fits into the interrogative, tagged box in the paradigm. The paradigm as a whole shows how the clause is related to others. So an analysis of an individual clause always involves implicitly relating that clause to others in the language.

Table 1.4   A paradigm for MOOD and TAGGING including function structure

	not tagged	**tagged**
declarative	*He was tickling the baby.* Subject^Finite...	*He was tickling the baby, wasn't he?* Subject^Finite ... ...Finite^Subject
interrogative	*Was he tickling the baby?* Finite^Subject	*Was he tickling the baby, was he?* Finite^Subject ... ...Finite Subject
imperative	*Tickle the baby!* –	*Tickle the baby, won't you?* – Finite^Subject

Paradigms as system networks

Once more than two dimensions of choice are brought into play, paradigms become rather cumbersome. You have to add a third dimension out the back and the three-dimensional cube you create in this way gets hard to read. A fourth dimension is

---

[6]Australians use a tag in this context, although most speakers of English do not have the option of a tag in interrogatives.

pretty much out of the question. In systemic functional linguistics – the linguistic theory behind the IFG – system networks are used to overcome this limitation (for a range of examples of this style of display, see IFG: 130, 169, 189, 214, 360). The two dimensions of choice outlined in the paradigm above can be represented in a system network as in Fig. 1.11.

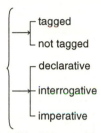

Fig. 1.11 A system network for MOOD and TAGGING

The network in Fig 1.11[7] says that, as far as choices for MOOD go, speakers of Australian English can choose among declarative, interrogative and imperative, and at the same time between having a tag or not. The square brackets set up the choices as alternatives: you have to choose tagged or not tagged, and you have to choose declarative, interrogative or imperative. The brace means that speakers must choose from both systems: from the choice of tagged or not tagged *and* from the choice of declarative, interrogative or imperative. The square bracket and its set of choices is referred to as a **system**. A set of systems is referred to as a **system network**. Fig. 1.12 identifies the different parts of a system network.

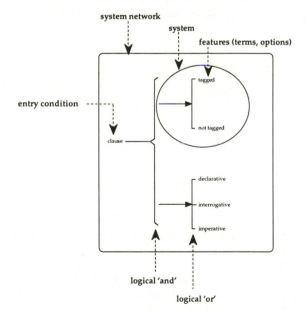

Fig. 1.12 Naming the parts of a system network

---

[7]For the actual MOOD network underlying the analyses presented in IFG, see Chapter 3.

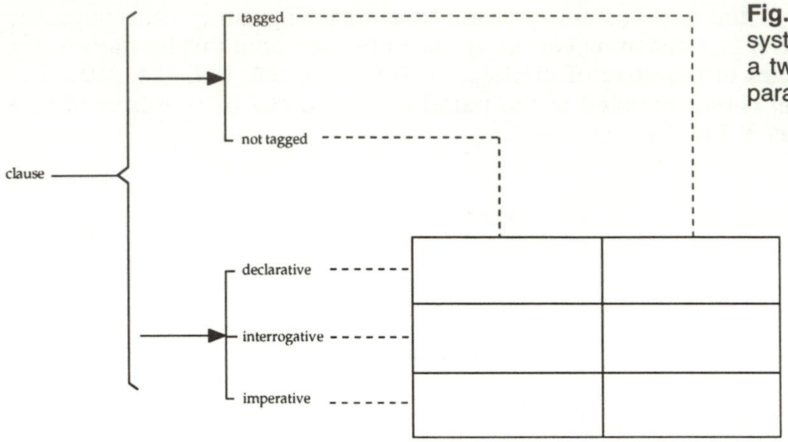

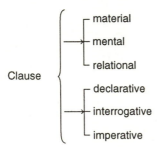

Fig. 1.13 Deriving a system network from a two-dimensional paradigm

A system network of this kind can be derived from any paradigm (including three-dimensional cubes) by turning names of rows and columns into sets of choices – systems of features. This translation process is outlined in Fig. 1.13 for the example we have been considering.

In this kind of display (the system network), there is no limit to the number of choices that can be considered. In considering MOOD and TAGGING, we have been considering interpersonal choices. Earlier on, we looked at the ideational structure of the clause *Quite recently the Norwegians were whaling off Greenland*, identifying functions like Actor, Process, Time and Place. These ideational functions embody choices from an ideational paradigm where the options relate to the kind of reality being constructed: doing (material process), thinking (mental process) or being (relational process). Choices for MOOD (IFG Chapter 4) and choices for PROCESS TYPE (IFG Chapter 5) combine freely in English, so we represent the choices as simultaneous, as in Fig. 1.14.

Fig. 1.14 A simple network for English PROCESS TYPE and MOOD

Just as the MOOD choice will be realized by a particular function structure, such as Subject followed by Finite (Subject^Finite), so the choice from PROCESS TYPE will be realized by the presence in the structure of particular functions like Actor and Process. An interpersonal function like Subject may therefore map onto an ideational function like Actor (as well as on to a textual function). Just as the configuration of Subject and Finite tells you the mood of a clause, the presence of an Actor role tells you what kind of process the clause is (material rather than mental or relational). The function labelling, in other words, is all about relating clauses and groups to one another according to the system networks on which IFG is based. If you want to see a full account of these networks, most of which are not presented in IFG, you can consult Matthiessen (1995).

As we extend our description of choices in any language, we may find that choices start to depend on each other. For example, if we kept working on MOOD in English, we would find we needed to include exclamative clauses (*What a fool he felt*). These could be grouped with declaratives on the basis that they share the sequence of the Subject and Finite functions (Subject^Finite for declaratives (both exclamative and non-exclamative), Finite^Subject[8] for interrogatives). Then interrogatives could be divided into the 'yes/no' (polar) type (*Is he a fool?*) and the wh- type (*Why is he a fool?*). Having got this far we would realize that the possibility of adding a tag is actually sensitive to MOOD. In Australian English you do not tag exclamatives or wh- interrogatives (**What a fool he is, isn't he?*, **Why is he a fool, is he?*[9]), but you can tag non-exclamative declaratives, polar interrogatives and imperatives. So TAGGING in fact depends on MOOD; it is not independent of it as implied by the simplified MOOD networks in Figs 1.11–1.13. The more complex picture of MOOD we have developed to this point is outlined in Fig. 1.15. The network now includes an 'or' bracket that faces left, to account for the fact that tags can be added to non-exclamative declaratives or polar interrogatives or imperatives. Note that our discussion has not had any repercussions for our PROCESS TYPE options, which freely combine with all the MOOD variations we have outlined.

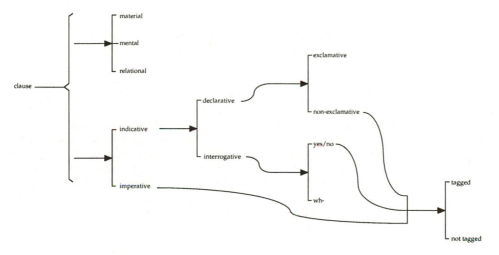

Fig. 1.15 A more developed network for English MOOD

This grouping together of systems of interrelated options is the basis for Halliday's functional interpretation of English grammar. Options related to PROCESS TYPE (clause as representation) are handled in IFG Chapter 5; options related to MOOD are handled in IFG Chapter 4 (clause as exchange); and options related to

---

[8]Except in Wh- interrogatives which ask about the Subject (see IFG: 45–6, 85).
[9]We follow here the convention in linguistics of placing an asterisk before an 'impossible' structure.

the distribution of information (what comes first and last in the clause – clause as message) are handled in IFG Chapter 3. These bundles of options reflect the 'metafunctional' organization of the grammar into experiential, interpersonal and textual components respectively.

Choice and constituency

Alongside bundles of choices organized by metafunction, we can also interpret constituency in terms of bundles of options. We will use an ideational focus to analysis to illustrate this, taking the clause *those shoes are wrecking my feet* as an example. Fig. 1.16 shows the ideational analysis of the clause and of its functional parts.

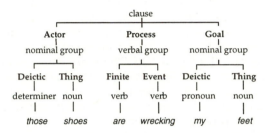

Fig. 1.16 Clause structure

We can see in this example that the layering in the tree diagram reflects the organization of grammatical choices. The top two layers are oriented to clause choices and the functional structures resulting from them (clause: Actor+ Process+Goal); the next two layers are oriented to group/phrase choices and the functional structures resulting from them (e.g. nominal group: Deictic^Thing); the final layer is oriented to word choices, whose functional structure is not developed. This way of organizing constituency with respect to layers of choices we have already referred to as organization by rank – so we speak of clause rank, group/phrase rank, and word rank, with a clause consisting of one or more groups and phrases (minimally a clause like *Help!*), and with a group consisting of one or more words (minimally a verbal group like *help*); and ultimately, if we went on beyond the IFG coverage, with a word consisting of one or more morphemes (minimally a noun like *man*). The relation of ranked layers of clause structure to bundles of choices is outlined in Fig. 1.17.

Fig. 1.17 Clause structure – in relation to underlying systems of choice

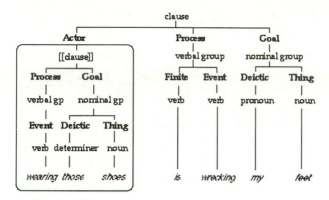

Fig. 1.18 Clause structure – showing an example of embedding

In bringing this discussion to a close, we will take two more steps. Both have to do with opening up choices again at places inside the clause hierarchy where we would not normally expect them. Consider the (ideational) analysis of the clause *wearing those shoes is wrecking my feet*. As we work through the analysis of this clause we find that the Actor is not a nominal group as we would normally expect, but is in fact another clause.[10] So, at the point where we might expect to have run out of clause choices and be making nominal group choices, we find the clause choices opened up again. See Fig. 1.18.

When choices are opened up again in this way, at a rank lower than we would normally expect them, we say that one unit has been **embedded** in another – in this case, a clause has been embedded inside another clause. This disturbs the normal layering we find in clause structure – instead of a clause consisting of one or more group/phrases and group/phrases consisting of one or more words, we have a clause consisting of another clause among the group/phrases. For more detail on embedding (also known as **rankshift** or **downranking**), see IFG Chapter 6, and Chapter 5 below.

Alongside embedding, the other way in which clause analysis gets more complicated as choices for meaning are opened up again is through complexing (discussed in IFG Chapter 7, including 7 Additional). For example, if we adjust the example we are working on slightly to read *those shoes are wrecking my feet and ankles* then it turns out that what is being wrecked consists of two nominal groups, not just one – two groups which are co-ordinated with each other. The second group expands the information in the first one, but is serving the same clause function. It is not that the clause has two Goals, but rather that the clause's Goal is a nominal group complex. An outline of this structure is provided in Fig. 1.19, where we have drawn an inter-dependency arrow between the first nominal group and the second. Note that, with complexing, we get more choices of the same kind of meaning – in this case, nominal groups choices followed by more nominal groups choices; this contrasts with embedding, where in the example above we had clause choices where we were expecting nominal group ones – choices of a different kind, rather than more of the same.

Complexing occurs at all ranks in the grammar. Suppose we adjust our example to read *those shoes are hurting my bruised and battered feet*. In this case, we have

[10]To simplify the discussion we will not deal here with the analysis that interprets the embedded clause as embedded as the Head of a nominal group functioning as Actor; see IFG Chapter 6 for discussion.

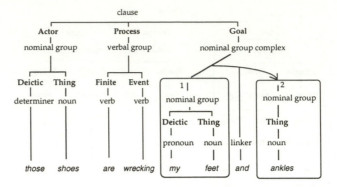

Fig. 1.19 Clause structure with a nominal group complex

an example of word complexing inside the nominal group describing my feet. Here, the description of my feet, its Epithet, consists of two adjectives, co-ordinated with each other. As with complexing in general, instead of one round of choices we have more of the same – two rounds of foot description instead of one. An outline of this clause structure, including word complexing, is shown in Fig. 1.20.

As well as words and groups, it is possible to have complexes of clauses. Suppose we change our example to *those shoes are hurting my feet so I'll throw them away*. In this case, we have a clause expanded by another one – a clause complex. Chapter 5 of this workbook focuses in particular on this phenomenon.

To sum up, grammatical choices made at clause and group/phrase rank create functional structures at those ranks. In the most straightforward case, clause rank choices will result in functions realized by groups and phrases while group/phrase rank choices will result in functions realized by words. In addition, however, there are two ways in which this constituency pattern can be disturbed to open up additional choices. One way is through embedding a unit of the same or higher rank into the structure. When this happens a particular function (like Actor in the clause or Deictic in the group) is realized not by a smaller unit but by a same size or larger one. In

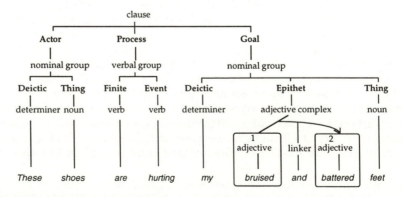

Fig. 1.20 Clause structure with a word complex

this situation we might, for example, find a clause functioning as part of another clause or even as part of a nominal group. A second way that additional choices are opened up is when, at any rank, a particular function is realized by a series of the same-sized unit, so instead of the Actor role in the clause taking the form of a nominal group, for example, it takes the form of two or more groups linked by conjunctions.

Learning to use IFG

The description of the language provided by IFG is a very rich one and can only be learned step by step. For example, you will need to focus on one of the three perspectives – ideational, interpersonal, textual – at a time, even though the goal of your study will be to bring all three perspectives to bear on any text. You will also need to focus on one grammatical rank at a time – clause or group/phrase – and on different kinds of groups separately. Wherever you start, you are likely at times to feel in need of understandings about the grammar that your present focus is not providing. This can be frustrating in the short term, but as you learn more you will have the satisfaction of seeing each new aspect of the grammar complementing and illuminating what you have already learned.

Another possible source of frustration when you first work with IFG is the amount of new terminology you will meet: compared with formal or traditional school grammars there are many more categories to learn in IFG. To familiarize yourself with these categories, it may help to photocopy summary tables from IFG and from this workbook and paste them up around your desk as a memory aid. If you are computer-oriented, there are also hypercard systems and other supportive resources available – you can get onto sysfling to hunt them down. If you are learning in a class, then it certainly helps to work on your analyses in a group with other students and develop your skills in grammatical reasoning as you argue for a particular analysis. We would also suggest that, as you concentrate on learning new categories and terminology, you practise your analytical skills with quite simple texts at first, such as those in the Phase I sections of this book. This lets you concentrate on what you are trying to learn at the time instead of getting distracted (or dismayed) by too many special cases and complications.

Once the labels are under control, then a whole new way of reading texts is opened up to you – one in which you see texts as semiotic entities that make meaning, rather than as formal entities that pass preformed thoughts and feelings (or even transcendental signifieds) from one human being to another. You will start to see language as having a far more central place in human experience than you may have imagined before, and may even go through a phase of thinking that after all language is all there is – since it shapes and categorizes everything around us the moment we try to say anything about anything at all. This radical Whorfian phase can be a trying one for peers from other disciplines; some of us never recover from it! However you react, we think you will find this grammar a new tool for thinking about human experience, in whatever professional context you use it in. It gives you a way of thinking grammatically about everything under the sun (and perhaps beyond).

Best of luck with your grammar learning. We hope this workbook gives you some new ways round at least some of the difficulties you might be experiencing without it.

References

Cope, W. and Kalantzis, M. (eds) 1993: *The powers of literacy: a genre approach to teaching literacy.* London: Falmer (Critical Perspectives on Literacy and Education) and Pittsburg: University of Pittsburg Press (Pittsburg Series in Composition, Literacy, and Culture).

Fairclough, Norman 1992: *Discourse and social change.* Cambridge: Polity Press.

Halliday, M.A.K. 1985: *Spoken and written language.* Deakin: Deakin University Press.

Halliday, M.A.K. 1994: *An introduction to functional grammar* (second edition). London: Arnold.

Iedema, R. 1995: *Administration literacy* (Write it Right Literacy in Industry Research Project – Stage 3). Sydney: Metropolitan East Disadvantaged Schools Program.

Iedema, R., Feez, S. and White, P. 1994: *Media literacy* (Write it Right Literacy in Industry Research Project – Stage 2). Sydney: Metropolitan East Disadvantaged Schools Program.

Kress, G. and van Leeuwen, T. 1996: *Reading images: the grammar of visual design.* London: Routledge.

Matthiessen, C.M.I.M. 1995: *Lexicogrammatical cartography: English systems.* Tokyo: International Language Sciences Publishers.

Matthiessen, C.M.I.M. and Bateman, John 1991: *Text generation and systemic-functional linguistics.* London: Pinter (Communication in Artificial Intelligence Series).

O'Toole, M. 1994: *The language of displayed art.* London: Leicester University Press (Pinter).

Rose, D., McInnes, D. and Korner, H. 1992: *Scientific literacy* (Write it Right Literacy in Industry Research Project – Stage 1). Sydney: Metropolitan East Disadvantaged Schools Program.

Rothery, J. 1994: *Exploring literacy in school English* (Write it Right Resources for Literacy and Learning). Sydney: Metropolitan East Disadvantaged Schools Program.

Thibault, P. 1991: *Social semiotics as praxis: text, social meaning making, and Nabokov's Ada.* Minneapolis: University of Minnesota Press (Theory and History of Literature 74).

2

Theme
clause as message

1 Orientation

1.1 Reading guide to IFG

IFG Chapter 3 (Clause as message)
    Section 2.5 (Subject, Actor, and Theme)
    Section 8.6 (Given + New, Theme + Rheme)

1.2 Characterization of Theme

The system of THEME belongs to the textual metafunction of the language. It is concerned with the organization of information within individual clauses and, through this, with the organization of the larger text. Thus the following versions of 'the same' clause-sized piece of information embody alternative THEME choices:

Your reporter repeatedly interrupted her replies.
Her replies were repeatedly interrupted by your reporter.
Repeatedly, your reporter interrupted her replies.

Every clause is organized as a message related to an unfolding text. The system of THEME organizes the clause to show what its local context is in relation to the general context of the text it serves in; the system is concerned with the current point of departure in relation to what has come before, so that it is clear where the clause is located in the text – how its contribution fits in. This local context or point of departure is called **Theme**. The rest of the message of the clause is what is presented against the background of the local context – it is where the clause moves after the point of departure. This is called **Rheme**. The clause as message is thus organized into Theme + Rheme. In English and many other languages such as Mandarin, this organization is 'realized' (expressed, signalled) positionally: Theme is realized by initial position in the clause and Rheme follows.

Theme:	Rheme:
Point of departure of clause as message; local context of clause as a piece of text.	Non-Theme – where the presentation moves after the point of departure; what is presented in the local context set up by Theme.
initial position in the clause	position following initial position

THEME is one of two systems that organize the information presented in the clause, the other being that of INFORMATION.[1] And, although our concern in this chapter is with THEME, it will be useful to distinguish it from that of INFORMATION and, at various points, to make links between the two systems.

While THEME uses position within the clause to organize information into an initial orientation followed by the Rheme, the system of INFORMATION uses intonation to highlight what is particularly newsworthy in the message. The **New** element in the clause is foregrounded by being 'stressed' as we speak (more technically, it contains a tonic syllable). For example:

A: Which one is Lindy's boy?
B: He   's the **tall** one.
     Theme   New

The information structure of the clause is discussed in IFG Chapter 8.

1.3 Thematic development within a text

The choice of Theme for any individual clause will generally relate to the way information is being developed over the course of the whole text. In the following text, the overall discourse theme concerns reptiles and their subtypes; clause by clause the Themes are selected to indicate the progression from reptiles in general to 'some reptiles', 'many reptiles', and so on:

Reptiles were the first animals with backbones that could live on land all the time. Some reptiles we know today are snakes, lizards and turtles. Many of the early reptiles grew very large. Two large, early reptiles were Edaphosaurus and Dimetrodon. They were each about ten feet long.

Edaphosaurus and Dimetrodon had *large fins* on their backs. These were held up by tall, bony spines...

This progression of Themes over the course of a text is referred to as the text's **method of development** (Fries, 1981).

2 Survey of options

We have described the Theme as providing the local context for the information in the rest of the clause. An important aspect to this is that the clause can be contextualized in terms of all three of its metafunctional perspectives – textually, interpersonally, and ideationally. The Theme of a clause can thus have textual,

[1]The domain of INFORMATION is really the information unit; see further IFG Chapter 8.

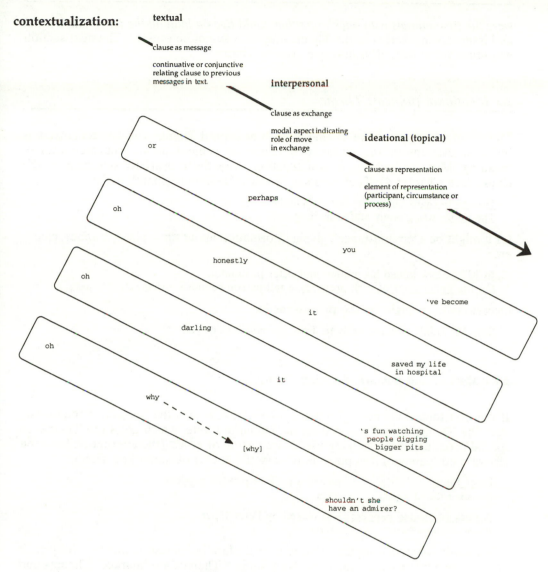

contextualization:

textual

clause as message

continuative or conjunctive
relating clause to previous
messages in text.

interpersonal

clause as exchange

modal aspect indicating
role of move
in exchange

ideational (topical)

clause as representation

element of representation
(participant, circumstance or
process)

or

perhaps

oh

honestly

you

oh

it

've become

darling

oh

saved my life
in hospital

it

why

's fun watching
people digging
bigger pits

[why]

shouldn't she
have an admirer?

Fig. 2.1 Metafunctional components to Theme

interpersonal, and ideational stages, as shown in Fig. 2.1. (The ideational stage to the Theme is known as **topical** Theme.) Fig. 2.1 exemplifies the way the Theme component in a clause may unfold from one metafunctional perspective to the next.

As the examples in Fig. 2.1 show, the Theme of the clause always concludes with a 'topical' element, and indeed there may only be a topical Theme, as in _Reptiles_ *were the first animals with backbones that could live on land all the time.* The textual and interpersonal stages to the Theme may or may not be present. The next section will illustrate in turn each different type of Theme.

2.1 Ideational (topical) Theme

The ideational stage of the Theme, known as topical Theme, can be recognized as the first element in the clause that expresses some kind of 'representational' meaning. More technically, it is a function from the transitivity structure of the clause (see Chapter 4). That is to say, it might be a 'participant', as in:

> George Bernard Shaw was born in Dublin.
> The house was gloomy and uninviting.

Or it might be a 'circumstance', giving information about time, place, manner, cause, etc.:

> In 1876, Shaw joined his mother and sister in London.
> On the upper floor of such premises, a tall person cannot stand erect.

Occasionally, it might be the process, as in:

> Says Mr Smith: 'It's too early to draw any conclusions yet.'

2.1.1 Marked and unmarked topical Theme

If the first topical element of a declarative clause is also the Subject of the clause, then the Theme choice is a neutral or 'unmarked' one, which gives the Theme no special prominence. By making use of the system of VOICE (the alternation between 'active' and 'passive') it is possible to vary the choice of unmarked Theme:

Peter Piper	picked a peck of pickled peppers
Unmarked Theme/Subject	Rheme

A peck of pickled peppers	was picked by Peter Piper
Unmarked Theme/Subject	Rheme

However, when the topical Theme of a declarative clause is not the Subject, it gains a greater textual prominence. Non-Subject Themes are 'marked' Themes and are often important in structuring the larger discourse. Here are some examples of marked Themes:

Someday,	you	'll understand that
	Subject	
Marked Theme	........Rheme............................	

Jasmine,	I	love the smell of
	Subject	
Marked Theme	........Rheme......................	

For discussion of unmarked Themes in relation to clauses other than declaratives, see Section 5.4 below.

2.2 Interpersonal Theme

The interpersonal part of the Theme, if present, includes one or more of the following (see Chapter 3).

(i) The Finite, typically realized by an auxiliary verb. Its presence in thematic position signals that a response is expected, as in:

<u>Should</u> they be doing that?
<u>Are</u> you coming?
<u>Don't</u> touch that!

(ii) A Wh- element, signalling that an 'answer' is required from the addressee:[2]

<u>Why</u> can't you come over tonight?
<u>How</u> did school shape up?

(iii) A Vocative, identifying the addressee in the exchange:

<u>Mr Wolf, Mr. Wolf</u>, may we cross your golden waters?

(iv) An Adjunct, typically realized by an adverb. It provides the speaker's comment, assessment or attitude towards the message. For example:

<u>Sadly</u>, it doesn't look like the old places will be around much longer.
<u>Perhaps</u> women make better vets.

One final type of interpersonal Theme consists of first and second person 'mental' clauses which express the speaker's opinion or seek the addressee's:

<u>I should think</u> there would probably be some of them that you'll never see.
<u>I don't suppose</u> you need Old English and Anglo-Saxon.
<u>Do you think</u> I should take an early play like the Prometheus?
<u>You know</u> bitter beer should be sharp.

Halliday regards these as 'interpersonal metaphors' of modality (IFG: 58, 354–63). That is, they can be regarded as comparable with Adjuncts like *probably* and treated as interpersonal Themes.

2.3 Textual Theme

Textual Themes almost always constitute the first part of the Theme, coming before any interpersonal Themes. They give thematic prominence to textual elements with a linking function.

i) Structural conjunctions, linking two clauses in a coordinating relation:

Jasmine, I love the smell of, <u>but</u> napalm I adore

or marking one clause as dependent on another:

The interviewer asked <u>whether</u> there would be a change in direction.
The Minister said <u>that</u> there was no need to amend the legislation.
Developers are also putting up huge office complexes, <u>while</u> the government is racing to complete infrastructure projects.
<u>When</u> you don't have enough police, the crime rate gets higher.

---

[2]A Wh- Theme is not exclusively interpersonal. It is simultaneously a topical Theme since, as well as its function as a 'question word', it is also a participant or circumstance in the clause.

ii) Relatives, relating a dependent clause to another clause:[3]

We heard Professor Smith's lecture, <u>which</u> was a great disappointment.
News of the scam alarmed customers, <u>who</u> in the following two trading days demanded to cash in an estimated $50 billion in securities.

iii) Conjunctives, providing a cohesive link back to previous discourse:

<u>Furthermore</u> this alternative would be far too costly.

Note that conjunctives may or may not be thematic depending on whether they occur first in the clause. For example, *two days later* is thematic in <u>*Later*</u> *the state-owned Taiwan Cooperative Bank took over Changhua*, but *later* is not thematic in *He later offered a brief, televised apology*.

iv) Continuatives, indicating a relationship to previous discourse:

<u>Well</u> there was a little bit of bakelite before the war, wasn't there?

2.4 Summary of types of Theme

All three metafunctions may contribute to the Theme of a clause; the last, and only obligatory, stage of a Theme as it unfolds from left to right in the clause, is the ideational (topical) part. If you analyse a clause for Theme from left to right, the most central question is how far the Theme extends to the right – i.e. where the boundary between Theme and Rheme can be drawn. Fig. 2.2 summarizes the information given in IFG. It shows that the Theme extends from the beginning of the clause to include any textual and/or interpersonal elements that may be present and also the first experiential element, that is a circumstance, process or participant.

2.5 Extending the thematic principle beyond the clause

The thematic principle of textual organization can also be seen operating with respect to units larger than the individual clause.[4] One such case is where two or more clauses are linked together within a 'clause complex' (the sentence of written English). Where a dependent (modifying, subordinate) clause precedes the main clause it can be interpreted as having thematic status for the clause complex as a whole, as in <u>*Although the play was well acted,*</u> *the characters ultimately failed to engage our sympathies*. (See 3.7 below.) In a similar way, the initial clause complex of a paragraph may be seen as functioning as a kind of 'paragraph Theme' (the Topic Sentence of traditional accounts), while the introductory paragraph itself has a thematic status *vis-à-vis* the text as a whole.

---

[3]Relative elements serve both as textual and topical Theme since, as well as relating the relative clause to a preceding one, they serve to specify a participant.
[4]Also for smaller units. See IFG Chapter 6.

and,　　　　secondly,　　　unfortunately,　　　in spring,　　　　the house is far too cold

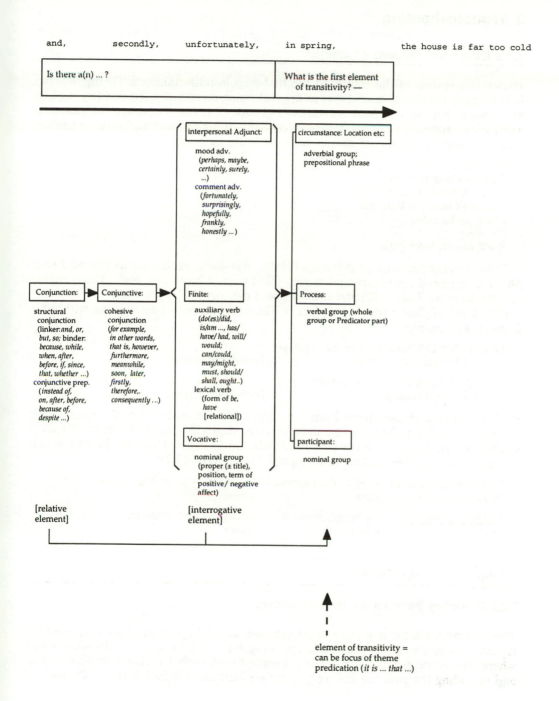

Fig. 2.2 The extent of the Theme element

3 Troubleshooting

3.1 Picking out the unit of analysis

THEME is a system of the clause, so the first step in undertaking a Theme analysis is to identify the clause boundaries in the text being considered. To divide your text into clauses you need to look for verbs or groups of verbs. These are the elements expressing processes of doing, saying, perceiving, thinking, feeling, being or having. Here are some examples of clauses with the verbs in bold:

Kiss me, my fool
I'**ll be waiting** for you
You **will tell** him, won't you?[5]
You **ain't heard** nothin' yet
I **vant to be** alone
It'**s** alive
We'**ll** always **have** Paris

Some utterances, such as greetings (*Hallo, Bye-bye*), exclamations (*Good Lord! Shit!*) or minimal conversational moves (*Oh*) do not have any verb. These **minor** clauses have no Theme-Rheme structure and can simply be set aside.

One kind of clause which may lack a Theme is the non-finite clause without a Subject. For example:

Old Mother Hubbard went to the cupboard
to fetch her poor dog a bone   (non-finite clause)

Little Jack Horner sat in the corner
eating his Christmas pie   (non-finite clause)

Such non-finite clauses have been backgrounded for interpersonal reasons (see Chapter 3) and this has affected their texture, depriving them of topical Themes, so that the whole clause can be counted as Rheme. In other words the Process which begins the clause does not serve as topical Theme (IFG: 62):

<u>Old Mother Hubbard</u>	went to the cupboard ‖	to fetch her poor dog a bone
Theme	Rheme	Rheme

<u>Little Jack Horner</u>	sat in the corner ‖	eating his Christmas pie
Theme	Rheme	Rheme

3.2 Identifying the Theme

3.2.1 Boundary between Theme and Rheme

Theoretically, Theme is a pulse of information at the beginning of the clause which tapers into Rheme; but practically speaking we need to make a decision about where Theme begins and stops. The principle to remember is that everything up to and including the first 'topical' (experiential) element will count as the Theme.

---

[5] A tag like *won't you?* counts as part of the clause and not as a separate unit.

3.2.2 Elliptical clauses

Where two clauses are linked by coordination – in a paratactic structure – the Subject of the second clause may be **ellipsed** or 'understood':

He roared in fury ‖ <u>and ( )</u> struggled with all his might

In such a case the ellipsed Subject of the second clause counts as the (ellipsed) topical Theme. Consequently, the Process (*struggled*) is not the Theme.

3.3 Identifying the metafunction

3.3.1 Textual or Interpersonal?

a) Yes and no   *Yes* and *no* may be interpersonal or textual in function. POLARITY is an interpersonal system, and when *yes* or *no* initiates a response to a yes/no interrogative, it functions as an interpersonal Theme:

A: Did you get a Herald today?
B: No, I didn't   *No* is interpersonal Theme

However, *yes* or *no* may also serve a continuative function, signalling a new move (by the same or a different speaker) simply by maintaining the current polarity. In these cases they will be phonologically weak and are textual Themes, linking the new move to what went before (see IFG: 92). Examples:

A: Bad news about Maxine's job.
B: Yes it is.   *Yes* is textual Theme

A: We won't go to the beach today.
B: No it's too windy.   *No* is textual Theme

Oh, well, now and *okay* are other textual continuatives, which similarly mark a response move in dialogue or a fresh initiation in monologue.

b) Adjuncts   It is easy to confuse initial Adjuncts which have a textual, linking function and those which have an interpersonal, modal function (see further Chapter 3). Some of the Adjuncts most frequently confused are given in Table 2.1 (see IFG: 49 for fuller lists).

Table 2.1   Examples of textual and interpersonal Adjuncts

Textual	Interpersonal
In fact	Evidently
Anyway	Broadly speaking
At least	Obviously
In conclusion	Provisionally

3.3.2 Interpersonal or topical?

a) Time expressions   Expressions of frequency ('usuality' Adjuncts) such as *sometimes* or *often* are interpersonal rather than experiential in nature (Table 2.2). (See IFG: 49, 89, 357–360.)

Table 2.2 Examples of interpersonal (modal) and experiential Adjuncts

Interpersonal (Usuality)	Topical (Temporal Location/Extent)
At times... Often... Usually... Occasionally...	In the mornings... On Saturdays... Three times a day... That particular year...

The Theme predication test is a useful way to discriminate topical Themes. In the following examples, the second version has the element in doubt as a predicated Theme (see IFG 3.7). Only a topical element can successfully function as a predicated Theme:

On Saturdays we used to go jogging
It was on Saturdays we used to go jogging

        On Saturdays is topical Theme

Usually Jeremy is too drunk (to drive home)
*It is usually that Jeremy is too drunk

        Usually is not topical Theme

b) Question words   Interrogative Wh- items[6] such as *Where, Why, When, How* are both interpersonal <u>and</u> topical (cf. IFG: 54 Table 3(7)). This is because they play a role both in the interpersonal structure of the clause – as the Wh- function – (see Chapter 3) and in the transitivity structure of the clause, as participant or circumstance (see Chapter 4). This is true both of direct and indirect (reported) wh-interrogative clauses. For example:

<u>Who</u>	'd even know	<u>who</u>	you were?
interp+ topical		interp+ topical	
Theme	Rheme	Theme	Rheme

3.3.3 Textual or topical?

a) Relative pronouns   Note that relative items (such as *who[m], which, whose*) play a role in the transitivity structure of a clause as well as performing a linking function; they are thus topical and textual Themes (cf. IFG: 54, Table 3(7)):

She spoke to Dr Jones, ‖ who	did his best to help her
textual + topical	
Theme	Rheme

b) Reference items   A reference item, such as ***this***, is sometimes mistakenly viewed as a textual Theme in an example like the following:

For many years, girls have fared worse than boys in mathematics and science subjects. <u>This</u> has resulted in a number of special programmes...

---

[6]Embedded clauses introduced by Wh- items, such as ⟦*whatever he did*⟧ *was wrong* are discussed in 3.6(iii).

However, although *this* is certainly textual in its function as a cohesive item, it counts as a topical Theme because it is a participant in the clause structure (see Chapter 4).

c) Temporal expressions   It is easy to confuse a textual linker combining two clauses or sentences in a temporal relation with a temporal circumstance specifying a time setting for its clause. Textual Themes are underlined in the following excerpts:

First I put my head on top of the gate – then the head's high enough – then I stand on my head – then the feet are high enough, you see – then I'm over, you see...

As he sat in the barn he watched Bern coming and going about his work. At last the beggar said...

Now look at circumstances functioning as topical Themes:

In 1925, the playwright was awarded the Nobel Prize for Literature. Between the ages of fifty-seven and sixty-seven, Shaw wrote such dramas as *Heartbreak House, Back to Methuselah, Androcles and the Lion, St. Joan*. During his lifetime he was besieged by offers to film his plays...

Further temporal examples are contrasted in Table 2.3. (See Chapter 4, 3.9 (iv) for further discussion.)

Table 2.3   Examples of textual and topical temporal expressions

Textual (see IFG 325-6)	Topical
Previously... Afterwards... Finally... Later...	Before breakfast... After many trials and tribulations... By the end of the race... At 5 o'clock...

3.4 Subject it *as unmarked topical Theme*

The grammatical item *it* is common as Subject and thus also as unmarked topical Theme. It will be helpful to distinguish different uses of *it* and to explain why *it* is analysed as topical Theme. Table 2.4 distinguishes three major cases.

In all these cases, the item *it* serves as the Subject of the clause. This is shown by the fact that it appears in the tag (the 'Moodtag'; see Chapter 3): *it's hot, isn't it?, it's raining, isn't it?, it is said that ... isn't it?, it seems that ... doesn't it?, it worries us that ... doesn't it?, it is irrelevant that ..., isn't it?, it was the dog that died, wasn't it?* Since the principle of THEME SELECTION in English is that the unmarked Theme keys into the mood of the clause, the Subject *it* will also be the unmarked topical Theme in declarative and yes/no interrogative clauses:

It	is	hot.
topical		
Theme	Rheme	

Is	it	hot?
interpersonal	topical	
Theme		Rheme

Table 2.4 Types of 'contentless' Subject *it*

type	subtype/use	example	agnate example
(i) ambient *it*		it's hot	The room's hot
(ii) non-representational *it*	meteorological *it*	it's raining	(rain's falling)
	impersonal projection *it*	it is said that he's a decent fellow it seems that he's a decent fellow	they say that he's a decent fellow : it is said to be the case that he's a decent fellow it seems to be the case that he's a decent fellow
(iii) anticipatory *it*	in mental and relational clauses with postposition	it worries us that he has disappeared	the fact worries us that he has disappeared : (the fact) that he has disappeared worries us
		it is irrelevant that she's a woman	the fact is irrelevant that she is a woman : (the fact) that she's a woman is irrelevant
	in Theme predication	it was the dog that died	the one that died was the dog : the dog died

That is, whether or not the item *it* has any representational value, it will always have the potential for serving as unmarked Theme and, when it does, it will give thematic status to the choice of mood – just as any other unmarked topical Theme does in a declarative or yes/no interrogative clause. (This is in fact part of the explanation why English uses *it* in the constructions we are dealing with here. Many languages have no equivalent item for some of these uses of *it*. For example, the Japanese for *It's hot* is *Atsui*, with an 'i-adjective' serving as Process and no Theme: the Japanese THEME system is not oriented towards the MOOD system in the way the English THEME system is.)

i) Ambient it   The ambient *it* serves as a participant in the transitivity structure of the clause in examples like *it's hot, it's humid, it's cloudy, it's stormy, it's windy, it's foggy, it's cooling down, it's clouding over, it's thawing*[7]. This *it* is thus representational: it represents the ambient conditions. Consequently, it can be probed with *what* in a wh-interrogative clause (*what's hot?, what's humid?, what's pleasant?*) and it alternates with fully lexicalized groups (*this room's hot, today's nice, the weather is pleasant, the air is humid*). For example:

It	is	hot.
What	is	hot?
The room	is	hot.

topical	
Theme	Rheme

[7]Ambient *it* is typically a Carrier in an attributive relational clause with an Attribute dealing with some feature of the environment such as temperature (e.g. *it's hot*), or else it appears as Actor in a material clause of qualitative change (e.g. *it's cooling down*).

Ambient *it* is thus a perfectly regular unmarked topical Theme: it serves as Subject and has a role in the transitivity structure of the clause.

ii) Non-representational it   However, there are uses of *it* where the item does not represent some phenomenon of experience and does not serve a participant role. This occurs in 'meteorological' clauses and in the 'impersonal' use of *it*.

In clauses construing precipitation, such as *it's raining/snowing/hailing*, the item *it* might at first glance look like ambient *it*. However, it differs from ambient *it* in that it does not represent some aspect of the environment and does not serve a participant role. Thus we cannot say (except jocularly) *what is it doing? – It's raining*, nor can we ask: *what's raining?* Nor are there any lexicalized alternatives: we cannot say *the sky's raining, the clouds are raining* or the like. The same considerations apply to the other non-representational use of *it*, the use of *it* in impersonal projections such as *it is said that he is very wealthy, it seems that he is very wealthy* (see IFG: 266).

From a textual point of view, clauses such as *it is raining* or *it seems that he is very wealthy* have *it* as unmarked topical Theme. This topical Theme is not prototypical: while it is quite regular in its orientation to the mood selection of the clause (*it [is] : is it*), it does not in fact serve a role in the experiential structure of the clause. Consequently, it is not open to special more marked thematic strategies – it cannot be theme-predicated (we cannot say *it was it that rained*) and it cannot be marked as an absolute Theme (we cannot say *as for it, it is said that he is very wealthy*). Further, it cannot be picked up textually by reference: if we say *it rained yesterday and it's snowing today*, the second *it* does not refer back to the first.

So why do we still interpret this non-representational *it* as topical Theme? On the one hand, as we have already noted, it is quite regular in its orientation to the mood selection of the clause: as unmarked topical Theme, it serves to give the mood selection thematic status:

| It | is | raining today. |
| It | is | said that he's wealthy. |

topical	
Theme	Rheme

| Is | it | raining today? |
| Is | it | said that he's wealthy? |

interpersonal	topical	
Theme		Rheme

On the other hand, it contrasts with marked topical Themes in the same way as prototypical, representational unmarked topical Themes do:

Henry is swimming today : Today Henry is swimming ::

It is raining today : Today it is raining

It is said nowadays that this substance is harmless :
Nowadays it is said that this substance is harmless

iii) Anticipatory it (mental and relational clauses)   The anticipatory *it* serves to anticipate an embedded clause occurring later in the structure. Unlike the impersonal projections, these structures have a variant where the embedded clause is Theme. For example:

> it worries me that he's not doing his homework :
> that he's not doing his homework worries me ::
>
> it is clear that he's not doing his homework :
> that he's not doing his homework is clear

iv) Anticipatory it *in Theme predication*   An anticipatory *it* also occurs with the special thematic strategy of Theme predication. This structure singles out one experiential element to serve as both Theme and New (see IFG 3.7). For example:

> It was **Rabbit** who saw Piglet first.
> It was in **Mathura** that the Divine Cowherd was exchanged with the infant daughter of Jasoda.

These examples differ from the use of anticipatory *it* described in (c) above. There is no variant where the embedded clause functions as Theme:

> *Who saw Piglet first was Rabbit.
> *That the Divine Cowherd was exchanged with the infant daughter of Jasoda was in Mathura.

Rather, the agnation is with a non-predicated version:

> It was Rabbit who saw Piglet first : Rabbit saw Piglet first.
> It was in Mathura that the Divine Cowherd was exchanged : In Mathura the Divine Cowherd was exchanged.

To indicate the marked status of a predicated Theme, the analysis can be shown as follows (see IFG: 60):

> It was Rabbit who saw Piglet first.
> Theme .... Rheme...............................

3.5 There's a ...: 'existential' clauses

There's always a long queue, There was trouble at the mill, There might come a time... are all examples of 'existential' clauses which introduce a participant into the text. An existential clause can be recognized by the presence of *there*, when *there* does not function to express a location. As with non-representational *it* (see 3.4 above), *there* functions as unmarked topical Theme, giving the mood choice (of declarative or interrogative) thematic status.

When interpreting such a Theme in the context of other topical choices, the meaning is simply that of 'existential' as expressed by *there* serving as Subject. In other words, the point of departure is precisely the fact that a participant (such as *a long queue* or *trouble at the mill*) is to be introduced. So although *there* does not itself function as a participant (or circumstance) it can still be regarded as topical Theme.

3.6 Recognizing longer Theme units

It is not difficult to recognise an unmarked Theme when that Theme is constituted by a pronoun, such as *They*, or a relatively short nominal group (i.e. noun phrase), such as *The big, bad wolf.* However, the Theme may be realized by a longer unit than this in the following cases.

(i) Nominal group in Theme position extends beyond the main noun:

<u>A large black wolf with yellow fangs</u> spoke to Red Riding Hood.
<u>The teacher who understood him best</u> was Marianne Fawley.

For an explanation of this structure, see IFG 6.2.

(ii) Group and Phrase complexes in Theme position. Sometimes more than one nominal group functions as the Theme:

<u>Jack and Jill</u> went up the hill.
<u>Nelson Mandela, the newly elected President of South Africa</u>, was invited.

Prepositional phrases may be similarly linked into 'complexes' functioning as Theme. For example:

<u>At Sezana, on the Yugoslav border</u>, they were very naughty, too.

For a discussion of complexing, see Chapter 5.

(iii) Embedded wh- clause as Theme. Another kind of long Theme occurs when a wh- clause is embedded into the Theme position as in [[*What he ate that night*]][8] *gave him terrible heartburn.* The most typical case is when a wh- clause is set up as Theme in a relational clause structure (see Chapter 4) of the following kind:

| <u>What he said</u> | is | nonsense |
| <u>What they lacked</u> | was | a business plan |

(iv) Embedded non-finite clause as Theme. It is not only wh- clauses that can be embedded into Theme position. Non-finite clauses are also common as topical Themes:

<u>Doing twenty sit-ups a day</u> will improve your tummy muscles
<u>To err</u> is human   ‖   <u>to forgive</u> (is) divine

It is also possible for a complex of clauses to be embedded in this way:

<u>Getting plenty of exercise and eating the right food</u> is important.

(v) Embedded 'that' clause as Theme. 'Fact' clauses such as *(The fact)* [[*that the food might not be fresh*]] are more commonly found in the Rheme, but do occur in Theme position:

<u>That the food might not be fresh</u> didn't occur to them.

3.6.1 Tests to check for longer Themes

In all the examples in this section, the size of the expression is quite irrelevant; it is its function in the clause that is at issue. You can often see that a long expression functions as a single element in a clause by trying one of the following tests.

---

[8]Square brackets [[ ]] signal that a clause is functioning in an embedded way as part of another clause.

(1) 'Replace' the expression with a pronoun, i.e. consider a version of the clause with a pronominal version of the Theme. If you can 'replace' the expression you're interested in with a pronoun, it serves as a single element in the clause; for example:

<u>Mice, elephants and humans</u> are some of the animals we know.
<u>They</u>   are some of the animals we know.

⟦<u>Doing twenty sit-ups a day</u>⟧ will flatten your tummy.
<u>It</u>   will flatten your tummy.

(2) Make the expression non-thematic, i.e. consider a version of the clause with a different thematic structure. For example:

<u>From house to house</u> I went my way : <u>I</u> went my way *from house to house*.

The alternation involves *from house to house* as a whole, not only say *from house*; that is, you can't normally get:[9]

<u>From house to house</u> I went my way : <u>From house</u> I went my way *to house*.

3.7 'Hypotactic' clause as Theme

A different kind of long Theme can be found if we extend the thematic principle beyond the clause to the 'clause complex' (the 'sentence' of the written language). This can be illustrated by comparing the following:

<u>Were you</u> lonely in Paris, ‖ <u>when I</u> was in the concentration camp?
<u>When I</u> was in the concentration camp, ‖ <u>were you</u> lonely in Paris?

The first example can be regarded as an unmarked ordering of clauses, where a 'main' clause is followed by a modifying clause. It will simply be analysed as shown above. In the second example, the *when* clause in its entirety can be regarded as functioning as an orienting context for the question *Were you lonely in Paris?* The *when* clause thus provides a marked Theme to which the second clause is Rheme (IFG: 56–57):

When I was in the concentration camp, ‖ were you lonely in Paris?
Theme.. Rheme...

At the same time, each individual clause has its own Theme-Rheme structure, so a double analysis is possible:

When   I   was in the concentration camp, ‖ were you lonely in Paris?
Text.   Top.   Interp. Top.
Theme.. Rheme.................................

Note that it is only 'hypotactic' (i.e. dependent, modifying) clauses which have the possibility of occurring in this initial position as a marked Theme of the clause complex. Non-finite clauses are one such type of hypotactic clause. Here are some examples of non-finite clauses functioning as marked Theme of a clause complex:

<u>To strengthen his knee</u>, he did the exercise routine twice daily.
<u>Blinking nervously</u>, he tried to think of something to say.

---

[9]As always in language, you have to treat analytical rules of thumb with care: note that you can have *from Athens to Madrid we flew with Olympic: From Athens we flew to Madrid with Olympic.*

4 Analysis practice

4.1 Phase I

4.1.1 Exercises

Examples are taken from M. Williams, *The Velveteen Rabbit.* Pall & Munk; P. Theroux, *The Great Railway Bazaar*; A.A. Milne, *The House at Pooh Corner.* E.P. Dutton & Co, 1950; W. Russell, *Educating Rita.*

Exercise 1 Identifying topical Theme (declaratives)   Follow the models provided and underline the Topical Theme in each clause.

> <u>He</u> was fat and bunchy.
> <u>I</u> am real ‖ <u>said</u> the little rabbit
> <u>The clock</u> was still saying five minutes to eleven...

1. He's out.
2. You're just in time for a little smackerel of something.
3. One mustn't complain.
4. That's a very good idea...   See Section 3.3.3(b)
5. Christopher Robin had spent the morning indoors...
6. The wind had dropped...
7. My mind's full of junk, isn't it?
8. This room does not need air.
9. A peaceful smile came over his face...
10. His argument just crumbled.

Exercise 2 Identifying marked topical Theme (declaratives)   Identify the Topical Theme and classify as unmarked or marked (see 2.1.1.) For example:

> <u>One summer evening</u> the Rabbit saw two strange beings creep out of the
> bracken.   M
> <u>By this time</u> they were getting near Eeyore's Gloomy Place...   M
> <u>I</u> shall have to go on a fast Thinking Walk by myself.   U
> (For practice in recognizing the Subject, see further Chapter 3, Section 4.1.1,
> Exercises 1 and 2)

1. Kanga's house was nearest...
2. For at least two hours the boy loved him...
3. Nobody sits out there at this time of year.
4. After a long munching noise, he said...
5. The Extract of Malt had gone.
6. For students they don't half come out with some rubbish.
7. The nearest house was Owl's...
8. To Owl's house he made his way.
9. For a little while he couldn't think of anything more.
10. Of its type it's quite interesting.

Exercise 3 Identifying textual Theme (declaratives)   Follow the models to identify textual and topical parts to Theme. Fill in the table below.

<u>So he</u> sang it again.
<u>And then we</u>'ll go out.
<u>Well, poor Eeyore</u> has nowhere to live.

1.   And Christopher Robin has a house...
2.   Anyway, this tutor came up to me...
3.   Because I care for you...
4.   Well any analogy will break down eventually.
5.   Afterwards, he had an idea.
6.   ...but one line is hardly an essay.
7.   If he'd been warned of the consequences ...
8.   ...but two thousand people had seen me...

	Theme		Rheme
	textual	**topical**	
	So	he	sang it again.
	And then	we	'll go out.
	Well,	poor Eeyore	has nowhere to live.
1.			
2.			
3.			
4.			
5.			
6.			
7.			
8.			

4.1.2 Texts for analysis

Identify the Themes in Text 1 and Text 2. (Boundaries between the clauses are indicated by ‖). Display the Themes in a table, discriminating between textual and topical components to the Themes and between marked and unmarked topical Themes.

Discuss and compare the method of development observed in each text (see Section 1.3).

Text 1 Descriptive report

The numbat is an unmistakeable slender marsupial with a pointed muzzle and short erect ears.‖ The body is reddish brown ‖ but the rump is much darker ‖ and has about six white bars across it.‖ The eye has a black stripe through it ‖ and the long bushy tail is yellowish. ‖ The toes are strongly clawed and very effective in digging out termites.‖ The tongue is extremely long, as in all mammalian ant or termite eaters.‖ Unlike most marsupials, the numbat is active during the day.‖ It shelters in hollow logs. ‖ It was once relatively common ‖ but now lives only in a small area of S.W. South Australia. ‖

(Adapted from *The Concise Encyclopedia of Australia* 2nd ed. Buderim, Queensland: Bateman, 1984, 459.)

Text 2 Explanation

After flash floods, desert streams from upland areas carry heavy loads of silt, sand and rock fragments. ‖ As they reach the flatter area of desert basins ‖ they slow down ‖ and their waters may soak quickly into the basin floor.‖ Then the streams drop their loads; ‖ first they drop the heaviest material – the stones, ‖ then [they drop] the sand ‖ and finally [they drop] the silt. ‖ Soon these short lived streams become choked by their own deposits ‖ and they spread their load in all directions.‖ After some time, fan or cone-shaped deposits of gravel, sand, silt and clay are formed around each valley or canyon outlet. ‖ These are called alluvial fans.‖

(Adapted from Sale, C., Wilson, G. and Friedman, B. 1980: *Our changing world Bk 1.* Melbourne: Longman Cheshire, 54.)

4.2 Phase II

4.2.1 Exercises

Exercise 1 Identifying interpersonal Theme (declaratives)   Follow the models to identify interpersonal and topical components to the Theme in each clause. Fill out the chart below.

<u>Maybe you</u> call them sparrows.
<u>Of course he</u> does.

1.   Perhaps he won't notice you, Piglet.
2.   Frank, it was fantastic.
3.   For God's sake, you had me worried.
4.   Honest to God I stood up...
5.   Sometimes I wonder...   See Section 3.3.2(a)

	Theme		Rheme
	interpersonal	topical	
	Maybe	you	call them sparrows.
	Of course	he	does.
1.			
2.			
3.			
4.			
5.			

Exercise 2 Identifying Theme (interrogatives)   Follow the models to identify interpersonal and topical components to the Theme in these interrogative clauses.

<u>Are you</u> sure?
<u>Don't you</u> know what Tiggers like?

1.   Can you hop on your hind legs?
2.   Aren't you clever?
3.   Were you a famous poet?
4.   Did I ever say that?
5.   Is that all?

	Theme		Rheme
	interpersonal	topical	
	Are	you	sure.
	Don't	you	know what Tiggers like.
1.			
2.			
3.			
4.			
5.			

Exercise 3 Identifying Theme (interrogatives)   Follow the models to identify interpersonal and topical components to Theme in wh- interrogative clauses.

<u>Where</u> shall we build it?   See Section 3.3.2(b)
<u>How</u> are you?

1.   What's the matter, Eeyore?
2.   Who lives there?
3.   What shall we do?
4.   Why are they at the station instead of in town?
5.   How old are you?

	Theme		Rheme
	interpersonal	topical	
	Wh...	...ere	shall we build it?
	H...	...ow	are you?
1.			
2.			
3.			
4.			
5.			

Exercise 4 Identifying Theme (imperatives) Follow the models to identify the Theme in imperative clauses.

<u>Look</u> at it.
<u>Take</u> your old bunny.
<u>Don't mention</u> it Pooh.

1. Come on.
2. Oh go away, Frank.
3. Don't be soft.
4. Listen to me.
5. Let's visit Kanga and Roo and Tigger.[10]

	Theme		Rheme
	interpersonal	topical	
		Look	at it.
		Take	your old bunny.
	Don't	mention	it Pooh.
1.			
2.			
3.			
4.			
5.			

Exercise 5 Identifying Theme, all metafunctions Follow the models to identify textual, interpersonal and topical stages to the Theme.

<u>Then perhaps</u> he'll say...   See Section 3.3.3(c)
<u>But darling, you</u> shouldn't have prepared dinner should you?

1. But sometimes I hate them.
2. Then why did it try to bite me?
3. But surely you can see the difference between Harold Robbins and the other two?
4. But don't you realize...?
5. In fact, Christopher Robin, it's Cold.   See Section 3.3.1(b)
6. We really should talk about you and Denny, my dear.

---

[10]Halliday (IGF: 87) treats *let's* as an anomalous form of the Subject; alternatively *let's* can be taken as Finite, since an explicit Subject is possible with *let's* as in *Let's <u>you and me</u> go*.

	Theme			Rheme
	textual	interpersonal	topical	
	Then	perhaps	he	'll say...
	But	darling,	you	shouldn't have prepared...
1.				
2.				
3.				
4.				
5.				
6.				

Exercise 6 Identifying Theme, all metafunctions   Identify – if present – textual and interpersonal Themes and classify topical Themes as marked or unmarked. Fill in the table below.

> ... <u>and here</u> it is as good as ever
> ... <u>when Pooh and Piglet</u> set out on their way half an hour later.
> ...<u>perhaps</u> I'll put a muffler round my neck...

1. And then we'll go out, Piglet...
2. So after breakfast they went round to see Piglet...
3. In criticism sentiment has no place.
4. ...because halfway through that book I couldn't go on reading it.
5. A crowd of us stuck together all week.
6. Frank, it was fantastic.
7. Well, look in my cupboard, Tigger dear...
8. And in a little while they felt much warmer...
9. ...and on the way they told him of the Awful Mistake they had made.
10. ...until suddenly a hundred miles above him a lark began to sing.

	Theme				Rheme
	textual	interpersonal	marked topical	unmarked topical	
	and		here		it is as good as ever
	when			Pooh and Piglet	set out on their...
		perhaps		I	'll put a muffler...
1.					
2.					
3.					
4.					
5.					
6.					
7.					
8.					
9.					
10.					

4.2.2 Texts for analysis

Text 1 Procedure

Paprika-Garlic Roast Chicken

1 medium whole frying chicken (2½–2¾ pounds)
1½ teaspoon garlic powder
1½ teaspoons paprika
3 tablespoons salad oil
salt and pepper

Preheat oven to 325°.

Remove giblets from inside chicken and save for chicken stew or soup. Wash chicken inside and outside. (Don't use soap!)

Rub chicken inside and out with garlic powder. Using a pastry brush or paper towel, coat chicken with oil and sprinkle with paprika to give a nice red tint. Salt and pepper lightly.

Place chicken in a deep oven pan, breast down, and cover tightly with aluminium foil. The juices will seep into the breast and keep the chicken moist.

Roast in oven for 40 minutes. At the end of this time, turn chicken breast up and cover again with foil. Return to oven for another 30 minutes. Then remove foil and continue roasting for 20–30 minutes more, or until chicken is fork tender and golden brown. Serve with Brown Rice or Bulgar Wheat.

(Cadwallader, S. 1974: *Cookup adventures for kids.* Boston: Houghton Mifflin.)

Text 2 Parent-child conversation   The first two clauses of this text have been analysed for you. Complete the Theme analysis for the rest of the text (M = mother, C = 4½ year-old boy)

C: <u>How</u> could birds die?

M: ... <u>like the one in the garden</u>, are you thinking of?
     Well, sometimes birds die just when they get very old, or maybe they got sick because they got some disease, or maybe a cat got it. Baby birds sometimes die when they fall out the nest, or, in the winter – if you were in a cold place – birds might die because they can't get enough food.

C: Yeah, but what happens if one bird falls out and then - and when it's just about at the ground it flies?

M: Yes, well if it's big enough to fly it'll be all right.
     And sometimes birds fall out the nest but they don't die...

Text 3 Exposition   The following text is analysed below. A rewritten version is then presented. Complete the analysis of the second version and compare their methods of development.

3a)

a   Although the United States participated heavily in World War I,

b   the nature of that participation was fundamentally different from what it became in World War II.

c   The earlier conflict was a one-ocean war for the Navy and a one-theatre war for the Army;

d   the latter was a two-ocean war for the Navy and one of five major theatres for the Army.

e   In both wars a vital responsibility of the Navy was escort-of-convoy and anti-submarine work,

f   but in the 1917–1918 conflict it never clashed with the enemy on the surface;

g   whilst between 1941 and 1945 it fought some twenty major and countless minor engagements with the Japanese Navy.

h   American soldiers who engaged in World War I were taken overseas in transports

i   and landed on docks or in protected harbours;

j   in World War II the art of amphibious warfare had to be revived and developed,

k   since assault troops were forced to fight their way ashore.

l   Airpower, in the earlier conflict, was still inchoate and almost negligible;

m   in the latter it was a determining factor.

n   In World War I the battleship still reigned queen of the sea,

o   as she had in changing forms, since the age of Drake.

p   and Battle Line fought with tactics inherited from the age of sail;

q   but in World War II the capital naval force was the air-craft carrier taskgroup,

r   for which completely new tactics had to be devised.

(Morrison, S.E. 1963: *The two ocean war*. Boston: Little Brown.)

	Theme			Rheme
	textual	marked topical	unmarked topical	
a	Although		the United States	participated heavily in World War I,
b			the nature of that participation	was fundamentally different from [[what it became in World War II.]]
c			The earlier conflict	was a one-ocean war for the Navy and a one-theatre war for the Army.
d			the latter	was a two-ocean war for the Navy and one of five major theatres for the Army.
e		In both wars		a vital responsibility of the Navy was escort-of-convoy and anti-submarine work.
f	but	in the 1917–1918 conflict		it never clashed with the enemy on the surface.
g	whilst	between 1941 and 1945		it fought some twenty major and countless minor engagements with the Japanese Navy.
h			American soldiers [[who engaged in World War I]]	were taken overseas in transports
i	and		"	landed on docks or in protected harbours;
j		in World War II		the art of amphibious warfare had to be revived and developed,
k	since		assault troops	were forced to fight their way ashore.
l			Airpower,	in the earlier conflict, was still inchoate and almost negligible;
m		in the latter		it was a determining factor.
n		In World War I		the battleship still reigned queen of the sea,
o	as		she	had in changing forms, since the age of Drake.
p	and		Battle Line	fought with tactics inherited from the age of sail;
q	but	in World War II		the capital naval force was the air-craft carrier taskgroup,
r	for which		for which[11]	completely new tactics had to be devised.

[11]Relative pronouns function as conflations of textual and topical Theme.

3b) A rewritten version

a   Although the United States participated heavily in World War I,

b   the nature of that participation was fundamentally different from what it became in World War II.

c   The earlier conflict was a one-ocean war for the Navy and a one-theatre war for the Army;

d   the latter was a two-ocean war for the Navy and one of five major theatres for the Army.

e   A vital responsibility of the Navy was escort-of-convoy and anti-submarine work in both wars,

f   but it never clashed with the enemy on the surface in the 1917–1918 conflict;

g   whilst it fought some twenty major and countless minor engagements with the Japanese Navy between 1941 and 1945.

h   American soldiers who engaged in World War I were taken overseas in transports

i   and landed on docks or in protected harbours;

j   the art of amphibious warfare had to be revived and developed in World War II,

k   since assault troops were forced to fight their way ashore.

l   Airpower was still inchoate and almost negligible in the earlier conflict;

m   it was a determining factor in the latter.

n   The battleship still reigned queen of the sea in World War I,

o   as she had in changing forms, since the age of Drake.

p   and Battle Line fought with tactics inherited from the age of sail;

q   but the capital naval force was the air-craft carrier taskgroup in World War II,

r   which completely new tactics had to be devised for.

Fill in the changes and compare the method of development (see Section 1.3) of 3a and 3b.

	Theme			Rheme
	textual	marked topical	unmarked topical	
a	Although		the United States	participated heavily in World War I,
b			the nature of that participation	was fundamentally different from ⟦what it became in World War II.⟧
c			The earlier conflict	was a one-ocean war for the Navy and a one-theatre war for the Army;
d				
e			A vital responsibility of the Navy	was escort-of-convoy and anti-submarine work in both wars,
f	but			
g				
h			American soldiers ⟦who engaged in World War I⟧	were taken overseas in transports
i	and		"	landed on docks or in protected harbours;
j			the art of amphibious warfare	had to be revived and developed in World War II,
k				
l				
m				
n				
o				
p				
q				
r	wh...		...ich	completely new tactics had to be devised for.

4.3 Phase III

4.3.1 Exercises

Exercise 1 Recognizing long Themes Follow the models to identify the long nominal groups realizing topical Theme. See Section 3.6(i).

The singers on the gate stopped suddenly.
The only person who was kind to him at all was the Skin Horse.

1. The Zoroastrian at the gate would not let me in...
2. The nature of that participation was fundamentally different...
3. The paint on the window frames had chipped...
4. The current interest in iconicity and related themes points to this issue as a palpitating one.
5. The history of American linguistics over the past 50 years is awash with acrimonious name-calling...

Exercise 2 Recognizing long Themes Follow the models to identify the group or phrase complex realising topical Theme. See Section 3.6(ii).

You and I make a good team, don't we?
Tehran, a boom town grafted onto a village, is a place of no antiquity...

1. Future historians, philologists, and lexicographers might find their labours lightened by being enabled to appeal to such a standard.
2. STC, with more than $200 million in annual sales, is only the seventh Korean enterprise to sell foreigners bonds that can be converted into shares.
3. Basilosaurus, an early whale, grew as long as 70 feet.
4. The bored, lazy and unruly are not the only kind of problem students that teachers have to tackle.
5. Matter, in all its forms, is endowed by the figurative genius of every language with the functions which pertain to intellect.
6. 'Fault', 'responsibility', and 'cause' are explicit references to causation.
7. Relative genericness, non-specificity, and emptiness is commonplace in noun phrases.
8. Mesoamerica, with its rich genetic and typological diversity, deserves attention...

Exercise 3 Recognizing long Themes Follow the models and underline the wh-embedded clause realizing topical Theme in the following. (See Section 3.6 (iii)):

What you have just said will be a great help to us...
What we want is a Trained Bloodhound.

1. What I've been thinking is this.
2. What people see on the screen is me.
3. What he did for a living was the best he could.
4. What you see is what you get.
5. What I am proposing about compounding is, rather conservatively, that there are a number of compounding rules.

Exercise 4 Recognizing long Themes Follow the model and underline the non-finite embedded clause Theme in the following (see Section 3.6(iv)).

Losing to such an inexperienced team gave the coach a real jolt.

1. Squeezing the spots may damage the skin permanently.
2. Rocking baby may help her to sleep.
3. To see him all by himself like that really upset them.

4. To have requested leave just now would have been a bit unreasonable.
5. Eating an occasional Mars bar won't do you any harm.

Exercise 5 'Empty' Subjects as Theme, predicated Theme Underline the topical Theme in the following examples, some of which are predicated Themes. (See Section 3.4).

> Actually, <u>it</u> is useful to know a bit about chemistry, here.
> <u>It was only yesterday</u> that he was told about it. (predicated Theme).

1. It is good to understand the natural order.
2. It astonished me that you should even suggest such a thing.
3. It is the parasitic mode of life that makes mites and ticks of economic importance.
4. It is probable that Mrs Kelly would have endured the strain of a divided family.
5. Naturally it is not the PSG's money that is at risk in this proposal.
6. It had occurred to him that this might be the result.
7. It is only recently that reasonable proposals for using and saving the wharves have come to the public's attention.
8. It excited him, too, that many men had already loved Daisy.
9. In fact, it was the husband and not the wife who got custody in that case.
10. It happened that we were there at the same time.

4.3.2 Texts for analysis

Text 1 Biographical recount Identify the Themes and consider the method of development of the text. Note the role of any marked Themes.

> George Bernard Shaw was born in Dublin, Ireland, on July 26, 1856. He attended four different schools but his real education came from a thorough grounding in music and painting, which he obtained at home. In 1871, he was apprenticed to a Dublin estate agent, and later he worked as a cashier. In 1876, Shaw joined his mother and sister in London, where he spent the next nine years in unrecognized struggle and genteel poverty.
>
> From 1885 to 1898, he wrote for newspapers and magazines as critic of art, literature, music and drama. But his main interest at this time was political propaganda, and, in 1884, he joined the Fabian Society. From 1893 to 1939, the most active period of his career, Shaw wrote 47 plays. By 1915, his international fame was firmly established and productions of *Candida, Man and Superman, Arms and the Man, The Devil's Disciple*, were being played in many countries of the world, from Britain to Japan. In 1925, the playwright was awarded the Nobel Prize for Literature. Between the ages of fifty-seven and sixty-seven, Shaw wrote such dramas as *Heartbreak House, Back to Methuselah, Androcles and the Lion, St. Joan*. During his lifetime he was besieged by offers to film his plays, but he accepted only a few, the most notable being *Pygmalion*, which was adapted (after his death) as the basis for the musical *My Fair Lady*. He died at the age of ninety-four at Ayot St. Lawrence, England, on November 2, 1950.

Text 2 Topographic procedure Identify the Themes and consider the text's method of development.

> Singapore's city centre straddles the Singapore River and runs parallel to the waterfront along Raffles Quay, Shenton Way, Robinson Rd and Cecil St. The

Singapore River was once one of the most picturesque areas of Singapore with old shops and houses along the river and soaring office buildings right behind them.

Sadly, it doesn't look like the old places will be around much longer. All the bustling activity along this stretch of river – the loading and unloading of sampans and bumboats – has ceased. The cranes are gone and the yelling, sweating labourers, too. All boats have been kicked out of the area and relocated to the Pasir Panjang wharves away from the city centre. You can still sit in the hawkers' centres by the river, but rather than watch all the activity you can bet on which building will be next under the wrecking ball.

On the Empress Place side of the river a statue of Sir Stamford Raffles stands imperiously by the water. It's in the approximate place where he first set foot on Singapore island. There is a second statue of Raffles in front of the clock tower by Empress Place. Nearby is the Supreme Court and City Hall, across from which is the open green of the Padang, site for cricket, hockey, football and rugby matches. There are also memorials to civilians who died as a result of the Japanese occupation and to Lim Bo Seng, a resistance leader killed by the Japanese.

If you continue up Coleman St from the Padang, you pass the Armenian Church and come to Fort Canning Hill, a good viewpoint over Singapore. Once known as 'Forbidden Hill', the hill is now topped by the old Christian cemetery which has many gravestones with their poignant tales of hopeful settlers who died young. There too is the tomb of Sultan Iskander Shah, the last ruler of the ancient kingdom of Singapura. At the mouth of the river, or at least what used to be the mouth before the most recent bout of land reclamation, stands Singapore's symbol, the Merlion.

Change Alley, Singapore's most famous place for bargains, has survived or rather adapted to modernization. It still cuts through from Collyer Quay to Raffles Place, but has become a pedestrian bridge and is known as 'Aerial Change Alley'. It's still lined with shops and money-changers although now it's air-conditioned! The older alley runs below.

Further along the waterfront you'll find large office blocks, airline offices and more shops. Here too is the popular Telok Ayer Transit Food Centre by the waterfront. Singapore's disappearing Chinatown is inland from this modern city centre.

(T. Wheeler et al. 1991: Malaysia, Singapore and Brunei:
Lonely Planet travel survival kit. Hawthorn, Vic: Lonely Planet Publications.)

Text 3 Advertisement

Be seen in all the right places.

From New York to Los Angeles to Atlanta to Dallas/Ft. Worth, the Delta system flies to all the top business centres in America. That's over 4200 flights a day to more than 260 cities around the U.S. and around the world. So next time business takes you to the States, book Delta. We'll make sure you're seen in all the right places. At all the right times.

Delta Air Lines.

We love to fly and it shows.

Text 4 Description within narrative   Identify the Themes and consider how they have been used to organize the description. Note any marked Themes.

The trail of the meat

The land was cold and white and savage. Across it there ran a thread of frozen waterway, with dark spruce forest looming on either side. Along this waterway toiled a string of wolfish dogs, hauling a sled of birch-bark. On the sled, along with the camp-outfit, was lashed a long and narrow oblong box. In front of the dogs, on wide snowshoes, toiled a man. Behind the sled came a second man. On the sled in the box lay a third man, whose life was at an end – a man whom the Wild had beaten down and conquered. The bodies of the live men were covered with soft fur and leather. Their faces were blurred and shapeless under a coating of crystals from their frozen breath. All around them was a silence which seemed to press upon them as water does upon a diver.

(J. London: *White Fang*, Abridged edition N. Farr, Pendulum Press 1977.)

Text 5 Casual conversation

B: Do you think it's worth going to see The Godfather?
C: Yes, [it's worth going to see] The Godfather Two, yes.
B: Darling, Murder on the Orient Express is now at the ABC Shaftesbury Avenue. [It's] on with The Godfather.
A: [It would] be a pretty good double bill, that, actually. We'd be out of the house all night, wouldn't we?
B: But you can't see both of them, can you?
A: Well, if it's the same price, ...
B: I mean there are two screens at the ABC Shaftesbury Avenue.
C: Oh sorry, yes, no no no no you're right. Yes, yes they are...
B: Les Enfants du Paradis, what about that?
D: Oh, that's nice.
C: That's a real classic. I do want to see that cos I never saw it ever, even when I was a student. [:m] The Pasolini Arabian Nights apparently[12] are rather fun.
B: Erotic Inferno and Hot Acts of Love, I don't think they're quite down our street.
A: That must be in the Tottenham Court Road ...
B: They love sex and lusty laughs. What rubbish! [i.e. What rubbish it is!]
A: What is that lovely cinema in Victoria? Have you ever been to it, the Biograph?

(R. Quirk and J. Svartvik (Eds) 1980: A corpus of English conversation.
Lund: CWK Gleerup.)

Text 6 Exposition

...The claims for the educational value of Show and Tell and Morning News sessions are at best rather questionable, however, for several reasons. In the first place, the commitment to promoting oral language as something independent of other areas of language development is itself very dubious. The notion of language development must involve development both in speech and in literacy, and no very useful distinction can be drawn between the two. They are necessarily very closely related.

Furthermore, even the children who are successful in Showing and Telling or Newsgiving will benefit from being given opportunities to use spoken language

---

[12]Note that the modal Adjunct *apparently* is not an interpersonal Theme here, since it does not precede the topical Theme.

in other ways in schools. The particular activity and genre are not uniquely suitable for the development of oral language abilities.

On the contrary, since the particular genre used at any time is itself dependent upon the activity concerned, it should be clear that the need is to generate a range of differing activities in schools, to enable children to master the associated range of genre types. Regrettably, Morning News and Show and Tell sessions frequently feature as the only concessions made to the development of oral language in daily school programs. Where this is the case, the language program is impoverished indeed. In a good language program children move easily through many learning activities of a kind designed to stimulate and extend abilities to speak, to read and to write....

(Christie, F. 1985 *Language education*. Geelong: Deakin University Press 20–21.)

Text 7 Taxonomizing report   Analyse Theme in the following text and consider whether or not the pattern of selections supports the structure of the report. This text is taken from a set of ESP materials, *English in Electrical Engineering and Electronics* (Glendinning, 1980), published by Oxford University Press as part of its 'English in focus' series. Stuart Holloway, a professional ESL teacher and writer of technical textbooks, who drew this text to our attention, has commented that students find it hard to understand and that it appears to have been written by someone who was an 'outsider' as far as electrical engineering and electronics were concerned.

Conductors, Insulators and Semiconductors
If we connect a battery across a body, there is a movement of free electrons towards the positive end. This movement of electrons is an electric current. All materials can be classified into three groups according to how readily they permit an electric current to flow. These are: conductors, insulators and semiconductors.

In the first category are substances which provide an easy path for an electric current. All metals are conductors, however some metals do not conduct well. Manganin, for example, is a poor conductor. Copper is a good conductor, therefore it is widely used for cables. A non-metal which conducts well is carbon. Salt water is an example of a liquid conductor.

A material which does not easily release electrons is called an insulator. Rubber, nylon, porcelain are all insulators. There are no perfect insulators. All insulators will allow some flow of electrons, however this can usually be ignored because the flow they permit is so small.

Semiconductors are midway between conductors and insulators. Under certain conditions they allow a current to flow easily but under others they behave as insulators. Germanium and silicon are semiconductors. Mixtures of certain metallic oxides also act as semiconductors. These are known as thermistors. The resistance of thermistors falls rapidly as their temperature rises. They are therefore used in temperature-sensing devices.

(Glendinning, E. H. 1980 *English in Electrical Engineering and Electronics*. London: Oxford University Press (English in Focus).)

5 Review and contextualization

5.1 Defining Theme

The system of THEME is a textual resource at clause rank for presenting the clause as a message (piece of text) in the unfolding text. It organizes the clause into two parts by specifying a point of departure for the addressee in his/her interpretation of the clause – for example:

[1] Stepping beyond cognitive science's new theory of 'connectionism', Gee formulates a dynamic social theory of mind and meaning. [2] **With penetrating analyses**, he illustrates how such psychological entities such as memories, beliefs, values, and meanings are not formed in isolation but in a social or cultural context that is inherently ideological or political....

The second clause in this text opens with the phrase *with penetrating analyses*. This phrase provides a local environment or context for interpreting the rest of the clause; that is, Gee's illustrations are to be read against the thematic background of his analytical method. The textual organization of this clause is:

With penetrating analyses	he illustrates how such psychological entitites such as memories, beliefs, values, and meanings are not formed in isolation but in a social or cultural context that is inherently ideological or political.
Theme	Rheme

The point of departure of the clause as message, its local environment – what is called Theme – is realized by initial position in the clause, and is followed by the non-Theme, the Rheme. The Rheme provides the information to be processed within the local environment specified by the Theme.

5.2 *The location of* THEME *within the grammatical resources of English*

If we pull back and take in the whole grammatical system of English, we can see that THEME is a resource for organizing information located at the intersection of the textual metafunction and the clause (see Fig. 2.3).

In this overall system, THEME is systematically related to other such subsystems – other grammatical resources for constructing meaning in wordings. All these subsystems are complementary, each providing a particular angle on the overall construction of meaning. As we noted above, THEME provides the resources for setting up a local environment (context) for the clause as a piece of text or message at a particular place in a text that is being developed. (This local environment can be seen as the point of departure for the process of interpreting the meanings presented in the clause.) The textual system of INFORMATION is complementary to THEME: in the default case, the Theme of the clause falls within the Given assigned by INFORMATION and the New assigned by that system falls within the Rheme (see IFG, Chapter 8). Within the clause, THEME is related to CONJUNCTION, a system providing the resources for making explicit the rhetorical relation between the

— metafunctional spectrum —

rank: constituency potential

		ideational	interpersonal	textual
clause		TRANSITIVITY Resource for construing experience of a quantum of change in the flow of events as a process configuration [process + participants + circumstances]	MOOD Resource for enacting exchanges (with role adoption by speaker and assignment to addressee) and assessments, comments (including MODALITY, POLARITY, MODAL ASSESSMENT)	THEME Resource for presenting [creating as information] interpersonal & textual meanings as a message [quantum of information] in text unfolding in context, setting up local environment for interpreting the message. VOICE Resource for giving one participant in a process configuration the status of unmarked Theme. CONJUNCTION Resource for making explicit a message's rhetorical relation to preceding text.
phrase/group	prep. phrase	MINOR TRANSITIVITY	MINOR MOOD	MINOR THEME
	adverbial	CIRCUMSTANCE TYPE, MODIFICATION (INTENSIFICATION)	COMMENT TYPE	CONJUNCTION TYPE
	nominal	THING TYPE, MODIFICATION (EPITHESIS, CLASSIFICATION, QUALIFICATION)	PERSON, ATTITUDE	DETERMINATION
	verbal	EVENT TYPE, TENSE	MODALITY	
word		DENOTATION (including lexical taxonomies); COMPOUNDING, DERIVATION	CONNOTATION	LEXICAL COHESION
morpheme				

information unit ↗ tone group			KEY Resource for enacting meanings between 'polarity known' and 'polarity not known' as further elaborations of MOOD.	INFORMATION Resource for differentiating between given and new information.

Figure 2.3 Location of the THEME system

clause and preceding text. It is also related to VOICE, a system which allows a choice as to which participant within the TRANSITIVITY structure will be assigned the status of unmarked Theme.

5.3 Theme and Metafunction

There are three possible components to the Theme of a clause: textual, interpersonal and topical (i.e. ideational). As a general principle, every major, finite clause in English will select an ideational function (typically participant or circumstance) as topical Theme. The first such element in the clause realizes the topical theme while any preceding textual or interpersonal elements constitute textual and interpersonal Themes. For example:

Well,	naturally,	most people	don't discuss these things in public
Textual	Interpersonal	Topical	
Theme..		Rheme..	

5.4 Theme and Mood

The nature of the unmarked choice of theme depends on the interpersonal status of the clause – is it dependent or independent, and, if independent, which type of MOOD selection characterizes it? The various unmarked Theme types are shown in Table 2.5.

Table 2.5 Unmarked Theme types

MOOD TYPE:	Theme		Rheme
	interpersonal	topical (ideational)	
declarative		Subject *You*	*woke up late today.*
interrogative: yes/no	Finite *Did*	Subject *you*	*wake up late today?*
interrogative: wh-	Wh– *Wh...* *Wh...*	Wh† *...o* *...y*	 *woke up late today?* *did you wake up late today?*
imperative	(Finite) *(Do/ Don't)*	Predicator *wake up*	*late today!*

†Wh-element in interrogative clauses are both interpersonal and topical Theme.

Note that exclamative clauses are like wh-interrogatives in that the Wh element is thematic:

<u>What an impetuous boy</u> he is!

In addition, there are further types of imperative clause that are also thematically distinct (e.g. with Theme underlined, <u>let's</u> wake up late today!, <u>lemme</u> wakeup late today!).

Further reading

Fries, Peter H. 1981: On the status of theme in English: arguments from discourse. *Forum Linguisticum* 6(1): 1-38. Reprinted in J. S. Petöfi and E. Sözer (eds) 1983, *Micro and Macro Connexity of Discourse.* Hamburg: Buske (Papers in Text Linguistics 45) 116–52.

────── 1995: Patterns of information in initial position in English. In P.H. Fries and M. Gregory (eds), *Discourse in society: functional perspectives.* Norwood, N.J.: Ablex (Meaning and choice in language: studies for Michael Halliday) 47–66.

Ghadessy, Mohsen (ed.) 1995: *Thematic development in English texts.* London: Pinter (Open Linguistics Series).

Halliday, M.A.K. 1985: It's a fixed word order language is English. *International Review of Applied Linguistics* 67–68: 91–116.

Hasan, Ruqaiya and Fries, Peter H. (eds) 1995: *On Subject and Theme: a discourse functional perspective.* Amsterdam: Benjamins. (*Current Issues in Linguistic Theory* 118).

Martin, J.R. 1992: *English text: system and structure.* Amsterdam: Benjamins, Chapter 6: Texture.

────── 1992: Theme, method of development and existentiality – the price of reply. *Occasional Papers in Systemic Linguistics* 6, 147–84.

────── 1993: Life as a noun. In Halliday, M.A.K. and Martin, J.R., *Writing science,* London: Falmer Press: 221–67.

Matthiessen, Christian 1992: Interpreting the textual metafunction. In M. Davies and L. Ravelli (eds), *New advances in systemic linguistics,* London: Pinter: 37–81.

────── 1995a: *Lexicogrammatical cartography: English systems.* Tokyo: International Language Sciences Publishers. Chapter 6 in particular – relationship to VOICE: Section 6.3.2; textual resources: Section 2.3.6.

────── 1995b: THEME as a resource in ideational 'knowledge' construction. In Ghadessy (ed), *Thematic development in English texts,* London: Pinter (Open Linguistic Series) 20–54.

3

Mood
clause as exchange

1 Orientation

1.1 Reading Guide to IFG

> IFG Chapter 4 (Clause as exchange)
>   Section 8.7, 8.8, 8.9 (systems of TONE and KEY)
>   Section 10.4 (Interpersonal metaphors of MOOD and MODALITY)

1.2 Characterization of MOOD

The system of MOOD belongs to the interpersonal metafunction of the language and is the grammatical resource for realizing an interactive move in dialogue. For example, each of the following alternatives has a different interactional status and each embodies an alternative MOOD choice:

Example	*Mood*
The spy came in from the cold.	declarative
Did the spy come in from the cold?	interrogative:yes/no
Who came in from the cold? Where did the spy come from?	interrogative:wh-
Come in from the cold!	imperative

If we look at each of these as a possible move in a dialogue, we can see that one difference between them lies in the role the speaker takes up – the speaker may be giving something to the addressee or demanding something of him/her. Moreover, the 'something' here, the 'commodity' being traded (to use Halliday's metaphor), will be either information or goods and services. While goods and services exist independently of language (and can be exchanged without accompanying language),

Table 3.1 SPEECH FUNCTION choices and MOOD realizations

	goods and services	**information**
giving	OFFER ↘ (various)	STATEMENT ↘ declarative *He will help me.*
demanding	COMMAND ↘ imperative *Help me!*	QUESTION ↘ interrogative wh- Who will help me? yes/no Will he help me?
	proposal	*proposition*

information is constituted in language and has no existence outside the symbolic exchange.

The key to a **semantic** understanding of dialogue, then, is Halliday's metaphor of (symbolic) exchange among the persons taking part, which gives us the two notions of (i) the role taken on by an interactant in the exchange and (ii) the nature of the commodity being exchanged – goods and services versus information. These are set out in Table 3.1. As you can see from the table, (i) and (ii) combine to define the traditional speech functional categories of statement, question, offer and command. Statements and questions involve exchanges of information and are called **propositions** while offers and commands are exchanges of goods and services called **proposals**. These semantic categories are **realized** by grammatical MOOD options.

In Table 3.1 the arrow represents the realizational move from semantic category (statement, question, command, offer) to grammatical one (declarative, interrogative, imperative). The grammatical realizations shown are **congruent** ones. Alternatively of course, the speech functional categories may be realized by means of interpersonal **metaphors**, as when a command 'Get me another beer!' is realized metaphorically by an interrogative clause – *Would you get me another beer?* – instead of congruently by an imperative one – *Get me another beer!* Such interpersonal metaphors expand the speech functional options, for example in the area of politeness. (See 2.5.1 below and IFG Section 10.4 for a discussion of interpersonal metaphor.)

So far we have been looking at single clause examples, but to understand interpersonal grammar it is important to focus on its role in realizing dialogue, which is essentially an interactive, collaborative process. To explore the role of the MOOD system further, then, let us look more closely at a minimal example of dialogue.

In the following dialogic exchange (extracted from Svartvik and Quirk, *A corpus of English conversation [CEC]*, p. 623), A demands information and B gives on demand:

A: What the hell is structuralism?
B: It's a form of analysis, dear.

The most central aspect of this passage of dialogue is that it is acted out as an exchange between A and B. The example above is, semantically, a demand for

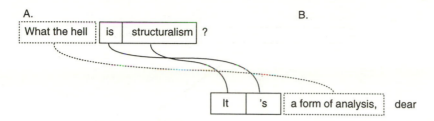

Fig. 3.1   Dialogic exchange

information (question) followed by a gift of information (statement), realized grammatically as 'interrogative: wh-' and 'declarative', respectively.[1] We can bring out the interactive nature and the implications for the interpersonal organization of the clause diagrammatically, as in Fig. 3.1.

Structurally, the exchange revolves around two parts: *is structuralism? – It is* and *What the hell – a form of analysis*. The first is the Mood element, here the combination of Subject and the Finite verb, while the other is the Residue element (which may involve one or more elements). You can see that the order of the Subject and Finite elements within the Mood element is interpersonally significant. In this exchange, it switches from Mood (Finite^Subject), indicating that the clause is interrogative, to Mood (Subject^Finite), indicating that the clause is declarative:

A: What the hell   is   structuralism?
.....Residue..........   ....Mood...............
                         Finite   Subject

B: It   's   a form of analysis, dear
......Mood....   ....Residue...............
Subject   Finite

The example above also illustrates other interpersonal choices. For example, B chooses to respond *it's a form of analysis, dear* rather than *it's a form of analysis*, thus naming the addressee with a **Vocative** embodying an interpersonal attitude, an endearment (*dear*).

Some further examples of exchanges revolving around the Mood element are given in Fig. 3.2.

In each example in Fig. 3.2, the arrow connects the Mood element of A's initiating declarative with the Mood element of B's response. You can also see that the part of a responding clause which is continuous with the clause it is a response to can be 'left out'. (More technically the Residue is presumed through ellipsis.) This use of ellipsis in responses effectively foregrounds the Mood element, the part of the clause embodying its dialogic contribution.

---

[1]Textually, the pattern is as follows (Theme underlined, focus of **New** in bold): <u>*What the hell*</u> is **structuralism** – <u>*It's*</u> **a form of analysis**, my dear. This is typical of an exchange revolving around a Wh-element: in the interrogative clause, the Theme is its information-demanding status in the exchange, plus the point of demand; the **New** is the element whose characterization is being sought, *structuralism*. In the declarative clause, the Theme is information-giving status in the exchange, plus the element whose characterization is being given, and the **New** is the characterization.

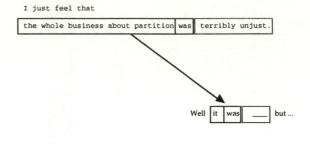

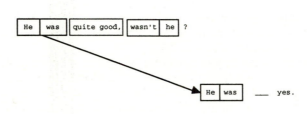

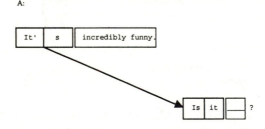

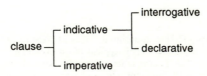

Fig. 3.2 Examples of dialogue

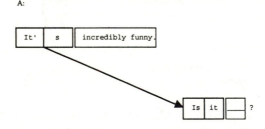

Fig. 3.3 Basic MOOD options

2 Survey of options

In this section, the different options within MOOD will be outlined, together with the clause structures that realize them. In addition a number of related interpersonal systems such as POLARITY, MODALITY, and VOCATION will be mentioned.

2.1 Basic MOOD types

The basic distinction within the grammatical system of MOOD is between imperative and indicative mood types, with the indicative type having the further distinction between declarative and interrogative types. These choices can be shown in the form of a simple 'system network' as shown in Fig. 3.3. The network is read from left to right as a series of options leading to further options.

Each of the three mood types - interrogative, declarative and imperative - can be further subclassified. For example, interrogatives may be of the yes/no type *(Was it cool?)* or the wh- type *(What was cool?)*, declaratives may be exclamative *(How cool it was!)* or non-exclamative *(It was cool)*, and there are various kinds of imperatives *(Stay cool; Let me stay cool; Let's be cool)*.

Each mood category is realized in English by a particular interpersonal structure, with one part of the structure being fundamental in discriminating the different types.

2.2 Overall interpersonal organization of the clause

Halliday assigns the clause an interpersonal function structure in two steps. First he identifies an overall organization of the clause into Mood[2] + Residue (+ Moodtag). See Fig. 3.4.

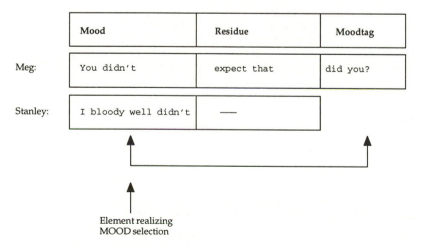

	Mood	Residue	Moodtag
Meg:	You didn't	expect that	did you?
Stanley:	I bloody well didn't	——	

Element realizing
MOOD selection

Fig. 3.4 Overall interpersonal structure

[2]Note that the term 'mood' is used by Halliday both for the interpersonal system in the grammar realizing speech function – written as MOOD – and for the interpersonal element of clause structure consisting of Subject and Finite – written as Mood.

One of the reasons for recognizing this kind of interpersonal clause structure is that, if a speaker wants to get a verbal response to a declarative or imperative clause, s/he can add a tag (Moodtag) that picks up only part of the clause – viz. the Mood element, but not the Residue. That is, if the Moodtag is present, it picks up the Mood element of the clause: *you didn't expect that, did you; they shoot* horses, *don't they*. Another reason for recognizing Mood and Residue as the major functions of the clause, when viewed interpersonally, is that the different mood categories (declarative, interrogative, etc.) are realized in English by the Mood element, while the Residue may in part or whole be involved in ellipsis in responding moves. To explore this further requires taking the second step in analysis, which is to identify the functional elements of the Mood, Residue and Moodtag.

2.2.1 Structure of the Mood element

The **Mood** element makes the clause 'negotiable' and consists of **Finite**, **Subject** and (sometimes) **modal Adjunct**(s). The Finite makes a clause negotiable by coding it as positive or negative and by grounding it, either in terms of time (*it is/it isn't: it was/it wasn't: it will/it won't*) or in terms of modality (*it may/it will/it must,* etc.) The Subject is the element in terms of which the clause can be negotiated. (See further 2.2.1.2 below.) Modal Adjuncts add meanings related to speaker judgement or to the positive/negative aspect of the Finite. Table 3.2 outlines the class of unit which typically realizes the functions within the Mood element.

Table 3.2 Functions within the Mood element

function	class of unit	example	IFG
(i) Finite	finite verb	*has*	p. 75
(ii) Subject	(typically) nominal group	*the girl*	p. 76
(iii) modal Adjunct	adverbial group	*already; unfortunately*	p. 81–3

For example:

Unfortunately	the girl	has	already	done it
Mood				Residue
modal Adjunct (comment)	Subject	Finite	modal Adjunct (mood)	

To probe for the Subject role, add a Moodtag. In the tag the Subject will be repeated as a pronoun, as in *The girl has already done it, hasn't she?* In a similar way, the Finite can be identified as the verb which (re-)appears in the Moodtag, as in *The girl has already done it, hasn't she?*

As shown in Table 3.2, there are two kinds of modal Adjunct: the mood Adjunct and the comment Adjunct. The mood Adjunct construes meanings most closely related to those of the Finite, while comment Adjuncts provide an attitude towards, or comment upon, the exchange itself or the information being exchanged.[3]

It is the structure of the Mood element which distinguishes the principal mood types (of declarative, interrogative, imperative), as shown in Table 3.3.

Table 3.3 Relation of MOOD selection to Mood structure

MOOD selection	Mood element	Example (Mood in bold)	
indicative declarative	present		
non-exclam.	**Subject^Finite**		**they^will** build the house.
exclamative	**Wh^Subject^Finite**	*how quickly^*	**they^will** build the house!
interrogative yes/no	**Finite^Subject**		**will^they** build the house?
wh-	**Wh^Finite^Subject[4]**	*what^*	**will^they** build?
imperative	------	------	build the house!

2.2.1.1 POLARITY and MODALITY

The Mood element of the clause is also where the interpersonal resources of POLAR-ITY (positive/negative) and MODALITY (probability etc.) are realized in English. These meanings can be expressed either as a feature of the Finite or as a separate mood Adjunct (see IFG: 82–3):

	Finite	mood Adjunct
polarity	*hasn't*	*not* [salient][5]
modality	*may*	*perhaps*

For instance:

he	may	be at home	:	he	is	perhaps	at home
..Mood....		...Residue....		..........Mood........			Residue
Su	Fi			Su	Fi	Adjunct	

(Note also the fusions of negative polarity and modality – as Finite: *won't, can't,* etc.; and as Adjunct: *rarely, seldom.*

---

[3]The first edition of Halliday (Arnold, 1985) treated comment Adjuncts as outside Mood-Residue structure, because they do not necessarily form part of the proposition being negotiated.
[4]Unless Wh = Subject, as **Who will build the house?**
[5]In addition, *not* may also occur as a non-salient variant of *n't*, in which case it is just part of the Finite: see IFG: 88.

Table 3.4 Kinds of modality

Kind of modality	Finite: modal	mood Adjuncts
(modalization) **probability**	may,[6] might, can, could; will, would; should; must	probably, possibly, certainly, perhaps, maybe
usuality	may, might, can, could; will, would; should; must	usually, sometimes, always, never, ever, seldom, rarely
(modulation) **obligation**	may, might, can, could; should; must[7]	definitely, absolutely, possibly, at all costs, by all means

readiness:
    inclination
    ability
	may, might, can, could;
	will, would; must; shall
	can, could[8]
		willingly, readily, gladly,
		certainly, easily

There are four main kinds of modality: **probability**, **usuality**, **obligation** and **readiness**. Halliday refers to probability and usuality together as **modalization**, which he associates with propositions (statements and questions); he refers to obligation and readiness as **modulation**, which is associated with proposals (offers and commands). See Table 3.4 and IFG sections 4.5 and 10.4.

2.2.1.2 The interpretation of Subject as an interpersonal function

Halliday interprets **Subject** as an **interpersonal function**, not as a textual or ideational one. He approaches it from **dialogue** in the first instance rather than just from monologue. Halliday's notion of 'modal responsibility' as the characterization of Subject may take a while to come to grips with; but it is very crucial to an understanding to the category of Subject in English. You can see it most clearly in clauses that express proposals – imperative clauses and indicative clauses with a modal auxiliary indicating obligation or readiness (modulated indicative clauses); for example:

proposal in the form of an imperative 'you do': (implicit) Subject *you*:

Oh **don't** (you) say that!
Mother, (you) take this hateful woman away.
Don't (you) touch me!
(you) be quick, will you?

proposal in the form of a modulated indicative clause: Subject in bold:

You mustn't mind what a sick person says.
You should go to bed.
You can go to sleep.
You really must allow me.

---

[6]Normally *may* in declarative, *can* in interrogative.
[7]In some dialects *shall* may be an option: cf. *thou shalt not kill.*
[8]Note that unlike the other modals, for ability, *could* is the past tense of *can*.

Could **you** lend me a hand?
Would **you** take me to the Strand?

Shall **I** pour you another glass?
Can **I** get you anything from the store?
Can **we** give you a ride home?

Here the Subject is responsible for the success of the proposal – it has to comply, etc. But you can also get a sense of Subject as the modally responsible element in propositions – indicative clauses negotiating information – when you consider the dialogic potential embodied in the combination of Subject and Finite (see also the example in IFG: 78):

MEG:	**The two gentlemen had** the last of the fry this morning.
PETEY:	Oh, **did they**?
PETEY:	**You slept** like a log last night.
MEG:	**Did I**?
MEG:	**I was** the belle of the ball.
PETEY:	**Were you**?
MEG:	Oh yes, they all said **I was**.
PETEY:	I bet **you were**, too.
MEG:	Oh, it's true. **I was**.
	I know **I was**.
MEG:	Well, I bet **you don't** know what it is.
STANLEY:	Oh yes **I do**.
STANLEY:	**They've** got a wheelbarrow in that van.
MEG:	**They haven't**.
STANLEY:	Oh yes **they have**.
MEG:	You're a liar.
STANLEY:	A big wheelbarrow. And when the van stops they wheel it out,
	and they wheel it up the garden path, and then **they knock** at the front door.
MEG:	**They don't**.
STANLEY:	**They're** looking for someone.
MEG:	**They're not**.

This example indicates that the Subject is also modally responsible in an indicative clause realizing a proposition. In propositions we might characterize the meaning of Subject in terms of that element of meaning which the speaker assesses to be most at risk – most likely to be a candidate for the listener rejecting the proposition. Thus characterized, the Subject is a kind of variable and the Residue a constant. Extended to proposals, this interpretation would imply that proposals are most at risk in terms of who is responsible for carrying them through, rather than whether they should be done in the first place.

In contrast to Halliday's dialogic approach to Subject, most recent linguistic work has tried to interpret it in textual terms as a grammaticalization of 'topic' in a monologic environment. But, as you have seen, (topical) Theme and Subject are only conflated in the unmarked case (in declarative clauses). Furthermore, the interpretation of Subject as a grammaticalization of 'topic' entirely fails to account for its contribution to Mood together with Finite and facts that follow from that, such as the following.

(i) As already implied, modulations (obligations and inclinations) are oriented towards the Subject of the clause, not towards any other elements. Thus in *you shouldn't say that word*, 'you' (Subject) rather than 'that word' (Complement) is vested with the obligation.

(ii) When a clause is negative, the negation normally starts with Finite and affects the whole of Residue, but Subject is not negated: it is the element with respect to which something is affirmed or denied, etc. – *he* – *has bought something for you/hasn't bought anything for you.*

2.2.2 Structure of the Residue

The Residue consists of **Predicator**, sometimes also of **Complement**(s), and sometimes also of **Adjunct**(s) (see Table 3.5).[9]

Table 3.5 Residue functions

	function	class of unit	example	IFG
(i)	Predicator	non-finite (part of) verbal group	*been given*	p. 79
(ii)	Complement(s)	(typically) nominal group	*my aunt*	p. 80
(iii)	Adjunct(s) with ideational role of circumstance	(typically) adverbial group/ prepositional phrase	*out of pity*	p. 80

For example:

These flowers have just	been given	my aunt	out of pity
	Predicator	Complement	Adjunct
Mood	Residue		

Whereas the Finite specifies the domain of arguability as through time or modality, the Predicator may specify features of temporality or modality (or other

---

[9]Traditionally, Complement was called Object (direct and indirect Object); but Complement also includes the 'predicative complement' of traditional grammar (as in *Cary Grant was* **a male war bride**). The term 'Complement' is preferable to 'Object' since it indicates the complementarity with Subject while 'object' suggests some kind of inappropriate ideational interpretation such as 'object of the action, acted upon'. Adjunct was called Adverbial, but the strict association with the verb is misleading, so the term Adjunct is preferable. Note the distinction between the term Predicator used in IFG and the traditional term Predicate. The Predicator is just those verbal elements of the clause that do not serve as Finite, whereas the 'Predicate' extends to cover Complements and Adjuncts as well (the Verb Phrase, VP, of many modern formal grammars). Thus in *these flowers have just given my aunt*, the Predicator is *been given*, whereas the Predicate would be *have just been given my aunt*. The Predicate is not a functionally motivated category in the description of English; it derives from an orientation towards logic in traditional grammar.

domains) that are related to whatever specification is made in the Finite. For example:

She	was	going to respond
Subject	Finite	Predicator

Here the primary tense in the Finite establishes arguability in terms of past (*was*) in relation to 'now', while the secondary tense in the Predicator specifies future (*going to*) in relation to that past.

The difference between Complements and Adjuncts is that Complements are potential Subjects, whereas Adjuncts are not. Thus alongside *she gave my aunt these flowers out of pity*, we have *my aunt was given these flowers (by her) out of pity* and *these flowers were given my aunt (by her) out of pity*, but not *out of pity was given these flowers my aunt*.

2.2.3 Wh: an itinerant function

One particular interpersonal clause function is sometimes found in Mood and sometimes in Residue. This is the Wh element, which always combines or 'conflates' with another function. If it conflates with the Subject, it becomes part of the Mood element, if it conflates with a Complement or Adjunct it becomes part of the Residue. For example:

Who	has	seen	the new Schwarzenegger movie?
..........Mood	....	............Residue	....
Wh/Subject	Finite	Predictor	Complement...

When	did	you	see	it?
Residue..	...Mood...		...Residue	
Wh/Adjunct	Finite	Subject	Predicator	Complement

2.4 Outside the Mood Residue structure

Some elements of clause structure fall **outside** the Mood + Residue (+ Moodtag) structure. These include (i) interpersonal elements which are not part of the proposition or proposal being negotiated and (ii) textual elements which have no interpersonal role at all.

(i) Interpersonal elements:

Vocative: Identifies the addressee in the exchange (see IFG: 85)

e.g. **Madam**, you'll look like a flower, won't you?

Vocative	Mood	.......Residue..............	Moodtag

Expletive: Expresses attitude towards the exchange itself or the information being exchanged[10]

e.g. **Heavens**, you'll look like a flower, won't you?

Expletive	Mood	........Residue............	Moodtag

---

[10]Note that attitudinal words will often occur as constituents of a group rather than a clause, in which case they will not have the function of Expletive within the clause. Thus *bloody* in *That bloody woman looks like a flower* is not an Expletive.

(ii) Textual elements:

Continuative: *yes, no* (see IFG: 89)
    e.g.   **yes**, it usually does   rain
        ....Mood.........   Residue

Structural conjunction, such as *and, but, or; when, while, if* (cf. IFG: 96)

Semantically, the fact that all these fall outside the Mood-Residue structure means that these elements are not part of the proposition or proposal being negotiated. They relate to it by indicating its textual relevance as a message (by means of continuatives and conjunctions) and by indicating the addressee (by means of the Vocative) and by indicating speaker stance (by means of an Expletive), but they do not form part of what is being negotiated.

2.5 Interpersonal grammatical metaphor

2.5.1 Mood metaphor

As noted in section 1.2 above, speech functions such as statement, command and question have both congruent and metaphorical realizations. With metaphorical realizations the grammar works as a metaphor for the relevant meaning - as when an imperative like *Tell me your name* is used to question (to demand information) (see Table 3.6).

Table 3.6 Examples of Mood metaphor

speech function	congruent realization	metaphorical realization
question	*What is your name?* [interrogative]	*Tell me your name.* [imperative] *And your name is...?* [declarative]
command	*Get me a drink.* [imperative]	*Could you get me a drink?* [interrogative] *I need a drink.* [declarative]

2.5.2 Modality metaphor

Metaphorical realizations are also found for modality, expanding the range of modal meanings beyond those realized by modal verbs as Finite and mood Adjuncts.

As far as probability is concerned, one kind of metaphorical realization involves first person,[11] present tense 'mental' processes of cognition (e.g. *I think, I reckon, I suspect*) or 'relational' processes of cognitive state (e.g. *I'm sure, I'm convinced, I'm uncertain*). Here, the modal assessment of probability is construed as a clause - as a proposition in its own right. This form of realization, known as **explicitly subjective**, makes the speaker explicitly responsible for the assessment. The contrast between what Halliday refers to as the congruent and the metaphorical realization of modalization is outlined in Fig. 3.5.

---

[11]First person in declarative or second person in interrogative, e.g. *do you reckon...?*

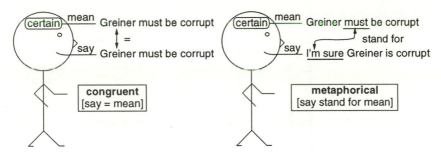

Fig. 3.5 Congruent and metaphorical realizations of probability

There is also the possibility of making modalization **explicitly objective** through nominalizations of probability and usuality, construing them either as a quality (adjective) or a thing (noun), as in *it is likely, there is no possibility*. Here, ideational resources for constructing participants are deployed to distance the assessment from the speaker and thus from negotiation. Adjectives such as *possible, probable, certain, usual, typical, common* are commonly used to construe modalizations objectively as qualities; nouns such as *possibility, probability, certainty, unusualness, regularity, typicality*, and so on are commonly used to construe modalizations objectively as things.

As far as inclination and obligation are concerned, the subjectivity of a speaker's assessment can be made explicit through first-person, present-tense mental processes of affection (e.g. *I want, I need, I'd like, I'd hate*). Again, a separate proposition is set up to symbolize assessments of proposals. The contrast between what Halliday refers to as the congruent and the metaphorical realization of modulation is outlined in Fig. 3.6.

Fig. 3.6 Congruent and metaphorical realizations of inclination

Modulation is also regularly made explicitly objective through nominalizations of inclination and obligation, construing these either as a quality or a thing. Adjectives such as *willing, keen, ardent, permissible, requisite, compulsory* and so on are commonly used to construe modulations objectively as qualities; nouns such as *intention, desire, determination, need, obligation, regulation, compulsion* and so on are commonly used to construe modulations objectively as things.

Table 3.7 Metaphorical realizations of modality

Kind of MODALITY	congruent realizations			metaphorical realizations	
	Finite	Adjunct (mood)	Predicator	mental clause	attributive clause
	implicitly subjective	**implicitly objective**	**implicitly objective**	**explicitly subjective**	**explicitly objective**
probability	can/could, may/might, will/would, should, ought to, must	possibly, probably, certainly ...		[cognitive:] I guess, I think, I know	it is possible... it is probable... it is certain...
usuality		sometimes, usually, always ...		–	It is unusual (for him to leave)
obligation		necessarily ...	be allowed to, be supposed to, be obliged to	[affective:] I'm willing for... I expect... I want... (him to leave)	it is permitted it is expected it is necessary (... for him to leave)
readiness: inclination		willingly, eagerly ...	be willing to, be keen to, be determined to	[verbal group complex:] I'd like to leave I want to leave	it'd be lovely to leave
readiness: ability	can/could		be able to	–	it is possible for him to leave

An outline of explicitly subjective and objective metaphorical realizations of modality is presented in Table 3.7.

3 Troubleshooting

3.1 The unit of analysis

Every 'major' clause in English will embody a choice from the MOOD system. Such choices are also inherent in elliptical clauses, where all or part of Mood or Residue may be absent. For example:

> A: Did you get a Herald today?
> B: No, I didn't [   ]   Elliptical declarative

There are, however, two kinds of clause which do not embody a MOOD choice, as follows.

(i) The 'non-finite' clause, as its name indicates, is characterized by its lack of finiteness; for example *to fetch her poor dog a bone, (without) fetching her poor dog a bone, having fetched her poor dog a bone,* etc. Such clauses are not grounded or bounded by the tense or modality meaning carried in a Finite element and are consequently not arguable or negotiable. They generally consist of Residue only, although sometimes a Subject is present, as in *her having fetched the dog a bone*.

(ii) Minor clauses are a second kind of moodless clause. They are 'minor' because they are not open to any of the major systems of THEME, MOOD or TRANSITIVITY. Such clauses as *oh*, *yuk*, *hi*, *thanks* may, however, fulfil a minor speech functional meaning and thus serve an interpersonal function as a greeting, or acknowledgement, or the like.[12] They thus have a semantic role in dialogue but can simply be ignored when analysing grammatically for MOOD.

3.2 *Identifying structural elements*

(i) Finite and Predicator realized together In the (simple) present and (simple) past tense, the Finite function is conflated with that of Predicator; this is shown in the analysis by writing Finite/Predicator, where '/' means 'is conflated with' (as for Wh/Subject, Wh/Complement or Wh/Adjunct in wh- interrogatives).

simple past:

Dawn	had	her baby
Subject	Finite/Predicator	Complement

simple present:

He	feels	angry
Subject	Finite/Predicator	Complement

Note that, for purposes of emphasis, negation and tagging, the Finite is realized separately from the Predicator, through the auxiliary verb *do*.

emphatic

Dawn	did	have	her baby,
Subject	Finite	Predicator	Complement

tagged

didn't	she?
Finite	Subject

negative

Dawn	didn't	have	her baby
Subject	Finite	Predicator	Complement

[12]See IFG: 95–96. For fuller analysis and discussion of speech function see Martin (1992).

Note the contrast with bare imperatives:

simple present

You	swim	well
Subject	Finite/Predicator	Adjunct

imperative

(You)	swim	well!
(Subject)	Predicator	Adjunct

Note also that, when the main verb in the clause is *be*, there is no Predicator function, but only a Finite (also with *have* in some dialects). Thus *are they happy?*, not *do they be happy?*, and *they aren't happy*, not *they don't be happy*.

(ii) Adjuncts: in Mood or Residue? Modal Adjuncts have meanings related to those of the Finite (e.g. *probably* relates to *might*) and/or involve a measure of speaker 'intrusion' through an expression of judgement (*presumably*), inclination (*gladly*), or the like (see IFG: 82–83). Adjuncts in the Residue lack this intruding function and differ in that they also carry ideational meaning (they may be mapped on to circumstances, and can be referred to as circumstantial Adjuncts; see IFG 4.3.2).

The modal Adjuncts most frequently confused with circumstantial Adjuncts in the Residue are the mood Adjuncts of usuality and time, as follows.

(i) Usuality: *always, often, sometimes, occasionally, never,* etc. Usuality is an interpersonal system because, like modality, it involves gradations between positive and negative (see IFG: 356 and following), thus involving speaker judgement and a close relationship to the meaning of the Finite.

(ii) Time: *yet, still, already, once, soon, just*. It may be less obvious that mood Adjuncts of time are purely interpersonal in function, since time is an area of meaning also prominent in circumstantial Adjuncts like *at 6 o'clock that evening* or *on January 2nd 1976*. What distinguishes the mood Adjuncts is that they are concerned with time from the perspective of speaker expectation and judgement. The mood Adjuncts of time - unlike circumstantial Adjuncts – are referenced to the moment of speaking and indicate the speaker's expectation concerning the timing or duration of the activity. Being purely interpersonal, they cannot become the focus of theme predication (e.g. *it was still/just/already that he came* is not possible).

(iii) *Yes* and *no*: modal Adjunct or conjunctive Adjunct? *Yes* and *no* may be either interpersonal or textual in function. (If textual, a 'conjunctive Adjunct' see IFG 4.3.3.) When *yes* or *no* constitutes or initiates a statement in response to a question, statement, command or offer, it is interpersonal in function and thus a modal Adjunct. The following examples illustrate; in all cases the *yes* or *no* will be phonologically salient:

A: Did you bring the keys?
B: Yes, I did.

A: Peter brought the keys.
B: No, he didn't.

A: Peter, bring the keys!
B: Yes, yes.

A: I'll bring the keys shall I?
B: Yes, do.

On other occasions, *yes* or *no* do not realize a polarity choice in a response, but function as continuatives with a purely textual function, simply linking the polarity with what has gone before. In such a case, no switch in polarity from the previous move is possible and the *yes* or *no* will typically be phonologically weak:

A: Peter's been having a really difficult time at work.
B: Yes he's had a bad year all round.

A: I didn't understand what all the fuss was about || No I really couldn't see why everyone was in such a state.

In the above examples, *yes* and *no* are textual rather than interpersonal in character (conjunctive rather than modal Adjuncts).

(iv) Phrasal verbs: how far does the Predicator extend? English is rich in 'phrasal verbs', which comprise a lexical verb plus an adverb or preposition, as with *look for, look at, go out, call up, give out*. In terms of the content - the ideational meaning being represented - these phrasal verbs function as a single unit (see Chapter 4). However, since this is not the strand of meaning we are concerned with when analysing Mood and Residue, it does not constitute a good reason for treating the adverb or preposition as part of the Predicator. On the contrary, Halliday prefers to treat the phrasal element as an Adjunct or part of an Adjunct (see IFG: 209).

We	didn't	give	the books	out
Subject	Finite	Predicator	Complement	Adjunct

He	won't	wait	for us	
Subject	Finite	Predicator	Adjunct	

They	didn't	give	in	to the union
Subject	Finite	Predicator	Adjunct	Adjunct

He	won't	be waiting	too long	for us
Subject	Finite	Predicator	Adjunct	Adjunct

This analysis allows for generalizations concerning the ordering of Adjuncts relative to each other. Thus a modal Adjunct that could precede a Complement, such as *unfortunately* in *They won't be borrowing, unfortunately, any good books* can also precede a prepositional phase serving as Adjunct, as in *they won't be waiting* [Adjunct:] *unfortunately for any good books*. However, this interpersonal Adjunct could not occur between the preposition and the noun in the prepositional phase serving as Adjunct – *they won't be waiting for, unfortunately, any good books*. The analysis suggests, in other words, that one Adjunct cannot interrupt another.

(v) Complement or Adjunct? The Complement is in a complementary role to the Subject; that is, it has the status of 'potential Subject'. That potential could be realized if the voice of the clause were active rather than passive or vice versa. As a potential Subject, the Complement is realized by a nominal group, while an Adjunct is realized by a prepositional phrase or adverbial group:

Peter She They He	didn't is may will	tell making sell send	Linda her father Sharon his mum	that a cup of tea the car some flowers	in the kitchen at a cheap price at Christmas
Subject	Finite	Predicator	Complement (nominal group)	Complement (nominal group)	Adjunct (prep. phrase)

The first Complement in the above examples also has the ideational role of Beneficiary (see Chapter 4). This particular ideational role can also be realized later in the clause in a prepositional form, as shown below:

Peter Angela They He	didn't is may will	tell making sell send	that a cup of tea the car some flowers	**to Linda** **for my father** **to Sharon** **to his mum**	in the kitchen at a cheap price at Christmas
Subject	Finite	Predicator	Complement (nominal group)	Adjunct (prep. phrase)	Adjunct (prep. phrase)

In its prepositional form a Beneficiary is treated as an Adjunct in IFG, on the grounds that it cannot be a Subject in this form. Nonetheless some analysts would argue for regarding it as a Complement here too. Although *to Linda* or *for my father* is not a potential Subject, *his mum* or *Linda* does have the potential for becoming Subject without the preposition remaining in the structure:

Linda wasn't told that by him
My father is being made a cup of tea by Angela in the kitchen
Sharon may be sold the car at a cheap price by them
His mum will be sent some flowers by him at Christmas

This suggests a difference from other kinds of Adjuncts where, if the nominal element becomes Subject, then the preposition is left as an Adjunct by itself:

The flower bed	was	trampled	on
Subject	Finite	Predicator	Adjunct

A similar argument applies to a *by* phrase which fills the ideational role of Agent, as in *Linda will be told that **by Peter*** or *His mum will be sent some flowers **by him***. In IFG these are treated as Adjuncts, indicating that when agency is expressed in this form it has a more peripheral status than when it is mapped on to the interpersonal Subject role, as in ***He** will send his mum some flowers*. (The fact that Beneficiaries and Agents can appear both as Complements and Adjuncts is an indication of their status as falling between the central participant roles and circumstantial roles. See further Chapter 4.)

(vi) Split Subject: Anticipatory *it* There may be textual reasons for placing the 'content' of the Subject role in a position in the clause where it will be 'news',[13] particularly when an embedded clause functions as Subject. To accommodate this, a 'contentless' *it* may hold the typical Subject position in the clause, letting us know if the clause is interrogative or declarative. For example:

[13]See Chapter 2.

It will upset her [[that they didn't give the job to Max]].
Was **it** a good thing [[to lose Max]]?
Was **it** fair [[Max getting overlooked]]?

There are agnate variants to these clauses where the embedded clause itself occurs first in the normal Subject position and no anticipatory *it* is needed:

[[That they didn't give the job to Max]] will upset her.
Was [[to lose Max]] a good thing?
Was [[Max getting overlooked]] fair?

To capture this agnation, clauses with an anticipatory *it* are analysed as having a discontinuous constituent as Subject. The *it* forms the first part of the Subject and the 'postposed' embedded clause forms the second part:

it	will	upset	her	that they didn't give the job to Max
Sub...	Finite	Predicator	Complement	...ject..

3.3 Ambiguous mood type

For various reasons, a given example may be structurally ambiguous in terms of its mood analysis. Here we will just point to a few examples.

(i) Yes/no interrogative or imperative?
   (1) When the clause is negative and the Subject is 'you', yes/no interrogative clauses and imperative ones may be structurally the same – Finite: *don't* ^ Subject: *you*, as in:

[imperative:]   Don't you ever go out!
[interrogative:yes/no]   Don't you ever go out?

They are distinct in their TONE selections so if you speak the examples you can hear the difference (cf. IFG Section 8.9). They also have different variants. The imperative clause is agnate with *Don't ever go out, you!*, *Don't you ever go out, will you!*; but the interrogative clause is agnate with e.g. *Doesn't she ever go out?* (with non-interactant rather than interactant subject-person), *Didn't you ever go out?* (with past rather than present tense).
   (2) When the clause is positive and the Subject is 'you', a yes/no interrogative clause may presume the Mood element (cf. IFG: 94) and in such cases it may be structurally the same as an imperative clause:

[You] Believe me!
[Do you] Believe me?

[Do you] Want any sugar?

In writing, yes/no interrogatives and imperatives are disambiguated by punctuation; in speech the distinction is made clear by the choice of TONE (cf. IFG Section 8.7). As with (1) above, you can probe the difference by looking at agnate clauses since they bring out the difference between the two mood types.

(ii) Yes/no interrogative or declarative? Declarative clauses normally select a falling tone; but they may also choose a rising one. If they do, they are likely to be interpreted as questions at the semantic stratum, as indicated by the question marks in the examples below:

You find a resemblance?
You got your paper?

But, grammatically, these are still types of declarative clauses.

(Note also cases where a negative clausal polarity is Theme, as in *At no time did he question our decision*. Since polarity and finiteness are closely bonded in English, the Finite immediately follows the negative Theme and so comes before the Subject:

At no time	did	he	question	our decision
Adjunct	Finite	Subject	Predicator	Complement

Although the order Finite^Subject suggests a yes/no interrogative clause, these clauses are declarative. This is clear from the version with unmarked Theme – *He didn't question our decision at any time* – and from the possibility (in all varieties of English) of a Moodtag — *At no time did he question our decision, did he?*).

(iii) Declarative or imperative? The two examples above also illustrate a possible ambiguity between 'declarative' and 'imperative', more specifically between declarative clauses with addressee (*you*) as Subject and (simple) present tense and 'jussive' imperative clauses with explicit Subject:

You find a resemblance.
You find a resemblance!

You can probe these in various ways, for instance by checking the nature of the Moodtag (declarative: *don't you?*; imperative: *won't you?*) and the possibility of leaving the Subject implicit in the imperative clause (*Find a resemblance*).

3.4 Ambiguous POLARITY

You can probe the polarity value of a clause by adding a Moodtag (if the clause is declarative or imperative; if it is interrogative, just check the related declarative instead). In the unmarked case, the Moodtag always reverses the polarity of the Mood. For example, *they **shoot** horses, **don't** they*; *you **haven't** got a clue, **have** you?* In the normal case, there will be little doubt as to the polarity value, of course. However, there are at least three types of situation that may cause some analytical problems, as follows.

(i) The negative polarity value combines with usuality or degree. The clause is still negative, even though you don't find a *not* or *n't* and even though the negative is scaled down from definitely 'no': *they **seldom come** here nowadays, **do** they?*; *he **is hardly** civil, **is** he?*

(ii) The negative is a feature of the Subject: *nothing upsets her, does it?*; *nobody believes him, do they?* (Contrast with negative Complements: *he believes nobody, doesn't he?*)

(iii) The negative polarity has been 'transferred' to a mental projecting clause serving as a metaphorical modality: *I don't believe this is the right move for us, is it?* Here the clause *this is ...* looks positive, but it is not; the negative polarity is realized within the metaphorical modality *I don't believe*.

3.5 'Will' : TENSE or MODALITY?

Will as a modal auxilliary may realize PRIMARY TENSE on some occasions and MODALITY on others. For example *Dan will know the answer* is ambiguous out of context. Actually, it may be ambiguous even in context. Whether the *will* is expressing future primary tense or median probability depends on whether it is related to *Dan is going to know the truth* (realizing tense) or *Dan must know the truth* (realizing probability).

Dan will know the truth: future tense
Dan is going to know the truth (tomorrow when he reads the paper).

Dan will know the truth: probability
Dan must know the truth (because he was there at the time):
I bet Dan knows the truth (because he was there at the time).

Similarly, whether *will* expresses future primary tense or inclination should be judged according to the most likely agnate clause:

I'll open the window: future tense
I'm going to open the window (when I paint the room).

I'll open the window: inclination
I offer to open the window.

4 Analysis practice

4.1 Phase I

4.1.1 Exercises (Examples based on Roddy Doyle 1992: *Snapper*. London: Secker & Warburg.)

Exercise 1 Practising the tag test Construct a related clause with a tag and underline the Subject and Subject tag. For example:

He isn't a black.   <u>He</u> isn't a black, is <u>he</u>?

1. You heard me.   1. ....
2. That's shocking.   2. ....
3. No one said anything.   3. ....
4. We could have done something about it.   4. ....
5. There's no need to be getting snotty.   5. ....
6. Jimmy's the one that should be getting snotty.   6. ....
7. Linda's hitting me.   7. ....
8. Your mammy and Sharon and me are having a chat.   8. ....
9. The hot shower refreshed them.   9. ....
10. Those two little kittens were chasing the ball.   10. ....

Exercise 2 Practising the tag test Construct a related clause with a tag and underline the Subject tag. For example:

Make us a cup of tea there, love.   Make us a cup of tea there, love, will <u>you</u>?

1. Now get out.   1. ....
2. Don't start that.   2. ....

3.   Ah Veronica, stop that.   3.   ....
4.   Mind yourself against the table there.   4.   ....
5.   Just tell us.   5.   ....

Exercise 3 Practising mood agnation Construct a related clause in the appropriate mood to complete the paradigm: For example:

Are you sure?   polar interrogative
You are sure.   declarative
Be sure.   imperative

1.   Did you go in by yourself?   polar interrogative
     ....   declarative
     ....   imperative
2.   ....   polar interrogative
     The old girl drives it.   declarative
     ....   imperative
3.   Will you tell them soon?   polar interrogative
     ....   declarative
     ....   imperative
4.   ....   polar interrogative
     ....   declarative
     Come for a drink, Sharon.   imperative
5.   Will I bring home a few chips?   polar interrogative
     ....   declarative
     ....   imperative

Exercise 4 Practising mood agnation Construct a related polar interrogative and then a related declarative clause. For example:

Why won't you tell us?   wh-interrogative
Won't you tell us because of that?   polar interrogative
You won't tell us because of that.   declarative

1.   How did that girl get there?   wh-interrogative
     ....   polar interrogative
     ....   declarative
2.   What do you mean, Veronica?   wh-interrogative
     ....   polar interrogative
     ....   declarative
3.   What will all those people say?   wh-interrogative
     ....   polar interrogative
     ....   declarative
4.   When's it due?   wh-interrogative
     ....   polar interrogative
     ....   declarative
5.   Where did the wretched man go?   wh-interrogative
     ....   polar interrogative
     ....   declarative

Exercise 5 Ellipting Residue Develop an elliptical response for the following clauses, as modelled in the first two examples.

First speaker utterance	*Elliptical response by second speaker*
Is he married?	No, he's not.
You're absolutely sure now.	Yeah, I am.

1. ...you can watch me hitting him.
2. Can Tracy watch?
3. Abortion's murder.
4. You don't care what that lot says.
5. Dawn O'Neill had her baby for Paddy Bell.

1. ....
2. ....
3. ....
4. ....
5. ....

Exercise 6 Identifying Subject and Finite Label the Subject and Finite elements in each of the following clauses, as modelled for the first example.

First speaker	*Second speaker response*
...you can watch me.	– Can I ?
Su Fi	Fi Su
....	....

1. Can Tracy watch?
....
....

– She can of course.
....
....

2. Abortion's murder.
....
....

– It is of course.
....
....

3. You don't care about that.
....
....

– Yes, I do.
....
....

4. Dawn has had her baby for Paddy Bell.
....
....

– She has of course.
....
....

5. Will all our friends be there?
....

– They will be.
....
....

6. Your little brother isn't going to like it.
....
....

– Isn't he?
....

Exercise 7 Identifying Mood and Residue Divide the clauses in Exercise 6 into Mood and Residue elements on the basis of the previous analysis, as in the example.

...you can watch me.	– Can I?

...you	can	watch me.	– Can	I?
Su	Fi		Fi	Su
Mood		**Residue**	**Mood**	

Exercise 8 Identifying modal Finites Underline the Finite and check whether it realizes PRIMARY TENSE or MODALITY. If modal, classify as probability or obligation. For example:

My perception <u>may</u> be heightened by pregnancy.　　probability ....
They <u>didn't</u> come that weekend.　　　　　　　　　primary tense ....

1. He might already know.
2. Excuse me a moment, I ought to say hello to someone over there.
3. You shouldn't speak to your mother like that.
4. Are you looking for someone?
5. Well, he certainly must have strained himself to get this menagerie together.
6. He hasn't begun yet.
7. Didn't he explain?
8. You mustn't drink so much, darling.
9. It couldn't be him driving.
10. They don't know the answer to that one.

1.　...
2.　...
3.　...
4.　...
5.　...
6.　...
7.　...
8.　...
9.　...
10.　...

Exercise 9 Identifying Mood Adjuncts Analyse the following clauses for Mood and Residue; divide the Mood element into Subject, Finite and mood Adjunct as appropriate. Label any mood Adjuncts according to whether they express polarity, probability, usuality, readiness or obligation. See 2.2.1.1. For example:

I　had　　not　　　　　　thought of that.
Mood_____　　Residue_____
Su Finite　Adjunct: polarity

1. I'm not telling.

2. She certainly wasn't kidding.

3. She'd always been like that.

4. Your mind's probably made up.

5. They might have told me before this.

6. He must necessarily be dismissed for the theft.

7. You're definitely not going to tell us.

8. Would the lads sometimes go out?

9. Maybe it's a bad idea.

10. I'll gladly do it.

1.

2.

3.

4.

5.

6.

7.

8.

9.

10.

4.1.2 Texts for analysis

Text 1 Explanation (for young children) Reproduced below are the first 31 clauses of a short pictorial information book for young children. For each line, label the mood of the main clause (i.e. as declarative, interrogative:polar, interrogative:wh-, imperative). Underline the Subject of each (non-embedded) clause. (Note: The main clause comes first in the line except for lines 10 and 17.)

Consider what role relations are established for the reader by the mood choices you have identified (and what view of learning is thereby implied). Consider what is most often 'at stake' in the text in terms of the 'modally responsible' element.

1.   Do you enjoy making sounds?
2.   What sounds do these things make ‖ if you bang them?
3.   What different sounds can you make with your body and your voice?
4.   Put your fingers on your throat ‖ as you talk ‖ or [as you] sing.
5.   What can you feel?
6.   Hold a ruler on the edge of a table.
7.   Press down the end ‖ and let go.
8.   Can you hear a sound?
9.   What do you see?
10. Whenever you hear a sound ‖ there is something moving.
11. This movement is called a vibration.
12. Try this with a rubber band ‖ and see.
13   You can make musical sounds with rubber bands of different sizes‖ or if you pluck the strings of a guitar.
14. Strike a triangle with a beater.
15. Touch the triangle ‖ while it is ringing.
16. What can you feel?
17. When something stops vibrating ‖ the sound stops.
18. How does someone's voice reach you?
19. The sound travels through the air as sound waves.
20. Throw a stone in a pool of water.
21. Watch [[the waves spreading out]].
22. Sound waves move through the air in a similar way.

(From Webb, A. 1987: *Talk about Sound*. London, Franklin Watts.)

Text 2 Parent–child conversation Identify any instances of modality you find in this text. Identify Subjects and Finites and reflect on how this compares with Text 1 as a piece of information exchange (M = mother, C = 4½-year-old boy). The text is set out in clauses. Angled brackets indicate an 'included' clause. (See further Chapter 5.)

C: How could birds die?

M: Like the one in the garden, are you thinking of?
Well, sometimes birds die when they get very old,
or maybe they get sick
because they got some disease,
or maybe a cat got it.
Baby birds sometimes die
when they fall out the nest,
or, in the winter –
<<if you were in a cold place>> –
    birds might die
because they can't get enough food.

C: Yeh, but what happens
if one bird falls out
and then – and when it's just about at the ground
it flies?

M: Yes, well if it's big enough to fly
it'll be all right.
And sometimes birds fall out the nest
but they don't die...
But that didn't look like a baby bird;
maybe there was something wrong with it;
maybe a cat killed it -
(hastily) I don't think it was our cat.

C: Perhaps it was on the ground
and then a cat got it.

M: Yeah, it was probably pecking something on the ground...
maybe it was just a very old bird.
    ...

C: (referring to dead bird in garden) But it looks as if it's alive.

M: Yeah, it does, doesn't it?

C: Perhaps its eye got blind

M: Could have been,
but it definitely wasn't alive.

4.2 Phase II

4.2.1 Exercises

Exercise 1 Recognizing Vocatives Label the Vocative and Subject functions as required in the following clauses.

    Robin,   you   have to leave now.
    Vocative   Subject

1. Darling, would you carry this for me?

2. All of you, get out of here.

3. Bruce was inspecting the lab.

4. Robin, let's go.

5. You really ought to leave straight away.

6. Chase had a thing for black rubber.

7. Mr Eliot disagreed.

8. You had better get ready Alfred.

9. Don't, Riddler, even think about it.

10. Look at you.

Exercise 2 Practising voice agnation Construct the active or passive clause related to the following clauses as modelled in the first two examples.

    She'd just told her father. (active)   Her father'd just been told. (passive)
    It would have been taken by them. (passive) They would have taken it. (active)

1. He'd have walloped her.   1. ....

2. Why won't you tell us?   2. ....

3. The door was shut by Jimmy.   3. ....

4. He squirted his tea back into the cup.   4. ....

5. She'd been won over by the arguments.   5. ....

6. Will I bring you home a few chips. [2 versions]   6. ....

                                          ....

7. My perceptions may be heightened by pregnancy. 7. ....

Exercise 3 Identifying Residue elements Divide the Residue in the examples in Phase I, Exercises 6/7, into Predicator, Complement (nominal group), Adjunct (adverbial group, prepositional phrase) as in the first two examples.

...you can watch me. –				Can I?
...you	can	watch	me.	
Su	Fi	**Pred**	**Comp**	
.....Mood..................		**Residue**		

Are you coming for a drink? –				No thanks, Daddy.
Are	you	coming	for a drink?	
Fi	Su	**Pred**	**Adjunct**	
.....Mood..................		**Residue**		

Exercise 4 Identifying Predicator Analyse the following clauses for Subject, Finite and Predicator. Conflate Finite and Predicator if necessary. For example:

She	had	been dreading	the meeting.
Su	Fi	Predicator	

I	wanted to go	down	to the stables.
Su	Fi/Predicator		

1. They are going to sell the house as soon as possible.

2. I was expecting to see you earlier.

3. He seemed to be perfectly cheerful.

4. He was beginning to get into the car.

5. Couldn't they have done something about it?

6. She might have stopped listening.

7. Didn't they try to understand you?

8. They started to listen.

Exercise 5 Analysing Mood Residue structure including Wh Analyse the following clauses for Subject, Finite, Predicator, Complement and Adjunct; conflate Wh with Subject, Complement or Adjunct and Finite with Predicator as appropriate.

Make	us	a cup of tea	there,	love.
Predicator	Complement	Complement	Adjunct	Vocative

1. Stop that.

2. How did it happen?

3. Don't start that.

4. Why won't you tell us?

5. What do you mean?

6. When's it due?

7. What a house this is!

Exercise 6. Identifying types of Modal Adjunct Analyse the Mood function of the following clauses for Subject, Finite, mood Adjunct and comment Adjunct as appropriate (see IFG: 82–83).

Personally,	I	don't	dislike	him.
comment Adjunct	Subject	Finite		

1. She was usually seen by someone.

2. Frankly, she'd hardly been anywhere.

3. She'd already visited some of the sights.

4. Apparently she'd barely seen any of the sights in any quarter of the town.

5. In general she shopped in some of the fashionable streets.

6. Surprisingly, she probably didn't see anyone any more.

7. Provisionally, we might plan for a whole day then.

Exercise 7. Identifying Residue elements (phrasal verbs) As in the models, analyse the following clauses for Mood and Residue. Divide the Residue into Predicator, Complement and Adjuncts as appropriate.

They looked for John.	They	looked		for John.
	Subject	Fi/Predicator		Adjunct
	Mood	Residue		

She plugged in the kettle.	She	plugged	in	the kettle.
	Subject	Fi/Predicator	Adjunct	Complement
	Mood	Residue		

She plugged the kettle in.	She	plugged	the kettle	in.
	Subject	Fi/Predicator	Complement	Adjunct
	Mood	Residue		

1. Lay off, Veronica.   1. ....

2. I'll sort this fella out.   2. ....

3. They won her over.   3. ....

4. They put her up to it.   4. ....

5. She saw through their plan. 5. ....

6. He watched over the baby.   6. ....

7. She chewed out the opposition. 7. ....

Exercise 8 Analysing non-finite clauses Analyse the following non-finite clauses for Subject, Predicator, Complement and Adjunct as required (the non-finite clauses are underlined in each example). (Some examples from *The Goodman of Ballengiech*, retold by M.C. Maloney, London: Methuen, 1987.)

He'd send one of the kids	to get	her	a choc-ice.
	Predicator	Complement	Complement
They heard	him	walloping	up the stairs.
	Subject	Predicator	Adjunct

1. It stood there,   rattling,

    its paws slipping on the formica.

2. Tracy came back in   with the pup clinging to the front of her jumper.

3. Drawn by only two horses,   the coach moved slowly down the road.

4. Jimmy Sr wished   for Sharon to go out in the hall first.

5. He quickly took the King's part, wielding his flail against the attackers.

6. Given my aunt by the Duke   the teapot remained a family heirloom for generations.

7. He would attempt to repay him   by showing him through the royal apartments.

8. To give him cause for rejoicing, he granted him sole possession of the farm.

Exercise 9 Identifying long Subjects In the following examples, the Subject may be realized by an embedded clause, a long nominal group or by a complex of nominal groups. Underline the Subject (of the non-embedded clause) in each case. (Some examples from Hunter I. *Rethinking the School*. Sydney: Allen & Unwin, 1994: 170.)

<u>What he did for a living</u> was the best he could.

1. The points that you made there surprised me.
2. Your mammy and Sharon and I are having a chat.
3. What chance gave, chance took away.
4. The increase of empirical knowledge, and more exact modes of thought, made sharper divisions between the sciences inevitable.
5. ...the increasingly complex machinery of the State necessitated a more rigorous separation of ranks and occupations.
6. The inner unity of human nature was severed too.
7. The near identity of these two criticisms of the governmental state can of course be attributed neither to Schiller's prescience nor to the belated character of modern critique.

Exercise 10 Identifying Mood-Residue Boundaries Analyse Mood and Residue in the following clauses, taking care to exclude textual and interpersonal elements which are outside the Mood and Residue functions (i.e. conjunctive Adjunct, Vocative and Expletive).

Fortunately,	he'd already	had dinner,	my dear.
Mood		Residue	xxxxxxx

And then	he would	leave for work.	
xxxxxxxx	Mood	Residue	

1. Gosh, I forgot.

2. Tracy, go up to your room.

3. I don't think so, Veronica.

4. Finally, they all left.

5. I didn't meet anyone though.

6. Personally, I don't like him.

7. Frankly, my dear, I don't give a damn.

8. They don't, as a rule, arrive before six.

9. They lost, surprisingly.

4.2.2 Texts for analysis

Texts 1–2 Classroom talk The following text extracts are taken from a sequence of lessons in an upper primary science class. Divide the text into clauses and note the mood of each clause (or label as minor). Note any mood metaphors (i.e. where mood choice is not congruent with the speech function choice). Analyse the interpersonal structure of each clause. Use the analysis to reflect on the range of speech roles adopted by the interactants, the use of modality and the significance of the choice of Subject.

Text 1 Extract from the exposé
(The class has recently watched a science film on the topic of mechanical advantage)

TEACHER:	Alright, a quick summary of what we have just seen. (*teacher writes the heading 'Summary' on the board.*) Quick.
ANDREW:	Lever. (*calls out to the teacher before he is ready*)
TEACHER:	Hold on.
DANIEL	Seesaw. (*another child calls out to the teacher*)
TEACHER:	Right. Just wait till we are all here. Have you got enough scrap paper on your desk please? You'll probably only need two or three pieces. (*children get organized*) Right, you may have to use the stand. (*the teacher is waiting for the class to settle before he begins*) Steven and Brad, the sun is shining inside (*reminding the boys to take their hats off inside*). Alright, thankyou. Solved your problem? (*gaining the attention of a child*) You'll probably need to see that film tomorrow, as an extra, to get you (*pause*) to get your ideas really sorted out. Right. Let's have a summary of what was the film basically about. They seem to mention two basic machines. Um, Andrew?
ANDREW:	Levers. (*pronounces the word with an American accent as in the film*)
TEACHER:	It has an Australian pronunciation.
SIMON:	Levers.
TEACHER:	Yeah, leave her alone. (*said as a joke and the class laughs*). Lever (*writes on the board*) and ...(*pause*)
BRAD:	An inclined plane.
TEACHER:	An (*pause*) inclined plane. (*the teacher repeats the word as he writes it on the board and a child calls out*) Hold on, hold on, now they extended these two basic machines, (*pause*) into five separate machines. In that movie they extended them out, they extended out some of the machines. They used the lever. Hold on, hold on. (*a child is calling out*)
TEACHER:	Joanne?
JOANNE:	Lever.
TEACHER:	No, we've done a lever.
BRAD:	Baseball bat.
TEACHER:	Baseball bat. (*pause*) Any bat really.
JOANNE:	Flying fox. (*said very quietly*)
TEACHER:	Pardon, flying fox? (*writes on the board*)
KANE:	Clothesline.

TEACHER:	And what with it?
KANE:	A wheel.
TEACHER:	A wheel. (*repeats out loud to the class and writes on the board*) Yeah, no you're right. Clotheslines. That was a... (*interrupted*) what did she use on the clothesline?
SEVERAL:	Pulley.
TEACHER:	A pulley, which is a type of (*pause*) lever. Except of course, you've got also a what with it? A (*pause*) wind (*prompting children*) lass. Anything else that wasn't mentioned that possibly uses the principles of a lever.
STEVEN:	Door handle.
TEACHER:	A door handle, good one, hey.
TEACHER:	Yep. (*writes on board*) Righto, let's have a look at an inclined plane one (*pause*) well actually that is a type of tool which you have seen in action, come to think of it. Maybe we can get six uses of an inclined plane. Um Aranthi?
ARANTHI:	Stairs.
TEACHER:	Stairs, right. Great answer. (*writes on board*)

Text 2 Extract from children in task collaboration

C:	Ok, we are doing this one.
A:	So we need that.
C:	OK.
K:	Hey, I got it. (*referring to a bottle*)
C:	Oh, excellent.
Y:	Looks good. (*there is a whispered group discussion about what comes next*)
C:	We need a heavy nut.
K:	There is one off the um...
N:	We need – (*interrupted*)
C:	Yeah, yeah.
N:	Go ask Bill. (*Katrina runs off*)
A:	We need a thin saw blade. (*reading off the sheet*)
C:	Use this. (*i.e. a stanley knife*)
N:	Oh yeah.
A:	Do you have a matchbox anywhere?
N:	Do you want me to ask Mr Kelly?
A:	Empty one. (*Naomi gets up to look for a matchbox*)
K:	We got a heavy nuts. (*hands it to Aranthi*)
K:	We need to tie some string.
A:	Now we need another matchbox.
N:	It doesn't, it doesn't need a matchbox, does it?
A:	Yeah.
K:	Now we need one string, (*pause*) we've got that. (*pause*) We've got this.
A:	OK, we need a cork.
K:	Where are we going to get some of those?
C:	What we need is wire and a cork.
A:	OK, could you ask for one cork and one wire? (*Katrina goes off*)

(Texts courtesy of Frances Christie.)

4.3 Phase III

4.3.1 Exercises

Exercise 1 Analysis of 'split Subject' Find a related clause which begins with *it*. Analyse the *it...that*, *it...to etc.* clause for Subject, Finite, Predicator, Complement and Adjunct as required. For example:

I was shocked that they left.

It	shocked	me	that they left.
Sub...	Finite/Predicator	Complement	...ject

That he was actually listening wasn't obvious.

It	wasn't	obvious	that he was actually listening.
Sub...	Finite	Comp.	...ject

1. To enjoy it would be difficult.

2. That they said that is surprising.

3. That they've left is a relief.

4. People often say that no good will come of it.

5. That they didn't apologize irritates me.

6. That they don't often come here is true.

Exercise 2 Existential clauses Analyse the following existential clauses labelling for Subject, Finite, Complement and Adjunct.

There	was	a collection of dolls in different national costumes.
Subject	Finite	Complement

1. There was one particularly repulsive specimen in spotted blue.

2. On another wall there was a smaller shelf holding an assortment of china cats.

3. There was a record player in a corner.

4. And beside it was a greetings card.

5. There was a large number of cushions of all sizes and colours.

6. Along the stream ran a worn path.

7. On the table was a vase, a book and a greeting card.

Exercise 3 Classifying mood Adjuncts Pick out the mood Adjuncts in the following clauses and classify them as realizing polarity, probability, usuality, readiness, obligation, time, typicality, obviousness, intensity or degree (IFG: 82–83)

She was **utterly** shocked   degree.

1.	Riddler was absolutely beside himself	1. ....
2.	Obviously he was smitten.	2. ....
3.	Robin had not even become his partner.	3. ....
4.	His parents were already dead.	4. ....
5.	By all means see it.	5. ....
6.	He readily agreed to join the firm.	6. ....
7.	In fact, he just hated it.	7. ....
8.	I scarcely think about it any more.	8. ....
9.	He mainly did it for fun, of course.	9. ....
10.	Possibly they just haven't yet arrived.	10. ....

Exercise 4 Identifying modality type Pick out the most plausible kind of modality realized in the following clauses (ability, inclination, obligation, probability, usuality).

(phone rings) That must be Jane.   probability

1.	You ought to get yourself a new car.	1. ....
2.	You just might see them there.	2. ....
3.	However hard I try, I can't do it.	3. ....
4.	He never arrives before six.	4. ....
5.	Am I allowed to go?	5. ....
6.	I might go to France or I might stay here.	6. ....
7.	(Look at the time!) I should finish this before six.	7. ....
8.	(Knock on door) Must we answer it?	8. ....
9.	Must you make so much noise?	9. ....
10.	(With so little traffic about) we should be there by six.	10. ....

Exercise 5 Identifying modality metaphors In the following examples, determine whether the projecting clauses are likely to be interpersonal metaphors of modality; where so, identify the kind of modality.

I'm inclined to think it was Moriarty.   I'm inclined to think   [probability]
– Perhaps so.

1.	That's only fashion.	
	– I suppose so.	1. ....
2.	He thinks he'll leave.	2. ....
	– Does he?	
3.	You're sure now he's not married?	3. ....
	– Yeah, he's not.	
4.	I promise I'll go.	4. ....
	– Please do.	
5.	Will he marry you?	
	– No. I don't think so.	5. ....

6. I'd love you to do it.   6. ....
    – Okay, I will.
7. Do you reckon he'll come?   7. ....
    – I doubt it.
8. I demand you leave.   8. ....
    – Okay, I will.
9. She said she was pregnant.   9. ....
    – Did she really?
10. I still think you should tell us who the dad is. 10. ....
    – You can think away then.

4.3.2 Texts for analysis

Text 1 Dialogue in narrative Identify all instances of modality in the following excerpt and classify according to type (probability, usuality, etc.) value (high, median, low) and orientation (subjective, objective).

"But why Turkish?" asked Holmes, gazing fixedly at my boots. I was reclining in a cane-backed chair at the moment, and my protruded feet had attracted his ever-active attention.

"English," I answered in some surprise. "I got them at Latimer's, in Oxford Street."

Holmes smiled with an expression of weary patience.

"The bath!" he said; "the bath! Why the relaxing and expensive Turkish rather than the invigorating home-made article?"

"Because for the last few days I have been feeling rheumatic and old. A Turkish bath is what we call an alternative in medicine – a fresh starting-point, a cleanser of the system.

"By the way, Holmes," I added, "I have no doubt that the connection between my boots and a Turkish bath is a perfectly self-evident one to a logical mind, and yet I should be obliged to you if you would indicate it."

"The train of reasoning is not very obscure, Watson," said Holmes with a mischievous twinkle. "It belongs to the same elementary class of deduction which I should illustrate if I were to ask you who shared your cab in your drive this morning."

"I don't admit that a fresh illustration is an explanation," said I with some asperity.

"Bravo, Watson! A very dignified and logical remonstrance. Let me see, what were the points? Take the last one first – the cab. You observe that you have some splashes on the left sleeve and shoulder of your coat. Had you sat in the centre of a hansom you would probably have had no splashes, and if you had they would certainly have been symmetrical. Therefore it is clear that you sat at the side. Therefore it is equally clear that you had a companion."

"That is very evident."

"Absurdly commonplace, is it not?"

"But the boots and the bath."

"Equally childish. You are in the habit of doing up your boots in a certain way. I see them on this occasion fastened with an elaborate double bow, which is not your usual method of tying them. You have, therefore, had them off. Who has tied them? A bootmaker - or the boy at the bath. It is unlikely that it is the bootmaker, since your boots are nearly new. Well, what remains? The bath. Absurd, is it not?"

(Conan-Doyle, A. 1981: *The Penguin Complete Sherlock Holmes*, Harmondsworth: Penguin, 942.)

Text 2 Written exposition Analyse the interpersonal structure of each clause in the following text written as a 'letter to the editor' by a high school student. Note and classify any instance of modality.

TV Violence
It is essential for the well-being of the Youth of Australia that we adopt a less tolerant attitude to violence in television. It has been known for some time that young children can be disturbed by the violent scenes presented by the television scene. No apparent effort however has been made by either the producers of children's programmes or the programmers of children's programmes to take this into account: one only has to look at the extraordinary popular cartoon 'Teenage Mutant Ninja Turtles'. At some schools it was necessary to ban the accessories associated with the programme because children were engaging in fights in the playground, emulating their cartoon heroes; this sort of situation is deplorable, this incident also highlights how impressionable young children are. There is a definite danger that children, after years of exposure to violence on television, come to accept that violence is an acceptable solution to conflict. It is of vital importance for the future of Australia that young people realize that violence is not to be condoned, nor applauded. It is also essential that young people do not associate violence with bravery and heroism, which is an inevitable outcome if we persist in allowing our children to be influenced by the garbage that fills our screens every afternoon and evening, and succeeds in passing for entertainment. It is possible that children come to accept violence as an inevitable, but vaguely unpleasant part of the world. If this unfortunate scenario becomes true, we will never combat violence. It is of utmost importance then, that the television industry assumes a sense of responsibility by carefully regulating the materials that appear in children's programmes.

(Text courtesy of Bill Crowley.)

Text 3: Dramatic dialogue Analyse the following extract from Harold Pinter's *Old Times* (opening of Act One) in his *Plays: Four*. London: Methuen. With reference to Fig. 3.8 on p. 96, show MOOD selections in the columns to the right, and underline the Mood element of structure. We have supplied elided elements in square brackets.

Speaker	Turn	Kate	Deeley
Kate	(Reflectively) [She was] Dark.	major: finite: indic: declar: non-exclam: untagged	
Deeley	[Was she] Fat or thin?		
Kate	[She was] Fuller than me, I think.		
Deeley	She was [fuller than you] then.		
Kate	I think so [she was fuller than me then].		
Deeley	She may not be [fuller than you] now.		
Deeley	Was she your best friend?		
Kate	Oh, what does that mean?		
Deeley	What?		
Kate	[What does] The word friend [mean] ...		
	when you look back ... all that time		
Deeley	Can't you remember what you felt?		
Kate	It is a very long time.		
Deeley	But you remember her.		
	She remembers you.		
	Or why would she be coming here tonight?		

Compare the types of interpersonal selections Kate and Deeley make in this passage. Comment on and interpret the division of dialogic labour between them.

5 Review and Contextualization

5.1 *Locating* MOOD

MOOD is an interpersonal resource at clause rank for constructing the clause as a proposition or proposal for negotiation in dialogue. MOOD is the grammaticalization of the semantic system of SPEECH FUNCTION associated with the dialogic move. Selections in MOOD are, in turn, realized phonologically by selections in TONE. For example, a move giving information (a statement) is realized by a declarative clause, which is, in turn, realized by a tone group with a falling tone. See Fig. 3.7.

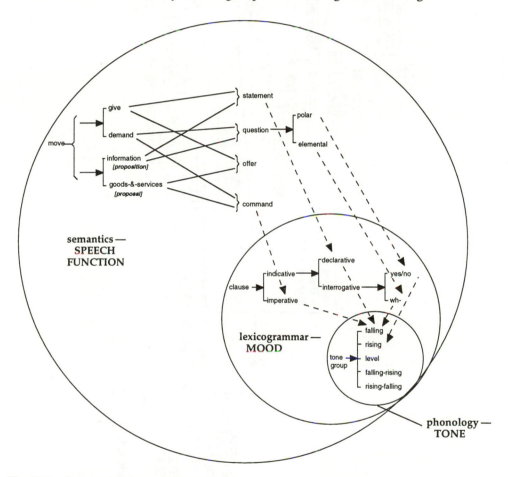

Fig. 3.7 SPEECH FUNCTION, MOOD and TONE

The basic options in the system of MOOD are set out as a system network in Fig. 3.8.

The options in the system of MOOD gain their realization in structures of the clause (see 5.2 below) and in selections in TONE (see IFG Section 8.9). Fig. 3.8

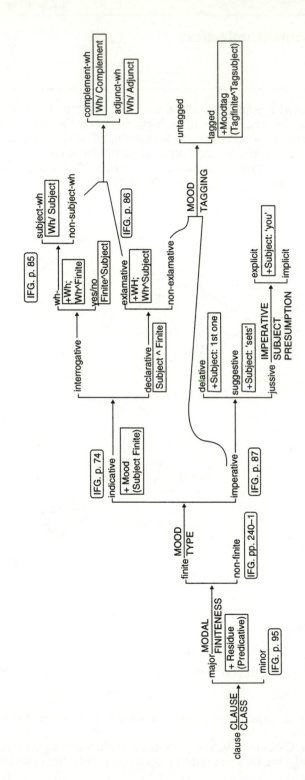

Fig. 3.8 MOOD system for English

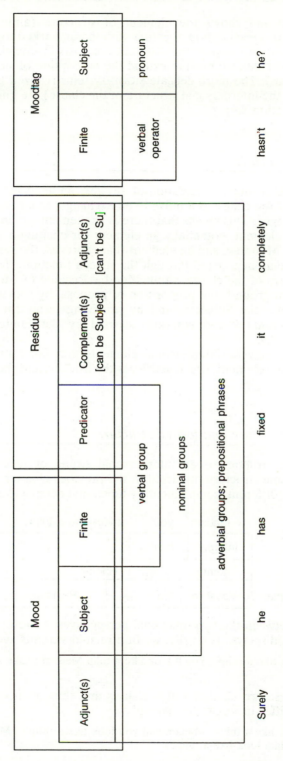

Fig. 3.9 Modal structure of the clause

displays the options and shows the element of structure (and/or ordering of elements) which realizes each option, together with the unmarked tone realizations. Note that, to differentiate between the different contrasts in meaning made available by the system of TONE, we need to extend the description of MOOD in delicacy (showing finer choices). The more delicate MOOD systems realized by selections in tone (rather than by the interpersonal structure of the clause) are known as the KEY systems (see IFG Section 8.9).

5.2 Interpersonal structure

We can now add add to our consideration of any text an analysis of the interpersonal organization of the clause as a move in an exchange, as a contribution to the development of dialogue. This means that there is an element for enacting a speech function, the **Mood** element, potentially an element for eliciting a response to the speech function, the **Moodtag**, and an element that expresses the rest of the proposition or proposal being negotiated through the speech function, the **Residue**. The interpersonal structure of the clause is thus Mood + Residue (+ Moodtag).

The Mood element grounds the proposition or proposal by providing a 'modally responsible' element - the Subject - and by providing terms for negotiation in choices of TENSE/MODALITY and POLARITY carried by the Finite and/or mood Adjunct(s). See Fig. 3.9.

In addition, there may be interpersonal elements that fall outside this modal structure: the **Vocative** element, which addresses the listener, and the **Expletive** (see Section 2.4 above).

5.3 Interpersonal structure and textual structure

The Mood^Residue structure is an interpersonal strand or layer alongside the textual Theme^Rheme structure discussed in the previous chapter. The two structures thus constitute different, complementary functional perspectives on the clause:

		Madam,	you'	ll look like a tulip.	
		Interp.	topical		
clause	textual	Theme		Rheme	
	interpersonal	Vocative	Mood	Residue	

The difference between the two functional perspectives is shown in the different set of variants each displays. Textually, we find related variants such as:

> Madam you'll look like a tulip : You'll look like a tulip Madam : Like a tulip you'll look Madam

Interpersonally, these are all declarative clauses and thus do not contrast. Interpersonal variants differ in MOOD; for example:

> Madam you'll look like a tulip : Madam will you look like a tulip? : Madam who'll look like a tulip? : Madam look like a tulip!

Textually, these clauses are all alike in having unmarked (topical) Theme.[14] Thus we need to recognize different patterns of meaning relating to different metafunctions, but simultaneously present in any clause.

Further reading

Caffarel, Alice 1995: Approaching the French clause as a move in a dialogue. In R. Hasan and P. Fries (eds), *On Subject and Theme: a discourse functional perspective*. Amsterdam: Benjamins 1–50.

Halliday, M.A.K. 1970: Functional diversity in language, as seen from a consideration of modality and mood in English. *Foundations of language* 6.3, 322–61.

_____1982: The de-automatization of grammar: from Priestley's 'An Inspector Calls'. J.M. Anderson (ed.) *Language form and linguistic variation: papers dedicated to Angus MacIntosh*. Amsterdam: Benjamins, 129–59. An extended discussion of modality, applied to the analysis of dramatic dialogue.

_____ 1984: Language as code and language as behaviour: a systemic-functional interpretation of the nature and ontogenesis of dialogue. R. Fawcett, M.A.K. Halliday, S. Lamb and A. Makkai (eds), *The semiotics of language and culture, Volume 1*. London: Frances Pinter (Open Linguistics Series) 3–35.

Hasan, Ruqaiya and Fries, Peter H. (eds) 1995: *On Subject and Theme: a discourse functional perspective*. Amsterdam: Benjamins.

Huddleston, Rodney D. 1965: A fragment of a systemic description of English. Working Paper. Reprinted in M.A.K. Halliday and J.R. Martin (eds) *Readings in systemic linguistics*. London: Batsford, 1981, 222–36.

Martin, J.R. 1990: Interpersonal grammatization: mood and modality in Tagalog. *Philippine Journal of Linguistics* 21.1 (Special Issue on the Silver Anniversary of the Language Study Centre of Philippine Normal College 1964–1989 – Part 2): 2–51. Discusses MOOD systems in Tagalog.

_____ 1992: *English text: system and structure – Chapter 2: Negotiation*. Amsterdam: Benjamins. On interpersonal semantics of exchange. Martin refers to recent work by M. Berry, E. Ventola, S. Eggins and others.

Matthiessen, Christian 1995: *Lexicogrammatical cartography: English systems*. Tokyo: International Language Sciences Publishers. Chapter 5; interpersonal resources: Section 2.3.5.

[14]We can add one further set of examples to bring out the difference between textual and interpersonal variation ('agnation', to use the technical term): interpersonally, *Madam you'll look like a tulip, won't you?* is related to *Madam you'll look like a tulip, you will*. In the first variant, the tag is concerned with eliciting an indication of the listener's state of agreement with the proposition in the dialogic interaction (e.g. *No, I won't!*), whereas in the second it serves to present a reminder of the Theme at the end of the clause (a strategy used in certain varieties of English).

4

Transitivity
clause as representation

1 Orientation

1.1 Reading guide to IFG

IFG Chapter 5 (main discussion of TRANSITIVITY)
Sections 7.4.5–6 (embedded expansions and acts)
Section 7.5 (projections, relevance to mental and verbal clauses)
Section 7A.4–6 (hypotactic verbal group complexes)
Section 10.3 (metaphors of transitivity)

1.2 Characterization of TRANSITIVITY

The system of TRANSITIVITY belongs to the **experiential**[1] metafunction and is the overall grammatical resource for construing goings on. It construes this flux of experience as quanta of change. These are represented as a configuration of a process, participants involved in it, and attendant circumstances. There are, of course, innumerable kinds of goings on and ways in which they may unfold, but the grammar construes out a small number of distinct types, each with its own particular characteristics. These constitute the process types.

Imagine you are looking up at the sky, with a number of things happening all the time (see Fig. 4.1). Out of this ongoing change (represented pictorially by repeated elements), you can construe a quantum of change as one process configuration, realized in the grammar as one clause; for example: *A kite is flying across the sky*. With this, you have turned experience into meaning, and into wording. Here it is constructed as a configuration of 'a kite' + 'is flying' + 'across the sky', or more abstractly in terms of the transitivity system, as Actor + Process + Location. This is a representation, one which imposes three constituent elements, viz. a participant (Actor: *a kite*), a process (Process: *is flying*), and a circumstance (Location: *across the sky*); and these are of a distinct kind (e.g. Actor, rather than Sayer; Location,

---

[1]The third metafunction is the **ideational** one; but it has two modes, the **experiential** and the **logical**. Within the clause, we find the experiential mode, manifested in the system of TRANSITIVITY (see below). The logical mode provides the resources for forming various kinds of complexes – clause complexes, group complexes, and so on (IFG Chapter 7), and it plays a role together with the experiential mode in the organization of groups (nominal groups, verbal groups etc. (IFG Chapter 6)).

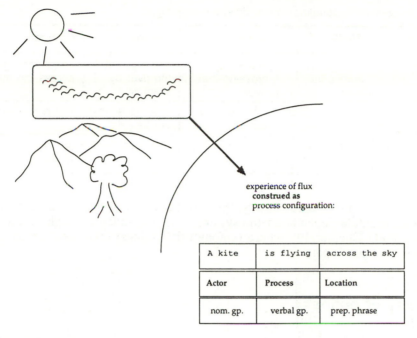

experience of flux
construed as
process configuration:

A kite	is flying	across the sky
Actor	Process	Location
nom. gp.	verbal gp.	prep. phrase

Fig. 4.1   Construing experience

rather than Cause). It may seem that this is the only way it could be; but it is not, of course: English might have given us the option of construing this as *it's winging across the sky* (cf. *it's raining*), *it's winging a kite across the sky* (cf. *it's blowing a gale*), *it's kiting across the sky*, or even *sky is winging a kite, the sky's crossing a kite*. Even without going outside conventional English, we can see there is always a choice in how to construe experience. For instance, we might separate out kite-hood, leaving it to be inferred from the manner of flying: *something is flying across the sky like a kite* or we might separate out the motion and the mode of motion: *a kite's traversing the sky by flying*.[2]

It is possible to get a sense of the choice involved by looking across languages and noting the alternative ways of construing some semantic domain such as directed motion. For example, see Table 4.1. When we look at the different ways different languages construe the same semantic domain, we find variation along the various dimensions of transitivity, e.g. in whether some phenomenon is construed as a process or a participant. However, such choices are also available <u>within</u> a given language. For example, we have alternatives such as *in May people bought more and more TVs, VCRs, etc.* and *May saw a sharp rise in consumer electronic*

---

[2]It is easy to fall into the trap of thinking that there is some mode of objective phenomenal world that can be reflected in different ways in language (especially given our somewhat simplistic diagram, where we actually move from one semiotic representation to another, the first one standing for the outside world experienced); but there is not. We construe our experience actively by imposing organization. An important aspect of this is treating things, events, etc. that are unlike one another as alike. It is perhaps easier to realize this if we consider more abstract domains of experience – social value systems, religious systems, scientific models.

Table 4.1   Semantic domains across different languages

Domain	English	Akan	Japanese	Chinese
Directed motion	she swam across the river	she swam crossing the river	she crossed the river by swimming	she swam, getting across the river
Possession	she has a car	with her is a car	s/he (location) car be:exist	she has a car
Precipitation	it's raining	water is falling	rain is falling	the sky's dropping water

purchases. These are complementary; they are both part of the overall system, but the second example depends on the system being expanded through grammatical metaphor (IFG Chapter 10), where (among other things) processes are construed as if they were participants.

2 Survey of options

We have described TRANSITIVITY as a resource for construing our experience in terms of configurations of a process, participants and circumstances. Such configurations are determined by two major systems, those of PROCESS TYPE and CIRCUMSTANTIATION.

(i) PROCESS TYPE is the resource for sorting out our experience of all kinds of events into a small number of types. These differ both with respect to the Process itself and the number and kind of participants involved. The system discriminates six different types of process in English. The three major ones are **material**, **mental** and **relational**, each with a small set of subtypes. In addition, there are three further process types, the **behavioural**, **verbal** and **existential**. These six kinds of clauses are illustrated in Table 4.2.

Table 4.2 Process types in English

Process type	subcategory	Example clause (processes in bold)
material	event (i.e. happening) action (i.e. doing)	*the sugar **dissolved*** *she **stirred** the coffee*
mental	perception cognition affection	*she **saw** the car* *she **forgot** his name/his name **escaped** her* *she **liked** his music/his music **pleased** her*
relational	attributive identifying	*Maggie **was** strong* *Maggie **was** our leader*
behavioural		*she **laughed***
verbal		*she **replied***
existential		*there **was** once a beautiful princess*

Table 4.3 Process types and nuclear participants

Process type	nuclear participants	Example (participants in bold)
material	Actor, Goal	*she* made *the coffee*
mental	Senser, Phenomenon	*she* saw *the car*
relational: attributive	Carrier, Attribute	*Maggie* was *strong*
: identifying	Token, Value	*Maggie* was *our leader*
behavioural	Behaver	*she* laughed
verbal	Sayer	*she* replied
existential	Existent	*there was* a beautiful princess

Each of the six types of process has its own small set of participant roles. For example, a material clause involves an Actor and possibly a Goal:

She	stirred	the coffee
Actor	Process:Material	Goal

Table 4.3 shows the central, or 'nuclear' participants associated with each process type.

Two further participants, generalized across process types, are introduced in IFG Section 5.6. These are Beneficiary and Range. These are still participants but closer to circumstances than the other participants.

(ii) Circumstances are discussed in Section 5.7 of IFG. They are general across process types (precisely because they are less centrally involved in the process than participants). Examples are given in Table 4.4.

The various process types differ according to the criteria summarized in IFG on p. 173. (See Troubleshooting section below for further discussion.) A brief outline of characteristics of each type is given below.

2.1 Material clauses

Material clauses construe doings and happenings (IFG Section 5.2). Prototypically, these are concrete: changes in the material world that can be perceived, such as motion in space (*she drove down the coast; she drove him down the coast*) and change in physical make-up (*the lake froze; he melted the butter*). However, such concrete material processes have also come to serve as a model for construing our experience of change in abstract phenomena. For example *Prices fell throughout this period* construes movement in an abstract space of measurement. Similarly, alongside *the wind destroyed the gazebo* we have *their arguments destroyed her theory*. 'Material' thus covers both concrete and abstract processes.

The one inherent participant is the **Actor** – the one doing the material deed. In addition, there may also be a **Goal** – a participant impacted by a doing (the one done to/with), and sometimes a **Beneficiary** – a participant benefiting from the doing (the one given to or done for), or else (in clauses without a Goal) a **Range** – a participant specifying the scope of a happening. Examples are shown in Table 4.5.

The **Goal** is either actually brought into existence by the doing (*build a house, bake a cake, compose a song*), or it exists prior to the doing, but is affected in some

Table 4.4 Types of circumstance in English

Circumstance type	typical probe	Example realization	Circumstance subcategory	subcategory probe
Extent	how___? at what intervals?	*for three hours every three hours*	temporal	for how long?
		every second step for six miles	spatial	how far?
Location	at what point?	*in September; before tea; recently; during the lesson*	temporal	when?
		in the yard; from Paris; miles away	spatial	where?
Manner	how?	*with a hammer; by trickery*	means	by what means?
		quickly	quality	how?
		as fast as possible; like a top	comparison	what like?
Cause	why?	*because of you; thanks to him; for lack of $5*	reason	why?
		for better results; in the hope of a good deal	purpose	for what purpose?
		on behalf of us all	behalf	on whose behalf?
Contingency	in what circumstances?	*in the event of rain; without more help (we can't do it)*	condition	under what conditions?
		in spite of the rain	concession	despite what?
		in the absence of proof	default	lacking what?
Accompaniment	together with?	*with(out) his friends*	comitative	who/what with?
		as well as them; instead of them	additive	and who/what else?
Role		*as a concerned parent*	guise	what as?
		(smashed) into pieces	product	what into?
Matter	what about?	*about this; with reference to that*		
Angle	says who?	*according to the Shorter Oxford*		

way. In the latter case, the Goal can be probed with *do to/with*, as in *what did she do with the chair?* or *what she did with the chair was move it*. Also, it can often be accompanied by a representation of the result of the impact, such as a new location (*she moved the chair into the corner*) or quality (*she scrubbed the chair clean*). In this, it differs from the **Range**, which cannot be probed with *do to/with*; thus we do not get: *what she did with* [Range:] *the mountain was climb it, she climbed* [Range:] *the mountain into fame*. This is because the Range is not impacted on by the performance of the Process.

Table 4.5 Participant roles in material clauses

type	Actor	Process	Goal	Beneficiary	Range
action	she	built	the house	(for the kids)	
	she	gave	the house	(to the kids)	
	she	moved	the chair		
event	the chair	moved			
	she	climbed			the mountain

The **Beneficiary** can be probed by looking at that version of a clause where it follows the Goal. In this case, it is realized with a preposition – either *to*, marking it as a recipient type of Beneficiary, or *for*, marking it as a client type of Beneficiary:

> She gave <u>his aunt</u> a teapot : She gave a teapot **to** <u>his aunt</u>
>
> She built <u>his aunt</u> a gazebo : She built a gazebo **for** <u>his aunt</u>

The Recipient appears when there is a transfer of existing goods represented, while the Client is involved when there is provision of service (including the creation of new goods).

2.2 Mental clauses

Mental clauses construe a person involved in conscious processing, including processes of perception, cognition and affection. The one inherent participant is the **Senser** – the participant sensing, i.e. involved in conscious processing. This participant is endowed with consciousness; nominal groups serving as Senser which denote non-conscious entities have to be construed metaphorically as 'personified'. In the following examples the Senser is underlined:

> <u>The man</u> knew too much.
> <u>The witness</u> heard her threatening them.
> <u>She</u> liked her job.
> Her tasks interested <u>her</u>.
> It surprised <u>him</u> to see her so happy.
> <u>My car</u> doesn't like hills.

In addition to the Senser, mental clauses may involve one further type of participant, the **Phenomenon** being sensed. This can be any kind of entity entertained or created by consciousness – a conscious being, an object, a substance, an institution, or an abstraction, but not only such 'things' but also acts (e.g. *I like <u>swimming early in the morning</u>*) and facts (*I like <u>the fact that he apologized</u>*). Grammatically, this means that a wide range of units can serve as Phenomenon. In the following examples, the Phenomenon is underlined:

> The man knew <u>too much</u>.
> The witness heard <u>her threatening them</u>.
> She liked <u>her job</u>.
> <u>Her tasks</u> interested her.

It surprised him <u>to see her so happy</u>.
My car doesn't like <u>hills</u>.

The Phenomenon may represent the 'content' of sensing. However, this content is not always represented as a participant within the clause. It may also be represented by a separate clause. For example:

David thought → the moon was a balloon.

The second clause here is a **projected clause** which represents an **idea** brought into existence by the mental processing (see IFG Section 7.5). Other examples:

She guessed → he would be late.
He wanted → them to leave.
He preferred → them to stay.[3]

2.3 Relational clauses

Halliday's category of relational clauses is a generalization of the traditional notion of 'copula' constructions. Relational clauses construe being and do this in two different modes – attribution and identification. There are thus two principal relational clause types, with different sets of participant roles: (i) attributive clauses with **Carrier + Attribute**, and (ii) identifying clauses with **Token + Value**.[4] For example:

Maxine	is	energetic	[attributive]
Maxine	is	an energetic type	[attributive]
Carrier		Attribute	

| Maxine | is | the goalie | [identifying] |
| Token | | Value | |

| The goalie | is | Maxine | [identifying] |
| Value | | Token | |

The fundamental difference between attributive and identifying is the difference between class membership (attributive) and symbolization (identifying). Carrier and Attribute are of the same order of abstraction, but differ in generality as member to class, subtype to type (*elephants are mammals; elephants are huge animals*). Token and Value are of different orders of abstraction; they are related symbolically (*elephants are my favourite animals; Mary is the leader; Olivier is (plays) Lear*). Typical kinds of meaning relations holding between Token and Value in an identifying clause are given in Table 4.6.

Table 4.7 shows some contrasting examples of attributive and identifying clauses.

2.3.1 Subcategories of relational clause

All the examples given above are of intensive relational clauses. It is also possible for relational clauses to involve an additional meaning feature, making them either

---

[3]See Troubleshooting Section 3.5(iv) below for guidance in discriminating a projected clause and an embedded clause functioning as Phenomenon within the mental process clause.
[4]In addition to the roles of Token and Value, participants in identifying clauses construe the roles of Identified and Identifier (see IFG: 122 and following).

Table 4.6 Examples of meanings of Token and Value roles

Token	Value	typical verb (other than *be*) realizing process	Example clause
expression	content	express, mean, represent, signify	*Knit brows signify thoughtfulness*
symbol	symbolized	betoken, stand for, reflect, spell	*Red stands for danger*
form	meaning	translate as, mean	*chien means dog*
name	referent	name, christen, call [causative]	*[they] named the baby John*
function	filler	function as, serve as, act as	*the reservoir functions as the city's emergency water supply*
position	holder of position	vote, elect [causative]	*[the people] voted him President*
actor	role	play, act as	*Jenny played Ophelia*

possessive or **circumstantial**. In such a case two participant roles may be 'conflated' in the one clause element (indicated by a /). Examples:

Max	has	lots of energy
Carrier/Possessor	Process: attributive and possessive	Attribute/Possession

Max	owns	the property
Token/Possessor	Process: identifying and possessive	Value/Possession

The trees	are	around Mary
Carrier	Process: attributive	Attribute/Location

The trees	surround	Mary
Token	Process: identifying and circumstantial	Value

Table 4.7 Attributive and identifying clauses

attributive (not reversible)	identifying (reversible)
Judy is/seems/sounds (like) a star	*Judy is the star of Cukor's movie; The star of Cukor's movie is Judy*
He's a friend	*He's the friend you met yesterday; The friend you met yesterday is him*
It's hot	*It's Wednesday; Today's Wednesday; Wednesday is today*
It's late	*It's 3 pm; The time is 3 pm; 3 pm is the time*

2.4 Verbal clauses

Verbal clauses represent processes of 'saying'; but this category includes not only the different modes of saying (*asking, commanding, offering, stating*) but also semiotic processes that are not necessarily verbal (*showing, indicating*). The central participant is the **Sayer** – the participant saying, telling, stating, informing, asking, querying, demanding, commanding, offering, threatening, suggesting, and so on. It can be a human or human-like speaker, of course; but it can also be any other symbolic source. For example:

> She told me a strange story
> He asked too many questions
> They asked me → whether I could leave at once
> They told me → to leave at once
> The paper says → there'll be another election
> The sign indicates → that Gates 40–62 are to the right
> The form asks → what other funding sources you have

In addition, a verbal clause may also represent the addressee of a speech interaction, as the **Receiver**. The Receiver is like a verbal Beneficiary, and can often (but not always) be marked by *to*:

> They told me → to leave at once
> They said to me → to leave at once

The 'content' of saying may be represented as a separate clause (a **locution**) quoting or reporting what was said (*she said → that she'd return in the morning; they told me → to leave at once; she asked → whether it was too late*). This quoted or reported clause is called a **projected** clause and is discussed in IFG Chapter 7 (in particular Section 7.5). It is not a constituent part of the verbal clause (cf. below), but is a separate clause in a projecting clause complex.[5]

However, in addition to being constituted in a projected clause, the content of saying may also be construed as a participant – the **Verbiage** of a verbal clause:

> They told me a story
> She asked him a question
> They said a few words

This is a kind of verbal Range, indicating the scope of saying in terms of a generic category (e.g. *story, fable*), a speech functional category (e.g. *lie, question*) or a lexico-grammatical one (*word, phrase*).[6]

2.5 Behavioural clauses: between material and mental/verbal

In addition to material clauses on the one hand and mental/verbal clauses on the other, each with their own grammatical characteristics (see Section 3 below), the grammar accommodates an intermediate type with mixed characteristics - the

---

[5]This is clear from the oddness of passive and theme-predicated variants such as *to leave at once was said to me by them, it was to leave at once that they said to me.*
[6]Note that IFG also includes examples where the clause is not an exchange of information and the content of saying is a non-linguistic commodity, e.g. 'She requested *a dance*'.

Table 4.8 Behavioural and mental processes of perception

behavioural	mental: perception
I'm looking at John	*I see John; I can see John*
—	*I see that John's already left*
I'm listening to John working	*I hear John working; I can hear John working*
—	*I can hear that John is working*
The cat's sniffing the flower	*The cat smells the flower*
—	*The cat smells that another cat's been in*
I'm tasting the wine	*I taste the wine in this; I can taste the wine in the sauce*
—	*I can taste that there's wine in the sauce*

behavioural clause. These construe (human) behaviour, including mental and verbal behaviour, as an active version of verbal and mental processes. That is, saying and sensing are construed as activity; for example: *chat, gossip*; *ponder, watch, listen, smile, grin*. Behavioural processes are like mental ones in that one participant is endowed with human consciousness. This is the Senser in the case of mental processes. We can call it the **Behaver** in the case of behavioural processes. However, behavioural processes are unlike mental and verbal ones but like material ones in that:

(i) the unmarked representation of present time is present-in-present (the present continuous/progressive); and

(ii) they cannot report (i.e. occur with a reported clause in a projecting clause complex).

Table 4.8 illustrates the differences between related pairs of behavioural processes and mental processes of perception.

Behaviourals include categories reflecting the mental and verbal ones: perception, cognition, affection, and verbal. See Table 4.9.

Behaviourals also include more material-like subtypes. The border area (see Section 3.1) between material processes and behavioural ones is covered by two main types, physiological processes – *twitch, shiver, tremble, sweat*, etc. – and social processes – *kiss, hug, embrace, dance, play* etc. Both of these shade into the verbal type, from different angles; physiologically: *cough, gasp, stutter* etc. and socially: *chat, talk, gossip* etc.

2.6 Existential clauses

Existential clauses resemble relational clauses in that they construe a participant involved in a process of being, but differ from relational ones in that there is only one participant, the **Existent**, which is thereby introduced into the text:

There	will be	a real bunfight	at the next meeting.
	Process: existential Process	Existent	Location: temporal

Table 4.9 Types of behavioural process

	behavioural	mental/verbal
perception	look at, watch, stare, gawk, view, look over, observe	see, observe
	listen to	hear, overhear
	sniff, smell	smell
	taste	taste
	feel	feel
cognition	ponder, puzzle, solve, work out, meditate, ruminate, think	think, know, believe
affection (subtype emotion)	smile, frown, laugh, pout, gasp, grin, scowl, shake, shudder, tremble,	fear, enjoy, like; frighten, scare, alarm, disgust, please, amuse, upset
verbal	whine, whinge, mumble, stammer, stutter, mutter, moan, chatter, gossip, talk, speak, sing; frown, grimace, snort, cough, slander, insult, praise, flatter, [These are treated as verbal processes with a Target in IFG.]	say, tell, ask

In an existential clause, the *there* signals the process type but does not function as a Location circumstance; nor does it represent a participant.

However, existential clauses frequently have a circumstance of Location and, if it occurs in thematic (initial) position, the existential *there* may be absent:

All around them	was	a silence
Along this waterway	toiled	a string of wolfish dogs
Location	Process: existential	Existent

2.7 Additional Agents

In addition to the participants so far discussed for each process type, there is often the possibility of an additional participant with a causing or agentive role, especially when there is a causative verbal group complex realizing the Process, such as *make → do*, *cause → to do*. Examples are given in Table 4.10.

The Initiator, Inducer, Assigner and Attributor roles can be generalized as representing the role of Agent in the various clause types (see further Section 2.8 below).

2.8 Ergative interpretation

In the discussion so far, we have been giving a **transitive** interpretation to the experiential grammar of English. However, according to Halliday, if we look carefully at

Table 4.10 Agents in different clause types

additional Agent				
You Initiator	*'ll help* Process: ...	*us* Actor	*monitor* ... material	*this* Goal
These programmes Inducer	*let* Process: ...	*parents* Senser	*understand* ... mental	*their responsibilities* Phenomenon
His experience Assigner	*makes* Process: ...	*him* Token	*(be)* (... identifying)	*the best judge* Value
The new school Attributor	*has made* Process: ...	*him* Carrier	*(be)* (... attributive)	*more rebellious* Attribute

the grammar, this perspective emerges as one of two complementary motifs as far as construing experiential reality is concerned. The transitive view is the more commonsense one, that we have inherited from Latin (via traditional grammar with its notions of nominative and accusative case). From this perspective, something involving an Actor and a Process happens (intransitive), and may optionally affect a Goal (transitive), as shown in Fig. 4.2.

From the transitive perspective, the question we are asking is whether the action carries over to affect an additional participant or not, and this provides the contrast between transitive and intransitive clauses. See Table 4.11.

The other perspective is the **ergative** one, in which a happening is conceived of as involving a Process and some central entity (Halliday's middle voice). This entity through which the process is actualized is called a **Medium**, as shown in Fig. 4.3.

The additional question we can ask from the ergative perspective is who or what brought the happening about (Halliday's effective voice). Example clauses are shown in Table 4.12.

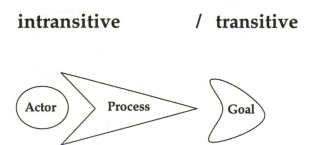

intransitive   / transitive

Fig. 4.2   The transitive perspective

Table 4.11 Examples of intransitive and transitive clauses

Actor and Process [intransitive]	action optionally extended to a Goal [transitive]
the troops attacked	*the troops attacked the capital*
the guerillas hunted	*the guerillas hunted the militia*
the police charged	*the police charged the rioters*
Alfie pushed	*Alfie pushed the forward*
Glen kicked	*Glen kicked the ball*

Table 4.12 Examples of effective and middle clauses

Process and Medium [middle]	Agent bringing about action [effective]
the baby bounced	*the father bounced the baby*
the pizza cooked	*Tim cooked the pizza*
the clothes dried	*Mac dried the clothes*
the news spread	*Sue spread the news*
the ship sank	*the storm sank the ship*

effective   /   middle

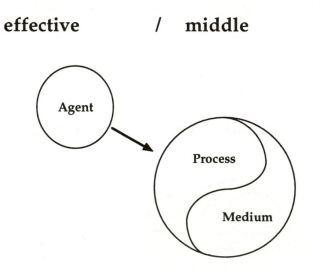

Fig. 4.3 The ergative perspective

Table 4.13 Ergative correspondences for transitive participant roles

PROCESS TYPE	transitive role	ergative role	example
material	Actor (intransitive)	Medium	***They*** *ran*
	Actor (transitive)	Agent	***They*** *moved the chair*
	Goal	Medium	*They moved **the chair***
	Recipient, Client	Beneficiary	*They gave **me** the book;* *They built **her** a sandpit*
	Range	Range	*They did **a dance***
mental	Senser	Medium	***They*** *like the movie*
(*like* type)	Phenomenon	Range	*They liked **the movie***
(*please* type)	Phenomenon	Agent	***The movie*** *delighted them*
	Senser	Range	*The movie delighted **them***
verbal	Sayer	Medium	***They*** *replied*
	Receiver	Beneficiary	*They told **me***
	Verbiage	Range	*They told **a story***
behavioural	Behaver	Medium	***She's*** *looking at you*
existential	Existent	Medium	*There was **a surprise***
relational: attributive	Carrier	Medium	***She*** *was happy*
	Attribute	Range	*She was **happy***
relational: identifying	Token	Agent or Medium	*(see IFG Table 5(19))*
	Value	Medium or Range	

Halliday suggests that all English clauses can be analysed from either a transitive or an ergative perspective, even though some clause types lend themselves to one analysis or the other,[7] as do some texts. The transitive categories can be 'translated' into ergative ones as in Table 4.13, which shows that, in addition to the Agent and Medium roles, the ergative model includes the Beneficiary and Range. You have already met these in their material manifestation (see Section 2.1 above), and the same generalized participant roles may occur in the other process types, as shown in the table. (Note too that all the differentiated 'additional Agent' roles exemplified in Section 2.7 above are Agents in effective clauses in the ergative interpretation.)

[7]For example, *the police attacked the militia* lends itself to a transitive analysis, pairing naturally with *the police attacked* – and could thus be challenged *no, the army attacked* since it is the police or army that are doing the attacking; *the sergeant marched the troops* on the other hand lends itself to an ergative analysis, pairing naturally with *the troops marched* – and cannot be challenged: *no, the corporal marched*, since it is the troops rather than the sergeant or corporal that are doing the marching.

3 Troubleshooting

3.1 A topology of processes

The four major process types – material, mental, verbal and relational – cover the grammatical-semantic 'space' of 'goings on' – happenings, doings, sensings, saying, being, havings etc.; and they constitute a particular 'theory' of this space – a framework for interpreting and representing it by means of clauses in English. There are prototypical cases of all the four major process types; these are the core types of doing and happening, saying, sensing, and being and having. The core types can be identified by means of all or most of the probes used to differentiate different transitivity types (see Section 3.2). But there are also more peripheral cases. These peripheral cases can all be located on scales or clines whose endpoints are the regions that constitute the core cases. For instance, there is a cline between prototypical material processes and prototypical mental ones and somewhere along this cline there is a region of processes with both material and mental properties. Such regions include the indeterminate cases. The same is true of other pairs of process types. The factors that determine where a particular process is located in the overall

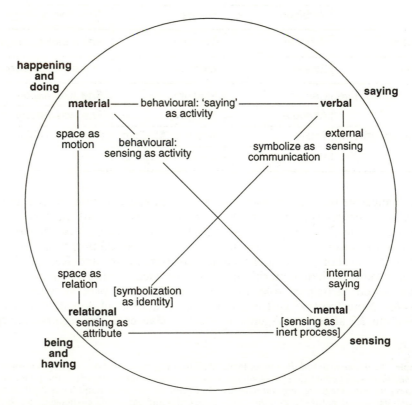

Fig. 4.4   A topology of process types

Table 4.14 Troubleshooting sections for distinguishing process types

	material	behavioural	mental	verbal	relational
material					§3.6 (i)
behavioural			§2.5	§3.7 (i)	
mental				§3.5 (ii),	§3.5 (iii)
verbal					§3.7 (iii)
relational					

space of process types include the degree of 'potency' of the participants (animacy, volitionality etc.), the degree of their affectedness (state, change), the degree to which the process can project another process, and so on; many of these factors are reflected in the transitivity probes to be discussed in more detail in this section.

Fig. 4.4 represents the three major process types, together with the verbal type, and shows several of the clines between pairs of them.

The clines are not all of the same type – some are more discrete than others, some clearly involve grammatical metaphor, and so on; but it is useful to bring them together for purposes of discussion and to explain why there may be different possible interpretations of 'borderline' examples. (Sometimes transitivity has been discussed in terms of a single scale running from high transitivity to low transitivity; but this is in fact only one type of consideration.)

To avoid clutter in the figure we have left out some clines. For instance, there is, arguably, a cline between receptive (passive) material (*it was broken by a stone*) and attributive relational (*it was broken and useless*) and a similar one between receptive (passive) mental (*he was excited by the prospect*) and, again, attributive relational (*he was happy and excited*). (See IFG: 121–2.)

Because the different process types 'meet' at certain points in the semantic-grammatical 'topology' illustrated above, some indeterminacy in assigning a particular text instance to a typological category is to be expected on occasion. None the less the 'core' instances can always be distinguished by checking for differentiating criteria, as discussed further below in the sections indicated in Table 4.14.

3.2 General probes helpful in analysing for TRANSITIVITY

Probes are questions you can ask which help you to explore the structure of the clause you are interested in. Three general probes for exploring transitivity structures are shown in Fig. 4.5 and discussed below.

(i) What are possible alternate verbs? To help determine the process type it is useful to ask what verbs other than the particular one used in the clause would function in the same way. This helps to sort out verbs that can be used with more than one type of transitivity. For instance, the verb *make* in *this makes a very good stuffing* is a member of a set that includes *be*, which indicates that it is relational; but *make* is a member of the set *cook, produce, create* when it is used in the clause *the chef makes a very good stuffing*.

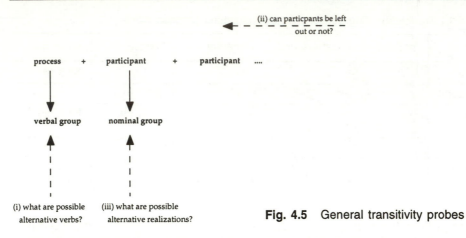

Fig. 4.5   General transitivity probes

(ii) Can participants be left out or not? To check whether a structure is related to another more familiar one, it is useful to see whether there are variations on the clause with more or fewer participants. For instance, this helps to show the difference between (behavioural) *he sang her a song* and (verbal) *he told her a story*:

> he sang her a song : *he sang her
> he told her a story : he told her

(iii) What are possible alternative realizations for participants? To discriminate between processes it is important to check what alternative realizations of the participants are possible. Are they constrained in terms of consciousness, fact-hood etc.? For instance, *that lonely child breaks my heart* might look like a material clause at first. But it is clearly closely related to (*the fact*) *that she is so lonely breaks my heart*. In the latter case, the Subject of the clause is a 'fact', which shows immediately that it is not a material clause. (It is rather a mental clause).

3.3 One process or two?

Very often there will be two lexical verbs in a single clause.[8] For example:

> they   will start → to enjoy   the camp   next week
> they   began → asking   questions
> they   ended up → explaining   my situation
> they   seem → to have   enough money
> they   practised → whistling
> they   were forced → to leave
> they   were allowed → to leave
>   ....Process.................

In all the above cases, there is a single clause, with a single Process element, but this element is realized by a complex of verbal groups. For example the Process *will start to enjoy* is realized by a complex of the two verbal groups *will start* and *to*

---

[8]We discuss cases with two lexical verbs here. But the potential for introducing additional expansions exists; e.g. *he seemed → to begin → to try → to study harder*. What we say here about the first verb applies to all in such a series except the last; the second verb in our discussion corresponds to the last in the series.

enjoy. In a Transitivity analysis, the second (non-finite) verbal group is the relevant one for PROCESS TYPE. Thus, *they will start to enjoy the camp next week* is a mental clause, *they began asking questions* is a verbal clause and *they seem to have enough money* is a relational possessive one. (See IFG Sections 7A.4–6.) In contrast the first verbal group elaborates the unfolding of the Process, for example in terms of phase (*begin/continue/stop* → *doing*). Note that these simple clauses with complex Processes are different from cases where there are two clauses – and hence two distinct Processes – such as the following (see further Chapter 5):

he	got up	‖ and ( )	turned on	the light
he	got up	‖	yawning	
he	got up	‖	to let in	the cat
he	left	‖	having told	them	his news
	Process	‖	**Process**	

Where there are two distinct proceses like this (i.e. two clauses), each can be associated with its own circumstances, as in *he left hurriedly at 3 pm, having told them his news quietly before the meeting*.

Less clear-cut is the analysis of examples similar to those in the first group above but where the first lexical verb has a mental or verbal meaning:

they	want → to change	their library books
they	'd like → to bring	their friends
they	claim → to know	the Minister

IFG recommends that these be analysed as a single transitivity configuration, in the same way as the earlier examples. Thus:

they	want to change	their library books
Actor	Process: material	Goal

This does not, however, foreground the fact that the choice of participant is restricted by the lexical verb in the first verbal group (i.e. only a conscious or semiotic entity can be construed as the major participant). An alternative analysis which gives equal status to both verbal groups by taking them to be processes of separate clauses may therefore be preferred:

they	want	→	to change	their library books
Senser	Process: mental		Process: material	Goal

The interpretation here is that there are two clauses forming a clause complex, just as in cases where each process has its own set of participants and circumstances, as in the following examples:

they	want	→	you to change	their books tomorrow
they	told us	→	they would change	their books tomorrow

See IFG Section 7A.6 for discussion of alternate analyses of such examples (clause complexes vs simple clauses with verbal group complexes).

3.4 Material clauses

(i) Material or non-material clause? An important test for distinguishing among the main process types is to check the unmarked tense selection used to represent

present time. Is it the simple present or the present-in-present (present continuous)? Of the three main types only material clauses favour present-in-present:[9]

Right now Janey **is digging** the garden	Material clause
At the moment Janey **likes** arty films	Mental clause
Right now Janey **has** no energy	Relational clause

In this respect, material clauses are like behavioural and many verbal ones.

A second crucial probe is whether the clause can project (i.e. report or quote) another clause or not. If it can, it is not material (but rather verbal or mental). Finally, it is important to realize that in certain types of text a material process may in fact be quite abstract in character (see Section 2.1 above).

(ii) Material or relational? See Section 3.6(i) below.

(iii) Material clauses with an Attribute In addition to the participant roles discussed in the Survey section (Actor, Goal, Beneficiary, Range, Initiator), we may also find an Attribute in a material clause which has a Goal. For example:

They	**left**	the bedroom	*happy*
Actor	Process: material	Range	Attribute (depictive)
They	**painted**	the bedroom	*pale green*
Actor	Process: material	Goal	Attribute (resultative)

Note the potential here for an interpretation according to the relational model of Attributor + Process + Carrier + Attribute. However in a material clause the Attribute can always be left out, which is not the case in an attributive relational clause. Thus material *we folded the paper flat: we folded the paper* but not relational *we kept the paper flat: we kept the paper.* (See further IFG: 157.)

(iv) Range or Goal? The difference between a Range and a Goal in a material clause is very clear in the prototypical case: the **Goal** is (as the name suggests) the participant that is impacted by the performance of the Process by the Actor. For example:

he squashed <u>the slug</u>; they felled <u>the tree</u>; they threw <u>the ball</u> into a corner; he mashed <u>the potatoes</u>; she repaired <u>the car</u>; he broke <u>the glass</u>.

The nature of the relationship between Actor-Process and Goal is thus very much a material one.

In contrast, the **Range** *elaborates* or *enhances* the Process.

(i) It elaborates the Process (a) by restatement (the traditional category of cognate object), as in:

he sang <u>an old melancholy folk song</u>; she laughed <u>the smoker's hoarse laugh</u>;

(b) by specification (of the 'lexical content'), as in:

he did <u>an exotic dance</u>; they made <u>a fatal mistake</u>; she took <u>a brisk shower</u>;

or (c) by exemplification (i.e. by giving a subtype of the process), as in:

they played <u>a game of tennis</u>; they listened to <u>stories</u>; they watched <u>TV</u>.

---

[9]But see Section 3.6 for 'change of state' attributive clauses which do take present-in-present. Note too that a material process can of course occur with a simple present tense choice, but will then have an habitual or generic sense, as in *young women smoke too much* – or else be registerially very restricted as in running commentary accompanying a 'demonstration'.

(ii) Alternatively, the Range may enhance the Process, typically, by a circumstantial feature of space (location or extent):

they climbed the nearest peak; the horse jumped the fence; they roamed the streets

The Goal and the Range thus differ in the degree and type of their involvement in the Process: the Goal is a real participant, actually affected by the performance of the process, whereas the Range is a restatement or further specification of the Process itself. From these differences follow differences in probes.

Goal (1) It is impacted (affected), so it can often be followed by an Attribute, a Role, a Recipient, or a Location of destination that represents the result of the impact[10] – *drive the car* [Attribute] *hot [the car is hot]*; *paint the wall* [Attribute] *pink*; *cut the onions* [Role:product:] *into cubes*; *kick the cat* [Location] *down the stairs*; *give* [Recipient] *the kid a car* etc.; (2) it is impacted, so it can be probed by *do to/with* (*what did he do to the wall? – he painted it pink*).[11]

Range It represents the scope of the performance of the Process, so it can often be preceded by a preposition that indicates the nature of this scope (*on, at, in* etc.) – *she climbed up the ladder*. When it is a restatement of the Process, there is typically an alternative wording with Process alone – *make a mistake* ~ *err; take a shower* ~ *shower*. Since the Range is not impacted, it can neither be construed with a result (Attribute etc.) nor be probed with *do to/with*. Ranges are contrasted with Goals in Table 4.15.

Table 4.15 Contrasting examples of Range and Goal

Process + Range	Process + Goal
play (on) the piano	*polish the piano (bright)*
scale the wall	*paint the wall (pink)*
reach the post	*shake the post (loose)*
climb (up) the steps	*wash the steps (clean)*
jump (over) the fence	*pull the fence (down)*
sing a song	*write a song*
visit churches	*build churches*
watch the slug	*squash the slug*
listen to the radio	*turn on the radio*
row the lake	*row the boat (across the lake)*

[10]This resultative Attribute may be 'incorporated' in the process itself – *kill* = '*cause to be dead*'; *break* = '*cause to be broken*'; *flatten* = '*cause to be flat*'; etc. – in which case it cannot be configured as a separate element.

[11]This probe with 'do to/with' does not apply to Goals in creative material causes, i.e. Goals that are actually brought into existence by the performance of the process; but the nature of the impact on them is clear enough – they actually result from the performance of the process: *he'll bake a cake tomorrow, Wren wants to build another gazebo, Danes design opera houses.*

As can be expected, there are a number of cases that are less clear than those represented by the examples given in Table 4.15. From one point of view, Goal and Range are really points on a cline between highly affected material participant (i.e. Goal) and non-affected material participant (i.e. Range). Various factors determine to what extent a particular participant approximates a prototypical Goal or a prototypical Range. For instance, affectedness is related to (textual) specificity: specific referents are more likely to be affected than generic ones. Thus the Goal in *farmers shoot ducklings* is arguably less affected and more range-like than the Goal in *the farmer shot the ugly duckling*; shooting ducklings is just one type of shooting just as hunting lions is just one type of hunting. Related to this is the fact that a Range is less likely to be a personal pronoun *her/him* than is a Goal. In fact, often the Range has no real referential existence independent of the Process – *play tennis, football*.

3.5 Mental clauses

(i) Mental or behavioural? Tests to distinguish these types of clauses were given in Section 2.5 above. (See also IFG: 139.)

(ii) Mental or verbal? Mental clauses are similar to some verbal clauses in their unmarked present tense selection – the simple present: *he thinks that would be a good idea, he says that would be a good idea*. They are also similar in that they may project another clause: *He thought → he was ambitious, he said → he was ambitious*. But, on the one hand, a mental projection is an idea, whereas a verbal one is a locution (and so can be quoted), and, on the other hand, while all verbal clauses can project, only certain mental ones can (namely, cognitive ones and certain affective ones).

In addition, mental and verbal clauses differ critically in that verbal ones can have a Receiver, whereas mental ones cannot. Thus we can get *he said to us → he was ambitious*, but not *he thought to us → he was ambitious*. (With 'think', a kind of interior voice can be represented – *he thought to himself → "that is the way to do it"* – but this borderline type is quite restricted; we do not get *he believed/knew/dreamed ... to himself.*)

See also discussion of 'judgemental verbs' in 3.7(i) below.

(iii) Mental or relational? Certain verbs can serve in relational attributive clauses as well as mental ones. One group comprises the verbs *taste, feel, smell*. Contrast:

The rabbit smelt the fox (mental): The rabbit smells good (relational)

In the first case, the rabbit is treated as a conscious being; in the second, an Attribute is ascribed to it and it is not necessarily a conscious being – indeed, it may have been turned into an inanimate stew. The verb *smell* belongs to different sets in the two cases; compare:

The rabbit smelt/saw/perceived/sensed the fox (mental):
The rabbit smells/seems/is good (relational)

Further, while the mental clause can be passive – *the fox was smelled by the rabbit*, the relational:attributive one cannot – *good is smelled by the rabbit* is not possible.

A second group involves verbs which may construe either a mental process of reaction or a relation of causality. Compare:

Violent TV programmes affect/influence our children (mental)
Temperature affects/influences humidity (identifying:causal)

Note that the first example, like many other mental clauses, has an alternative active version where the Senser is Subject as in *Our children respond to violent TV programmes.*

Mental and relational clauses both construe emotion. Very often the same emotion may be construed either as a mode of conscious processing or as an attribute. For example:

Who fears Virginia Woolf?   (mental)
Who's afraid of Virginia Woolf?   (relational)

Her story depressed me   (mental)
I felt unhappy   (relational)

Since both clause types construe emotion, it may be hard to know whether a particular example is a mental or relational clause. The pairs above are clearly distinct. For instance, relationally fear or misery can be intensified by *very* (as in *he's very afraid of Virginia Woolf*; *I felt very unhappy*), and mentally they can be passive (as in *Virginia Woolf is feared by him*; *I was depressed by her story*). However, with clauses such as *he is scared*, it is harder to tell:

	He	is	scared
mental	Senser	Process:passive	
relational	Carrier	Process	Attribute

The mental interpretation relates the example to *he is scared by large dogs: large dogs scare him, he got scared*, and so on; the relational interpretation relates it to *he is very scared, he seems scared, he became scared*, and so on.

(iv) Phenomenon or projected idea? It is not always easy to judge whether a clause is embedded into the Phenomenon role or whether it is 'projected' as a separate clause by the mental process (see further Chapter 5). The first thing to consider is what category of mental clause is involved, since perception clauses do not project and nor do affection clauses of the 'reaction' type, such as *enjoy* or *dislike*. See Table 4.16.

Where a cognition or affection mental process is involved, then, it may be necessary to discriminate an embedded fact clause functioning as Phenomenon from a projected clause. One test is to see whether the element in question can function as Subject in a passive variant of the clause. If it can, it is a participant (Phenomenon). Consider the following examples:

The supervisor wanted them to leave.
Jem thought the idea was preposterous.
Did you find out who was responsible?
He accepted that he would not get sole custody.
They all understood that there would be a cancellation fee.

If we explore the possibility of passive variants we find that this is only possible for the final two examples:

*(For) them to leave was wanted by the supervisor.
*(That) the idea was preposterous was thought by Jem.

Table 4.16 Mental process types

Mental Process	Projection possible?	Type of idea projected	Example
perception	No[12]		
cognition	Yes	proposition (statement, question)	*he knew → that it was too late* *he wondered → if it was late*
affection: desire	Yes	proposal (command)	*he wishes →us to leave* *we'd like → them to play sport*
reaction	No		

*Was who was responsible found out by you?
(The fact) that he would not get sole custody was accepted by him.
(The fact) that there would be a cancellation fee was understood by them all.

Thus *them to leave* and *that the idea was preposterous* are projected clauses, not participants.

Another test that can be applied in doubtful cases is that of Theme predication (see Chapter 2). As a participant, a Phenomenon is available for a Theme predicated variant of the clause, whereas a projected clause is not. Thus:

*It was (for) them to leave that was wanted by him.
*It was (that) the idea was preposterous that was thought by Jem.
*Was it who was responsible that was found out by you?
It was (the fact) that he would not get sole custody that was accepted by him.
It was (the fact) that there would be a cancellation fee that was understood by them all.

(v) Projecting clause complex or verbal group complex? See Section 3.3 above and IFG Section 7A.6.

3.6 Relational clauses

(i) Relational or material? Certain verbs can serve in both relational and material clauses. In particular, the semantic domains of location, possession and change of state can be construed either relationally or materially.

Location A number of locative verbs occur either in relational clauses, simply denoting relation in space, or in material clauses, denoting movement in space (verbs of motion). The following example is relational even though the verb is *go*:

The idea of relativity goes back, certainly, as a principle to Newton and Galileo.

If you consider what the unmarked present tense is, the analytic decision is usually easy: here it would not be possible to use the choice, present-in-present (the so-called present progressive or continuous), which is the unmarked choice in a material clause. Thus we would not expect to find:

The idea of relativity is going back, certainly, as a principle to Newton and Galileo.

[12]Note that a perception verb like *see* may also function as a (projecting) cognition process, as in *he saw that no amount of discussion would make any difference.*

This correlates with the fact that the idea of relativity is not construed as moving back to Newton and Galileo. As usual, we can also probe by exploring agnate verbs. Here we would have *the idea of relativity **dates** from Newton and Galileo*, which is clearly relational (cf. the impossibility of *the idea is dating from Newton and Galileo*); but we cannot relate the example to *the idea of relativity moves back to Galileo and Newton*, which would be material; nor can a circumstance of Manner be added to represent the rate of motion: we cannot say *the idea of relativity is going back **quickly** to Newton and Galileo*.

Similarly contrast:

The road runs along the river (relational) :
The jogger is running along the river (material)

The fence surrounds the White House (relational) :
The protesters are surrounding the White House (material)

Possession Although *have*, in its meaning of possess, is a relational process, the meaning of possession may be construed materially where it involves some dynamic aspect such as getting, taking, obtaining, giving, receiving. Thus:

The young man has high qualifications (Carrier + Process + Attribute)
The young is obtaining high qualifications (Actor + Process + Range)

(Note also the material use of *have*, as in *the young man is having dinner*.)

Change of state A state of being is typically represented in a Carrier + Process + Attribute structure such as in *the porridge was cold*. In addition, a change of state can be represented relationally, as in *the porridge became/got/turned cold*. This latter set of attributives is distinctive, however, in selecting present-in-present as the unmarked choice for present time: *it's getting late, it's turning cold* etc. In this they reflect a greater semantic proximity to the material process type. In fact a change of state can also be construed as a material process with no Attribute element, as in *she paled, the sky brightened, the water boiled*.

(ii) Relational or mental? See Section 3.5(iii) above.

(iii) Relational or verbal? See Section 3.7(iii) below.

(iv) Attributive or identifying? (a) The most important test is that of reversibility. Compare:

Border is short : *Short is Border   [attributive]
Border is the captain : The captain is Border [identifying]

Attributive clauses really have only one participant that can serve as Subject – the Carrier. Consequently, these clauses have no passive variants and are thus not reversible.

The reversibility test distinguishes easily between 'quality' type attributive clauses and identifying ones, but is not so successful if the clause is a nominal type attributive. Compare:

Border is short : *Short is Border   [attributive]
Border is a good batsman : A good batsman is Border   [?]

This last example is tricky because its reversal still makes sense. The clause needs to be considered in context; for example:

A: Tell me something about Border
B: Border is a good batsman

In this case, B's answer is an attributive clause (and B could not reply *A good batsman is Border* here). However, the following exchange shows the clause in a different context:

A: Tell me the name of (an example of) a good batsman
B: Border is a good batsman/A good batsman is Border

B's reply is an identifying clause and therefore reversible. The question is whether the clause assigns class-membership or gives an example of something. If it assigns class membership, it is attributive; if it exemplifies, it is identifying.

(b) In general, it is best to replace the unmarked intensive verb *be* with another more specific verb when using the reversibility test to distinguish between attributive and identifying clauses. If the reversal makes sense in the context then the clause can be taken as identifying. This can be done with *Border is a good batsman*:

Border exemplifies a good batsman : A good batsman is exemplified by Border

(v) Token or Value? Token and Value differ in meaning along the lines suggested in Section 2.3 above. If you have difficulty in a particular case in determining which participant is Token and which Value, you can apply the following rule. If the clause is active, as in *Border exemplifies a good batsman*, then the Subject[13] is the Token. If the clause is passive, as in *A good batsman is exemplified by Border*, then the Subject is Value. To apply the test when the relational verb is *be*, simply replace *be* with another relational verb and see whether the clause is then active or passive. For example *This piece of work is our best effort*: (Subject/Token:) *This piece of work represents* (Value:) *our best effort*.

(vi) Relational clauses sometimes not recognized There are some relational clause types that differ from the typical Carrier + Process + Attribute or Token + Process + Value structure in some respect – (i) they have an Agent (Assigner, Attributor), or (ii) a Beneficiary, or (iii) the Process itself embodies the Attribute role. These types are sometimes not recognized in analysis so we are drawing attention to them here with a few examples of each.

(a) Causative relational clauses (IFG: 171)

identifying

They	christened	the girl	Victoria
She	calls	him	uncle
They	elected	her	President
They	voted	him	man of the year
This	proves	(that)	my point
Assigner	Process: identifying	Token	Value

attributive

She	made	him	a good citizen
This	proves	him	wrong
Attributor	Process: attributive	Carrier	Attribute

[13]See Chapter 3 for identification of the Subject role.

Note that these should not be confused with material processes which include a 'resultative' Attribute. See Section 3.4(iii) above.

(b) Benefactive (attributive) relational clauses (i.e. with Beneficiary role)

He	owes	**her**	three dollars
He	makes	**her**	a good husband
The room	cost	**me**	fifteen dollars

Note: the ambiguity of an example such as *she made him a good friend*:

	she	made	him	a good friend
(i)	Attributor	Process	Carrier	Attribute
(ii)	Carrier	Process	Beneficiary	Attribute
(iii)	Actor	Process	Beneficiary: Client	Goal

(i)   means 'she caused him to be a good friend'
(ii) means 'she was a good friend to him'
(iii) means 'she made (produced) a good friend for him'. The third reading is material and is not very reasonable with this particular example, but is perfectly straightforward with something like *she made (baked) him a cake*.

(c) Clauses with Process/Attribute (i.e. a quality normally represented as an Attribute is inherent in the Process)

It doesn't matter ('it is not important')
That figures
That stinks
Doctors and treatments differ the world over. ('are different')

(vii) Attribute or part of process? Certain adjectives such as *eager, keen, willing, unwilling, happy, loath*; *able, unable*; *afraid, scared*; *ready*; *quick, slow* can occur as Attributes in attributive clauses:

Maxine	is	afraid
Rover	is	slow
Carrier		Attribute

They can also, however, function to modify the meaning expressed by the verb in examples where the process is not relational:

Maxine *is afraid to play* against that team
Doctors *are quick to prescribe* antibiotics...

Compare *doctors are quick to prescribe antibiotics : doctors prescribe antibiotics quickly/willingly*. In both cases the process being construed is the behavioural *prescribe*. But, in the second case, an additional meaning feature has been added to create a 'verbal group complex' (see IFG Chapter 7 Additional). The additional meaning is modal in character, relating to inclination or ability. Compare:

| Janey | is eager to please | her professors |
| Phenomenon | Process: mental | Senser |

| Professor Beech | is | easy [[to please]] |
| Carrier | Process: attributive | Attribute |

3.7 Verbal clauses

(i) Verbal or behavioural? Note that there are a number of processes representing verbal behaviour – *talk, chatter, gossip, speak*; *lie* – that are behavioural rather than verbal; they cannot project. For example, we cannot say *they gossiped that their neighbours had had a wild party.* (Note that while behavioural process can, in a written narrative, project by quoting: *'I enjoyed it thoroughly', he lied,* a true verbal process can project both direct and indirect speech in all contexts.)

Included in this behavioural group are processes which concern the creation of a symbolic representation. Verbs such as *characterize, outline, describe, portray* are used here, but again projection is not possible (e.g. *they outline the plot* is normal, but *they outlined that the heroine was kidnapped* is not possible) and these are behavioural rather than verbal.

We can also include on the behavioural borderline such 'judgemental' verbal processes as *flatter, insult, praise, malign, slander, abuse* which have the peculiarity of allowing for an additional participant role, the Target. These are analysed in IFG: 141 as follows:

They	praised	her	to her parents
Sayer	Process: verbal	Target	Receiver

But, as noted in IFG, they cannot project reported speech and are towards the material end of a cline. Because they cannot project, these too could be taken as behavioural and analysed in the following way:

They	praised	her	to her parents
Behaver	Process: behavioural	Range	Receiver

One final borderline case is when a sound is 'quoted', usually with *go* realizing the process. For example:

the tyres went 'screech!'
the little engine went 'wheeee!'
the car went 'bang'!

It is not possible to have a Receiver in these clauses since the sound is simply a sound and not a piece of language being addressed to anyone. They are therefore moving towards the material end of a cline and are best treated as behavioural.

(ii) Verbal or mental? See Section 3.5(ii) above.

Note too that a small set of 'verbal judgement' verbs – see Section 3.7(i) above – such as *condone, criticise, excuse, applaud* may also occur with an embedded fact clause: *The press applauded the fact that no violence occurred; The press condoned the fact that some violence occurred.* In these contexts, no Receiver is possible and such verbs are functioning as mental processes of affection: reaction.

(iii) Verbal or relational? There are a number of verbs (*show, indicate, suggest*) that can serve either in verbal clauses or in identifying relational ones. Contrast:

She showed (told, convinced) us ‖ that the substance was potassium (verbal)
The result showed (meant, was) ⟦that the substance was potassium⟧ (relational)

They emphasized/highlighted/underlined (said clearly) to the union ‖ that there would be no further negotiations on the pay offer (verbal)[14]
The stripes emphasize/highlight the width of the material (relational)

[14]Note that *he took the pen and highlighted/underlined the main points in the chapter* is an example of these verbs functioning in a material clause.

One difference between the two process types illustrated by these examples is that a verbal clause will usually admit a Receiver whereas a relational one will not.

3.8 Behavioural clauses

(i) Behavioural or mental? Tests to distinguish these types of clauses were given in Section 2.5 above. (See also IFG: 139.)

(ii) Behavioural or verbal? See Section 3.7(i) above.

(iii) More than one participant Most behavioural clauses have only one participant role, the Behaver. However, there may, in some instances, be candidates for a second participant role. Consider, for example: *they solved **the problem**, they stared at **the doctor**, they watched **the cricket**, they described **the new project***.

Because this second participant is a Range in an ergative analysis, this label may be adopted as a general term to cover this element. Alternatively, it may be preferable to highlight the mental or verbal process that the instance in question relates to. This can be done by giving the second participant a more specific label as Phenomenon or Verbiage:

they	solved	the problem
they	stared at	the doctor
they	watched	the cricket
Behaver	Process: behavioural	Phenomenon

| they | described | the new project | (to the Board) |
| Behaver | Process: behavioural | Verbiage | (Receiver) |

3.9 Discriminating circumstance type

Use the probes provided in Table 4.4 to help you.

3.10 Distinguishing between circumstances and other elements

When you identify a unit as a circumstantial element of clause structure, you have to make sure that it does not actually serve another function. In particular, circumstances have to be distinguished from:

(i)   participants;
(ii) Qualifiers in nominal groups;
(iii) dependent clauses in clause complexes;
(iv) conjunctive Adjuncts (textual).

(i) Circumstance or participant?

Circumstance or participant with phrasal verb? Because of the prevalence of phrasal verbs in English, it may sometimes be difficult to decide whether to interpret a structure as process + circumstance or process + participant. For example, which is the best analysis of the following?

They	got off	the old bus	OR	They	got	off the old bus
Actor	Process: material	Range		Actor	Process: material	Location

We	looked at	the snail	OR	We	looked	at the snail
Behaver	Process: behavioural	Phenomenon		Behaver	Process: behavioural	Location

They	weren't worrying about	it	OR	They	weren't worrying	about it
Senser	Process: mental	Phenomenon		Senser	Process: mental	Matter

Often it will be obvious that the preposition must count as part of the process realization. For example:

They	ran down	the boy	They	ran	down the lane
Actor	Process	Goal	Actor	Process	Location

They	called for	change	They	called	for a chat
Sayer	Process	Verbiage	Actor	Process	Cause

If in doubt, the best test is to check the 'circumstance' as the focus of Theme predication.

> ??It was off the old bus they got
> ?It was at the snail we were looking
> It wasn't about the strike (that) they were worrying
> It was for a chat they called

Where the prepositional phrase is feasible as a predicated Theme, as in the last two cases, it is likely to be functioning as a circumstance.

Location or Beneficiary? Examples:

> She sent the parcel *to New York*   Location
> She sent the parcel *to her aunt*   Beneficiary

If an expression like *to New York* or *to her Aunt* is Beneficiary then it can also occur in an alternative position in the clause without the preposition *to*. Thus:

> *She sent New York the parcel
> She sent her aunt the parcel

Manner or Attribute? Examples:

> Last year, the term went by *faster*   Manner
> Maybe it is *a bit like reading a book*   Attribute
> He is *luckier than most*   Attribute

The Attribute is always inherent in an attributive clause, whereas Manner is not inherent in any transitivity types. Consequently, you can probe the difference by leaving out the element in question. Further, while you cannot tell with *faster* whether it is adjectival or adverbial, you can check a related lexical item to see whether it is adjectival (and hence Attribute) or adverbial (and hence Manner). For example: *Time goes more quickly when you're having fun.*

Manner: means or Agent? Examples:

> His jaw was broken *by a particularly savage blow* Agent
> He was chosen for that task *by chance*   Manner

An Agent is a participant in the clause, although when it appears as a *by* phrase in a passive clause it may be hard to distinguish from a Manner circumstance.

However, only the participant can take on the Subject role in an active variant of the clause. Thus the active form of *his jaw was broken by a particularly savage blow* is *A particularly savage blow broke his jaw* whereas the active variant of *He was chosen for that task by chance* is *They chose him for that task by chance* (rather than *Chance chose him for that task*).

(ii) Circumstance or Qualifier? A prepositional phrase may function as a circumstance in the clause, as in *the cop hit the man* [Manner:means] <u>*with his baton*</u>. But prepositional phrases may also be embedded as the 'Qualifier' part of a nominal group, as in *the cop beat the man with red hair*. In this case *the man with red hair* functions in its entirety as the Goal. It is essential to pay attention not only to the form of a unit, but also to its function. If unsure about a particular prepositional phrase, check whether it actually represents the circumstance of the process, answering *where, when, how, what like* etc. with respect to the process. For example:

> The children *[from local schools]* were missing out on athletics.
> The Council sent information to *all residents [near the development]*.
> The report commented on *a number of inconsistencies [in their stories]*.
> For the clock on the space ship was showing *a different time [to the clocks on earth]*.

In all these examples, the prepositional phrases in square brackets are embedded into the nominal groups functioning as participants. Thus *from local schools* defines the children; it does not provide the location of the process of missing out. Similarly, *near the development* is part of the participant *all residents near the development*, it does not tell where council sent the information. Because they are part of a nominal group, these phrases cannot by themselves function as Theme. For example:

> *Near the development the Council had sent information to all residents.
> *In their stories the report commented on a number of inconsistencies.

Compare now the circumstances in the following:

> Sixty children travelled *from local schools* || to participate.
> Several protesters set up camp *near the proposed development site*.
> The commission criticised a number of officials *in its report*.

In these clauses the prepositional phrases can be read as providing the 'setting' for the process. Because they function as circumstances, they can readily occur as marked theme, as in *In its report the commission criticised a number of officials*.

(iii) Circumstance or dependent clause in clause complex? Meanings of location, manner, cause and so on can appear as <u>part of</u> the clause in the form of a circumstance. However, these meanings can also occur as a separate clause with its own process configuration, such as *when she was a young girl, by transmitting information* or *where angels fear to tread*. Such clauses are 'secondary' or 'dependent' in character, with respect to a main or 'alpha' clause (see further Chapter 5). Here are some examples of clauses that are dependent in clause complexes but might be mistaken as circumstances. Processes are picked out in bold:

> α H. Hertz **had demonstrated** the truth in the theory ||
> β by **transmitting** radio waves over a short distance.
>
> α Newtonian physics **used** this argument ||
> β in **developing** the special theory of relativity.
>
> β As well as **committing** funds to this new highway
> α we **should be upgrading** public transport in our cities...

(iv) Circumstance or textual Conjunctive? Circumstances and conjunctives are metafunctionally distinct, but there can be areas of overlap within the semantic domain of space-time. First let us look at a Conjunctive example:

Earlier, several attempts had been made to cross the Blue Mountains.

Here *earlier* marks a temporal relation in construction of the narrative – a flashback. Such relations in text are conjunctive and if they are made explicit, they are marked by elements serving as Conjunctives within the textual layer of the clause. By contrast, circumstances of time construe time as an aspect of the process configuration itself, representing a location in time, in terms of some time interval (*in the morning, on Monday, after midnight, before Easter, during the Middle Ages*), in terms of the now of speaking (*now, then; yesterday, tomorrow*), or in terms an event (*after the meeting, at breakfast, before the war*).

In principle, you can probe the difference by checking whether the element in question can be the focus of Theme predication. For example, *it was before 1820 that several attempts had been made to cross the Blue Mountains* is perfectly fine, whereas *it was earlier that several attempts had been made to cross the Blue Mountains* is not so good. This is clearer outside the domain of space-time. For instance, *it was however/nevertheless/consequently/furthermore that several attempts had been made to cross the Blue Mountains* are all impossible.

The border between conjunctives and circumstances is hazier in the domain of space-time, as shown in the Table 4.17.

Table 4.17 Temporal conjunctives and circumstances

Conjunctive Adjuncts	Circumstantial Adjuncts (experiential)	
	nominal groups	Prepositional phrases
Earlier...	*The previous year*	*Before the war*
Later...	*The following week*	*After six weeks*
Next...	*A few minutes later*	*In a few minutes*
Afterwards; after this		*After the meeting*

There are unambiguously textual items with a clear anaphoric sense: *earlier* means 'earlier than this', *previously* means 'before this', *afterwards* means 'after this'; all these relate the current clause to previous text. Then there are circumstances which provide a time reference within the clause in which they occur, such as *earlier than 1942, before the war, after the meeting*.

In between these are those items which have a noun representing a period of time (*year, day, hour, minute, month, period*, etc.) as the central ('Head') element and which are modified by an item with conjunctive implications in the text: (*next, previous, subsequent, following* etc.) – *The previous year they had made several attempts; the following day they would try again*. On the grounds that these can be the focus of Theme predication - only available to 'topical' Themes - they can be analysed as circumstances.

4 Analysis Practice

4.1 Phase I

4.1.1 Exercises

Exercise 1 Practising the tense test Write a clause agnate to each of the following examples which would be used to comment on action or states concurrent with the moment of speaking.

A small boy **stood** bravely on the ramparts.	A small boy **is standing** bravely on the ramparts.
He **had** a crown on his head.	He **has** a crown on his head.

1. He **will have** a sceptre in his hand.
2. The young king **calmed** the crowds.
3. The lad **was** James V of Scotland.
4. His father **had fallen** in battle.
5. James **wanted** his uncle's sword.
6. Only his closest attendants **knew** his identity.
7. The farmer **saw** the battle on the bridge.
8. He **said** that his name **was** 'The Goodman of Ballengiech'.

1. ....
2. ....
3. ....
4. ....
5. ....
6. ....
7. ....
8. ....

Exercise 2 Practising the 'do to/do with' probe Write a clause related to the example, which asks a question focusing on the process (formed with *do to* or *do with*).

The farmer **was wielding** his flail against the attackers.	What did the farmer do with his flail?
The man **led** James to the barn.	What did the man do with James?

1. The farmer **had been threshing** corn.
2. They **admitted** the bondsman immediately.
3. James **led** Willie through the palace.
4. He **removed** his hat.
5. He **gave** him the farm.
6. Feuding **divided** the country.
7. Ruffians **attacked** the king.
8. He **brought** water to the king.

1. ....
2. ....
3. ....
4. ....
5. ....
6. ....
7. ....
8. ....

Exercise 3 Practising the projection test Find a clause related to the example which reports or quotes, as in the models.

James **heard** things that normally would not have reached his ears.

James **heard** that there was trouble in the land.

The king **asked** the labourer a question.

The king **asked** the labourer, 'Who are you?'

1. He **answered** quickly.
2. James **saw** the castle.
3. James **knew** the answer.
4. The king **replied**.
5. The king **smiled** to himself.
6. James **assured** him of his welcome.

1. ....
2. ....
3. ....
4. ....
5. ....
6. ....

Exercise 4 Discriminating process types Label the following clauses appropriately as material or mental. See Section 3.4(i).

The boy **stood** bravely on the ramparts.   material

Only his closest attendants **knew** his true identity.   mental

1.   The ruffians **robbed** him.
2.   The king **retreated** to a nearby bridge.
3.   The farmer **saw** the battle.
4.   The farmer **wanted** a farm of his own.
5.   Kinsmen **performed** the service for 300 years.
6.   The king **was amused** by his wonder and comment.
7.   Nothing **could please** me more.
8.   ...whenever the king should **pass** over the land.
9.   How will I **recognize** the king?
10. Willie suddenly **realized** the true rank of the man.

1.   ....
2.   ....
3.   ....
4.   ....
5.   ....
6.   ....
7.   ....
8.   ....
9.   ....
10. ....

Exercise 5 Discriminating process types Label the following clauses appropriately as mental or verbal. See Section 3.5(ii).

The sight of their young king **calmed** the crowds below.   mental

Willie **said** so.   verbal

1.   James **wanted** his uncle's sword.
2.   Willie eagerly **agreed**.
3.   James **asked** a question.
4.   James **decided** on peace.
5.   Willie **answered** slowly.
6.   James **heard** things about the feuding chieftains

1.   ....
2.   ....
3.   ....
4.   ....
5.   ....
6.   ....

7. He **liked** the simple pleasures.
8. "Easily", **replied** his companion.
9. Willie suddenly **realized** the true rank of the man.
10. "His hat", **repeated** his escort.

7. ....
8. ....
9. ....
10. ....

Exercise 6 Discriminating process types Label the following clauses appropriately as material or relational:

Willie **had been threshing** corn.	material
He **must be** either you or me.	relational

1. All but the two of us **are** bareheaded.
2. Willie **had rescued** the king.
3. He **had** a crown on his head.
4. He **became** king.
5. Willie **fell** to his knees.
6. My name **is** Willie.
7. He **was** content with his lot.
8. This promise **was kept**.
9. He **was attacked** by ruffians.
10. Who **are** you?

1. ....
2. ....
3. ....
4. ....
5. ....
6. ....
7. ....
8. ....
9. ....
10. ....

Exercise 7 Identifying clause elements Find the process, and each participant and circumstance in the following clauses, as shown in the example.

Long ago	a small boy	stood	on the ramparts.
circumstance	participant	process	circumstance

1. The sight of their king calmed the crowds.

2. This lad was James V of Scotland.

3. Shortly after his birth his father had fallen in battle.

4. Disorder spread throughout the kingdom.

5. In the hall, Mum took off his boots.

6. One day he was attacked by a band of ruffians.

7. He retreated to a nearby bridge.

8. Jamie put on his thickest jersey.

9. The farmer had been threshing corn in his barn.

10. He travelled with the king.

Exercise 8 Discriminating process types Label the following clauses as material, mental, verbal or relational.

That was awful.	relational

1. It was Christmas Eve.   1. ....
2. Josie had played in the car almost all the   2. ....
   way to Grandma's.
3. "Yes", answered Dad.   3. ....
4. Now it was bedtime...   4. ....
5. From the landing she could see the   5. ....
   decorations in Grandma's hall
6. ...and she was wide awake.   6. ....
7. Have some hot milk and a biscuit.   7. ....
8. No one will notice.   8. ....
9. Josie grew more and more excited.   9. ....
10. This Josie knew.   10. ....
11. In the porch, the ringers said goodnight   11. ....
    to each other.
12. She curled up tight.   12. ....
13. She counted sheep.   13. ....
14. The present delighted her.   14. ....

Exercise 9 Discriminating process types Label the following clauses as relational or existential.

There was a sudden noise.	existential
The noise was loud.	relational

1. She is a very tall woman.   1. ....
2. There will be a storm soon.   2. ....
3. Once upon a time, there was a   3. ....
   beautiful princess.
4. This is ridiculous.   4. ....
5. Her favourite colour was red.   5. ....
6. In the lane there was a new sports car.   6. ....
7. There are many different kinds of   7. ....
   toadstool.
8. Many toadstools are poisonous.   8. ....
9. This time there can be no excuse.   9. ....
10. Her father is going to be furious.   10. ....

Exercise 10 Discriminating circumstance types Label the underlined circumstance in the following clauses, as in the examples. See Table 4.4.

Jamie had slept <u>in the car</u>.	Location: place
He lay <u>with open eyes</u>.	Manner: quality

1. ...and they exploded <u>to bits</u>.   1. ....
2. Are you going <u>out</u>?   2. ....
3. You can come <u>with me</u>.   3. ....

4. Some of the people were standing in a ring, holding the ropes.	4. ....
5. They pulled the ropes again.	5. ....
6. They rang for several minutes.	6. ....
7. Now the bells were ringing sweetly again.	7. ....
8. See you in the morning.	8. ....
9. Dad had to carry him the last bit.	9. ....
10. Nobles feuded among themselves over land and power.	10. ....
11. James dressed as a yeoman.	11. ....
12. ...wielding his flail against the attackers.	12. ....
13. He wanted to own the farm for himself.	13. ....
14. Willie prepared for his important journey.	14. ....
15. You will know him by his hat.	15. ....
16. He played a trick for a laugh.	16. ....
17. According to Willie, he was just a yeoman.	17. ....
18. He laughed in spite of himself.	18. ....
19. It seemed odd to him.	19. ....
20. ...pleasures he could not have shared as king.	20. ....

Exercise 11 Discriminating circumstances from textual and interpersonal elements
(See Chapters 2 and 3.) Pick out the circumstances in the following examples.

Unfortunately, they could not get away **quickly**.

1.   However no-one followed him into the valley.

2.   We hurried || but did not arrive until the evening.

3.   While they were taking the boxes into the yard || they were singing loudly.

4.   They were probably working the whole week.

5.   They just came with their friends || although they were uninvited.

6.   The men often travelled away from home.

7.   Next they opened the presents with great excitement.

8.   During the long drought, he lost much of his crop.

9.   Although she disliked him || she quickly offered him a drink.

10. Perhaps he will be noticed at the hunt by some of the others.

4.1.2 Texts for analysis

Identify the process types and circumstance types in texts 1 and 2, which were earlier presented in Chapter 2. Write the labels in the table below the text. To help you, processes are in bold and circumstances underlined. What comparisons can be made between the two texts? How do the selections of PROCESS TYPE and CIRCUM-STANTIATION reflect the purposes of the texts?

Text 1 Descriptive report

1. The numbat **is** an unmistakeable slender marsupial with a pointed muzzle and short erect ears.|| 2. The body **is** reddish brown || 3. but the rump **is** much darker || 4. and **has** about six white bars <u>across it</u>.|| 5. The eye **has** a black stripe <u>through it</u> || 6. and the long bushy tail **is** yellowish. || 7. The toes **are** strongly clawed and very effective in digging out termites.|| 8. The tongue **is** extremely long, <u>as in all mammalian ant or termite eaters</u>.|| 9. <u>Unlike most marsupials</u>, the numbat **is** active <u>during the day</u>.|| 10. It **shelters** <u>in hollow logs</u>. || 11. <u>It</u> **was** <u>once</u> relatively common || 12. but now **lives** only <u>in a small area of S.W. South Australia</u>. ||

(Adapted from *The Concise Encyclopedia of Australia* 2nd ed. Buderim, Queensland: Bateman, 1984: 459.)

	PROCESS TYPE	CIRCUMSTANTIATION
1.		
2.		
3.		
4.		
5.		
6.		
7.		
8.		
9.		
10.		
11.		
12.		

Text 2 Explanation

1. <u>After flash floods</u>, desert streams from upland areas **carry** heavy loads of silt, sand and rock fragments. || 2. As they **reach** the flatter area of desert basins || 3. they **slow down** || 4. and their waters **may soak** <u>quickly into the basin floor</u>.|| 5. Then the streams **drop** their loads; || 6. first they **drop** the heaviest material - the stones, || 7. then (they **drop**) the sand || 8. and finally (they **drop**) the silt. || 9. Soon these short lived streams **become choked** by their own deposits ||10. and they **spread** their load <u>in all directions</u>.|| 11. <u>After some time</u>, fan or cone-shaped deposits of gravel, sand, silt and clay **are formed** <u>around each valley or canyon outlet</u>. || 12. These **are called** alluvial fans.||

(Adapted from Sale, C., Wilson, G. and Friedman, B. *Our changing world Bk 1.* Melbourne: Longman Cheshire 1980: 54.)

	PROCESS TYPE	CIRCUMSTANTIATION
1.		
2.		
3.		
4.		
5.		
6.		
7.		
8.		
9.		
10.		
11.		
12.		

Text 3 Taxonomizing report Identify the processes in the following text and label according to type. What semantic work is achieved by the different types of process and how do the choices compare with those of text 1?

There are many species of whales.* They are conveniently divided into toothed and baleen categories. The toothed whales are found worldwide in great numbers. The largest is the Sperm whale, which grows to about the size of a boxcar. Other species familiar to Canadians are the Beluga or white whale, the Narwhal with its unicorn-like tusk, the Killer whale or Orca, the Pilot or Pothead whale, which is commonly stranded on beaches, the Spotted and Spinner Dolphins that create a problem for tuna seiners, and the Porpoises which we commonly see along our shores.

There are fewer species of the larger baleen whales*, that filter krill and small fish through their baleen plates. The largest is the Blue whale which is seen frequently in the Gulf of St Lawrence. It reaches a length of 100 feet and a weight of 200 tons, equivalent to about 30 African elephants. The young are 25 feet long at birth and put on about 200 lbs a day on their milk diet. Other species are: the Fins which at a length of 75 ft blow spouts of 20 ft, the fast swimming Seis, the Grays so commonly seen on migrations along our Pacific coast between Baja California and the Bering Sea, the Bowheads of Alaskan waters, the Rights, so seriously threatened, the Humpbacks, enjoyed by tourists in such places as Hawaii and Alaska, the smaller Bryde's whales, and the smallest Minke whales, which continue to be abundant worldwide.

As with the growing interest in birding, increasing numbers of whale watchers now notice the differences between the various species of whales.

(Adapted from Martin, W.R. 1989: 'Innovative fisheries management: international whaling.' A.T. Bielak (ed) *Innovative fisheries management initiatives*, Ottawa: Canadian Wildlife Federation, 1–4.)

*An 'existential' clause, used to introduce something into the text.

Text 4 Magazine feature (excerpt) Pick out and classify the processes, writing them into the table below. (A longer version of the text will be analysed and discussed in Phase 2.) Note: You can ignore for now a process in an 'embedded' clause - one enclosed in square brackets - since it forms part of a participant role.

Dangerous liaisons

Women [[who form relationships with prisoners]] often believe they alone understand the men, and can reform them. 'They say, "I *know* this guy; I *know* he's good". It's partly a nurturing instinct, but some prisoners are also very physically attractive and charming,' notes Sister Janet Glass, who works with a Catholic chaplaincy team at Sydney's Long Bay jail.

'Often, these women are attracted to prisoners because they have just ended a relationship,' Glass adds. 'They're empty, and want some sort of emotional fillip. The prisoners are probably telling them lies, but they appear gallant and masculine and women believe them.'

(Adapted from box inset into large feature by F. Robson 'Prisoners prey'. *Sydney Morning Herald. Good Weekend magazine* 24/6/95: 24.)

material	verbal	mental	relational

4.2 Phase II

4.2.1 Exercises

Exercise 1 Identifying participant roles Go back to Phase I, exercise 4, and label the Actor, Goal, Senser and Phenomenon participants. For example:

The boy	**stood**	bravely	on the ramparts.	material
Actor				

Only his closest attendants	**knew**	his true identity.	mental
Senser		Phenomenon	

Exercise 2 Identifying participant roles Go back to Phase 1, exercise 5, and label the Senser, Phenomenon, Sayer and Verbiage participants.

The sight of their young king	**calmed**	the crowds below.	mental
Phenomenon		Senser	

Willie	**said**	it.	verbal
Sayer		Verbiage	

Exercise 3 Distinguishing Beneficiary and circumstance Identify the underlined phrase in the following clauses as either a circumstance or a participant (Recipient, Client in a material clause or Receiver in a verbal one). Note that if it is a participant there will be a related clause in which the underlined phrase appears without a preposition, as in the example. See Section 3.10(i): Location or Beneficiary?

They made some food <u>for their Royal guest</u>.
They made their Royal guest some food.   participant (Client)

1. He granted sole possession of the farm <u>to Willie</u>. 1. ....
2. All the children ran up <u>to her</u>. 2. ....
3. She was thirsty <u>for a drink</u>. 3. ....
4. He poured a glass of milk <u>for her</u>. 4. ....
5. Father Christmas's box of clothes was 5. ....
   brought <u>to your house.</u>
6. She made a good dinner <u>for her</u>. 6. ....
7. And I shall creep very quietly <u>to the spare room</u>. 7. ....
8. She trained hard <u>for the race</u>. 8. ....
9. She sang a song <u>for her sister</u>. 9. ....
10 He sent some money <u>to his friend</u>. 10. ....
11. She worked hard <u>for her mother</u>. 11. ....

Exercise 4 Differentiating identifying and attributive clauses Label the following clauses as attributive or identifying; if identifying, formulate an agnate clause in reverse sequence. See Section 3.6(iv). For example:

He had a crown on his head.   attributive

This lad was James V of Scotland.
James V of Scotland was this lad.   identifying

1. His mother was the regent.   1. ....
2. The lion represents courage.   2. ....
3. James became adventurous and resourceful.   3. ....
4. At 16 he was an experienced fighter.   4. ....
5. He was both wise and good.   5. ....
6. His name was Willie.   6. ....
7. That was only a foolish dream.   7. ....
8. Who are you?   8. ....
9. The king must be either you or me.   9. ....
10. All but the two of us are bareheaded.   10. ....

Exercise 5 Existential clauses Underline the Existent role in the following examples.

There were <u>his carrots</u> in a sack and on the table (there) was <u>a fine cooked goose</u>.

1. In his hand there was a royal sceptre.
2. There will be a continuing struggle.
3. In the townships, there had been a riot.
4. There was a rose in the vase.
5. On the table lay some tattered books.

Exercise 6 Practising tests to differentiate mental from verbal processes Identify the following clauses as verbal or mental by checking whether a Receiver role is possible (verbal) and whether the 'active' participant must be conscious (mental).

Mary **told** an exciting tale of her adventures.
Mary told <u>us</u> an exciting tale of her adventures.
<u>The diary</u> told an exciting tale of her adventures.   verbal

1. They didn't **explain** that we needed to pay in   1. ....
   advance.
2. We always **hope** for a quick response.   2. ....
3. Please **consider** all the options carefully.   3. ....
4. They **suggested** that there were alternative   4. ....
   flights.
5. They **promised** that there would be a short   5. ....
   interval.
6. We **believe** it's the best idea.   6. ....
7. They **understand** that they won't be able to stay. 7. ....
8. They **insisted** that portable computers would   8. ....
   not be covered.

Exercise 7 Practising tests to discriminate behavioural from mental processes Fill in the following grid for each of the clauses given by answering the questions.

(i) What is the unmarked tense for commenting on ongoing activity? (If present, mental)
    present   e.g. hears
    present in present e.g. *is hearing

(ii) Can the process in question report what was thought? (If yes, mental)
    yes   e.g. They thought he'd left.
    no   e.g. *They meditated he'd left.

		unmarked present?	can report?	PROCESS TYPE
	They thought he'd left.	present	yes	mental
1.	The baby was watching me.			
2.	No one will notice.			
3.	She suddenly heard movements.			
4.	He pondered the situation.			
5.	Jamie hadn't remembered.			
6.	Listen to this.			
7.	They all looked round.			
8.	Jamie could smell the holly and the ivy.			

Exercise 8 Differentiating behavioural from verbal processes Identify the process in the following examples as behavioural or verbal by checking whether or not the process can report another clause (if yes, verbal).

Jamie explained everything.
Jamie explained that he was coming.   verbal

Jamie laughed.
*Jamie laughed that he was coming.   behavioural

1. They all talked at once.   1. ....
2. They were singing at the top of their lungs. 2. ....
3. Jamie agreed.   3. ....
4. The barometer says rain.   4. ....
5. The baby was screaming.   5. ....
6. Everyone praised him.   6. ....
7. They stated their beliefs.   7. ....
8. She spoke loudly and firmly.   8. ....

Exercise 9 Identifying participants (behavioural clauses) Analyse the following clauses for Behaver, Range and Target as required (see Section 3.7(i)).

They	praised	Caesar.
Behaver		Target

They	sang	a carol.
Behaver		Range

1. She took a bow.

2. He insulted his audience.

3. He did a poo.

4. She drove the car.

5. They scaled the wall.

6. He slandered his rival.

7. She blamed the judges.

8. She gave a speech.

9. He smiled a most compelling smile.

10. He pondered the problem.

Exercise 10 Discriminating mental from attributive clauses Identify the following clauses as mental or relational attributive. See Section 3.5(iii).

Joanna was very excited.   relational attributive
I don't believe it.   mental

1. I didn't know.	1. ....
2. The play upset him.	2. ....
3. I wasn't aware of that.	3. ....
4. The children could see from a distance.	4. ....
5. Joanna was very upset.	5. ....
6. But I did see him.	6. ....
7. None of the children believed it except Sylvia.	7. ....
8. Sylvia always had good ideas.	8. ....
9. I've never felt so irritated.	9. ....

Exercise 11 Discriminating material from attributive clauses Identify the following clauses as relational attributive or material. See Section 3.6(i): change of state.

The night grew cold.	relational attributive
Stranger things happen.	material

1.	The play begins at six.	1. ....
2.	She became upset.	2. ....
3	The paint turned brown.	3. ....
4.	The term ends in November.	4. ....
5.	A problem arose with that solution.	5. ....
6.	It gets bad sometimes.	6. ....
7.	It goes sour in the heat.	7. ....
8.	A bridge appeared in the distance.	8. ....

Exercise 12 Discriminating Range from Goal Pick out a Range or a Goal in each of the following examples. See Section 3.4(iv).

He never gave it <u>a thought</u>.	Range
He picked up <u>a stone</u>, threw <u>it</u> and hit <u>the little robin</u>.	Goal(s)

1.	We're doing 'The Coventry Carol'.	1. ....
2.	I'll have to find a place to rest.	2. ....
3.	I will sing you beautiful songs.	3. ....
4.	He pulled his little broken wing along.	4. ....
5.	Why would they do that to such a little bird?	5. ....
6.	He made a nest.	6. ....
7.	He smelled that smell in every nook and cranny.	7. ....
8.	They had a game of catch.	8. ....
9.	They licked their fingers.	9. ....
10.	I can taste prunes.	10. ....
11.	The Sergeant kicked another cannon ball.	11. ....
12.	They climbed the wall.	12. ....
13.	He had the best dinner ever.	13. ....

Exercise 13 Discriminating Token and Value Label the Token and Value functions in the following relational identifying clauses, as in the examples. See Section 3.6(v).

She	's	the one.
Token	Value	

The last thing we want		**is**	for something to go wrong.
Value			Token

1. What **was** the last item on the programme?

2. The student's response **is** a site for surveillance.

3. Now **was** the time for everyone to join in.

4. The basic mechanism **is** one where the teacher surveils the student.

5. It's his fault.

6. The view of English that I have developed **represents** a minority position.

7. It **was** the best concert ever.

8. One of the results **is** that real differences are obscured.

9. What is immediately striking **is** the manner in which it works.

10. The exercise **doesn't involve** composing a written response.

11. My birthday **is** today.

Exercise 14 Types of attributive clause Label the Carrier and Attribute in the following relational attributive clauses; also note whether the clause is intensive, possessive or circumstantial. See Section 2.3.1.

| I | have | plenty of carrots. | possessive |
| Carrier | | Attribute | |

| It | wasn't | any use. | intensive |
| Carrier | | Attribute | |

1. He was in the phone booth.   1. ....

2. It was a tracksuit.   2. ....

3. He grew thoughtful.   3. ....

4. Has he got a plan?   4. ....

5. The fare seems exorbitant.   5. ....

6. That's easy.   6. ....

7. He had a sore head.   7. ....

8. Where's our lunch?   8. ....

9. Here are his paw marks.   9. ....

Exercise 15 Discriminating projected ideas and locutions from participants Label all participants and circumstances in the following clauses; remember that separate clauses are not participants unless embedded. See Sections 3.5(iv), 3.7(i).

"We	're	home!",		they	said.
locution			‖	Sayer	
Carrier		Attribute			

No one	saw	⟦them	opening	the kitchen window	with a jemmy⟧.
Senser		Phenomenon			
		Actor		Goal	Manner:means

1. They love ice-cream.

2. They don't like us doing this.

3. I want you to have it.

4. She repeated the answer.

5. I wish there was someone to talk to.

6. Are you quite sure I'm not dreaming?

7. We've all been wondering where you disappeared to.

8. "But we'll get cold," said Rachel.

9. I told everyone to leave.

10 The toy amused her.

11. I don't even know if her family has gifts at Christmas.

12. It was wonderful to be wrapped in paper with pictures on it.

Exercise 16 Discriminating circumstances from other elements Label the participants and circumstances in the following clauses. See Table 4.4.

As	the snowflakes	fell,	the two girls	danced.
	Actor		Actor	

1. On Christmas eve, he crept out to his woolshed.

2. He ran away out of fear.

3.   He had a surprise for them all.

4.   The sledge began moving, because the ground sloped down.

5.   They saw some toys in the sack.

6.   In no time at all, he made a top.

7.   They ate the icing on the cake.

8.   They ate the icing off the cake.

9.   What did the youngsters say on your arrival?

10. Can I see the presents you got from Santa?

4.2.2 Texts for analysis

Text 1 Explanation (for young children) Consider again the following text from Chapter 3. Analyse it for TRANSITIVITY, subcategorizing mental and behavioural processes (see Sections 2.5; 3.8(iii)). What patterning can you observe to the choices and – if you analysed it in Chapter 3 – how does this relate to the MOOD choices?

1.   Do you enjoy [[making sounds]]?
2.1   What sounds do these things make || 2.2 if you bang them?
3.   What different sounds can you make with your body and your voice?
4.1   Put your fingers on your throat || 4.2 as you talk || 4.3 or [as you] sing.
5.   What can you feel?
6.   Hold a ruler on the edge of a table.
7.1   Press down the end || 7.2 and let go.
8.   Can you hear a sound?
9.   What do you see?
10.1 Whenever you hear a sound || 10.2 there is [[something moving]].
11.   This movement is called a vibration.
12.1 Try this with a rubber band || 12.2 and see.
13.1 You can make musical sounds with rubber bands of different sizes ||
13.2 or by plucking the strings of a guitar.
14.   Strike a triangle with a beater.
15.1 Touch the triangle || 15.2 while it is ringing.
16.   What can you feel?
17.1 When something stops vibrating || 17.2 the sound stops.
18.   How does someone's voice reach you?
19.   The sound travels through the air as sound waves.
20.   Throw a stone in a pool of water.
21.   Watch [[the waves spreading out]].
22.   Sound waves move through the air in a similar way.

(From Webb, A. 1987: *Talk about Sound*. London: Franklin Watts.)

Text 2 Children's story (opening) Divide the following excerpt into clauses. Identify and label the processes, participants and circumstances. How do the choices made relate to the concerns of the book?

1988

My name's Laura and this is my place. I turned ten last week. Our house is the one with the flag on the window. Tony says it shows we're on Aboriginal land, but I think it means the colour of the earth, back home. Mum and Dad live here too, and Terry and Lorraine, and Aunty Bev, and Tony and Diane and their baby Dean. He's my nephew and he's so cute! We come from Bourke, but Dad thought there'd be more jobs in the city. This [picture] is me and Gully. I have to keep her on a lead because she chases cars. She comes from Bourke too. I guess she thinks they're sheep. This is a map of my place. We've got a McDonalds right on the corner!

(From Wheatley, N. 1989: *My place*. Blackburn: Collins Dove.)

Text 3 Parent-child conversation Revisit the following text from earlier chapters. Identify and label processes, participants and circumstances. Be careful not to confuse circumstances with elements that are purely interpersonal or textual in function (see Chapters 2 and 3) (M = mother, C = 4½-year-old boy).

C: How could birds die?
M: ...[One] Like the one in the garden, are you thinking of?
   Well, sometimes birds die ‖ when they get very old, ‖
   or maybe they get sick ‖ because they got some disease, ‖
   or maybe a cat got it. ‖ Baby birds sometimes die ‖
   when they fall out the nest, ‖ or, in the winter – <<if you were in a cold place>> – birds might die ‖ because they can't get enough food. ‖
C: Yeh, but what happens ‖ if one bird falls out ‖
   and then – and when it's just about at the ground ‖ it flies?
M: Yes, well if it's big enough to fly ‖ it'll be all right.
   And sometimes birds fall out the nest ‖ but they don't die...
   But that didn't look like a baby bird; ‖
   maybe there was something wrong with it; ‖ maybe a cat killed it – ‖
   (hastily) I don't think ‖ it was our cat.
C: Perhaps it was on the ground ‖ and then a cat got it.
M: Yeah, it was probably pecking something on the ground...
   Maybe it was just a very old bird. ‖ ...
C: (referring to dead bird in garden) But it looks as if it's alive.
M: Yeah, it does, doesn't it?
C: Perhaps its eye got blind.
M: Could have been, ‖ but it definitely wasn't alive.

Text 4 Magazine feature Text 4 from Phase I is reproduced here in a longer version and without one simplification included in Phase I. Analyse the text again, this time including participant and circumstantial roles. Reflect on the patterning of process choices through the text and the roles construed for the various people mentioned in the text.

Dangerous liaisons

Women ⟦who form relationships with prisoners⟧ often believe they alone understand the men, and can reform them. 'They say, "I *know* this guy; I *know* he's good". It's partly a nurturing instinct, but some prisoners are also very physically attractive and charming,' notes Sister Janet Glass, who works with a Catholic chaplaincy team at Sydney's Long Bay jail.

'Often, these women are attracted to prisoners because they have just ended a relationship,' Glass adds. 'They're empty, and want some sort of emotional fillip. The prisoners are probably lying to them*, but they appear gallant and masculine and women believe them.'

Prison Fellowship (see main story) is an interdenominational organization with its own programs and volunteers. Although seen as independent, PF has received financial support from the Baptist Church and its director, Ross Coleman, was a welfare worker with Baptist Community Services. Coleman says PF volunteers must provide character references and undergo a training program before starting the work. Volunteers use pseudonyms in letters and prisoners' replies are sent to PF headquarters and then redirected. The forming of emotional attachments with prisoners is forbidden.

Coleman admits that volunteers ⟦who transgress⟧ 'would only be detected if they told us, so sometimes that could happen and we were oblivious to it, which is always a risk...' He says PF is 'particularly concerned' ⟦with Christian prisoners, or prisoners ⟦who have found Christ whilst in prison.⟧ ⟧

Not unexpectedly, mainstream churches often criticise the influence of pentecostal or charismatic Christian groups within the penal system. 'Some PF volunteers want to baptise prisoners after one week,' says Sister Glass. 'Some pentecostal types raise emotional levels to an extraordinary degree, then leave prisoners to deal with** the realities of prison life, which can be dangerous,' says Sister Glass. 'Born again prisoners believe they can wipe out all memory of their crimes, because Jesus has forgiven them.'

> (Adapted from box inset into large feature by F. Robson 'Prisoners prey'. *Sydney Morning Herald. Good Weekend magazine* 24/6/95: 24.)

*Note: This clause was edited slightly in the Phase I version of the text.
***They leave prisoners to deal with the realities* is a causative structure agnate to *They make prisoners deal with the realities. Leave ... to deal with* can be regarded as a single causative material Process with *prisoners* as Actor and *they* as Initiator... See Section 2.7.

For further practice in analysing texts for transitivity, Texts 5 and 6 are provided. The Key will include analyses for embedded clauses.

Text 5 Procedure

Blackbirds take the heaviest toll of raspberries. They are more troublesome in gardens where there is plenty of cover to nest in, and fewer plants to feed from, than in large open raspberry fields. Unless you can devise a really efficient way of scaring them, you will have to net. To support the net, make a framework of wires or canes fixed to posts over the row. Cover the tops of the posts with polythene or jam jars so that the net can be pulled smoothly over them without snagging. Alternatively, buy more expensive supports which slot together to form a rigid frame. The net should be high enough above the row to prevent birds sitting on the top and pecking through; it must hang well clear of the sides as fruit is carried on side shoots growing out from the canes.

(From Spiller, M. *Growing fruit*. Harmondsworth: Penguin Books: 155)

Text 6 Biographical recount

George Bernard Shaw was born in Dublin, Ireland, on July 26, 1856. He attended four different schools but his real education came from a thorough grounding in music and painting, which he obtained at home. In 1871, he was apprenticed to a Dublin estate agent, and later he worked as a cashier. In 1876, Shaw joined his mother and sister in London, where he spent the next nine years in unrecognized struggle and genteel poverty.

From 1885 to 1898, he wrote for newspapers and magazines as critic of art, literature, music and drama. But his main interest at this time was political propaganda, and, in 1884, he joined the Fabian Society. From 1893 to 1939, the most active period of his career, Shaw wrote 47 plays. By 1915, his international fame was firmly established and productions of *Candida, Man and Superman, Arms and the Man, The Devil's Disciple* were being played in many countries of the world, from Britain to Japan. In 1925, the playwright was awarded the Nobel Prize for Literature. Between the ages of fifty-seven and sixty-seven, Shaw wrote such dramas as *Heartbreak House, Back to Methuselah, Androcles and the Lion, St. Joan*. During his lifetime he was besieged by offers to film his plays, but he accepted only a few, the most notable being *Pygmalion*, which was adapted (after his death) as the basis for the musical *My Fair Lady*. He died at the age of ninety-four at Ayot St. Lawrence, England, on November 2, 1950.

4.3 Phase III

4.3.1 Exercises

Exercise 1 Relational clauses Analyse the following clauses as attributive or identifying, assigning Carrier, Attribute or Token, Value labels as appropriate.

| The red | stands for | our mother earth. | identifying |
| Token | | Value | |

1. It was the best movie I'd ever seen.

2. It was pretty good.

3. Isn't he just the cutest little thing!

4. One good batsman is Lara; another's Tendulkar.

5. If Scully's a babe ‖ is Mulder a fox?

6. (Give an example of a Range.) – *A dance* is a Range in *Do a dance.*

7. "You're the greatest", (he exclaimed.)

8. He's a good player.

9. That has to be the slowest century ever scored.

10. Dolphins are toothed whales with a clear dorsal fin, some cervical vertebrae fused and spatular teeth.

Exercise 2 Differentiating verbal and identifying clauses Analyse the following clauses as verbal or relational, assigning Sayer or Token Value labels as appropriate. See Section 3.7(iii). For example:

He   said hello.
Sayer   verbal

1. *Ulan* means 'rain'.

2. The report reflected their intelligence.

3. The last item on the programme said Secondary School Choir – Carol.

4. Our protest shows we're against apartheid.

5. It means peace in our time.

6. It indicates the lack of consensus on the issue.

7. The clouds suggest rain.

8. The report revealed they're intelligent.

9. He indicated he'd be there at six.

Exercise 3 Distinguishing facts from ideas (mental and relational clauses)
Determine whether the projections in the following examples are embedded or
projected; enclose embedded projections in [[ ]] and underline projected ideas (see
Section 3.3, 3.5(iv) and Table 5.11 in Chapter 5).

> I heard that she'd arrived.
> I heard [[that she'd arrived]].   embedded

1. I wondered if she was winning.

2. It struck me that she was late.

3. She had been upset she hadn't won.

4. She expected him to leave.

5. He rejoiced that she'd arrived.

6. He was angry that she'd arrived.

7. It piqued him that she'd won.

8. He is hopeful that she'll pass.

Exercise 4 Causative mental and verbal clauses Analyse the following clauses as
verbal or mental, including Sayer, Receiver or Inducer, Senser roles as appropriate.
For example:

He	convinced	her	(to go.)	i.e. 'he told her persuasively'
Sayer		Receiver		verbal

He	made		her believe (that the proposal was genuine.)
Inducer		Senser	mental

1. They tried to convince them that resistance was futile.

2. He'd have liked Data to take charge.

3. He satisfied them that victory was possible.

4. She had them consider that Tokens were Subject in the active.

5. She implored them to leave.

Exercise 5 Causative relational processes Label the following agentive clauses as involving an Assigner or Attributor, including as appropriate either Carrier, Attribute or Token, Value functions. See Section 3.6(vi a). For example:

You must make it a good one.

You	must make	it	a good one
Attributor		Carrier	Attribute

1. I'm keeping my windows shut.

2. Dad had called their cat Sally.

3. It would make her feel better.

4. You can consider it done.

5. They elected her chairperson.

6. I declare the games open.

7. I want it well done.

8. I pronounce him the winner and new champion.

Exercise 6 Resultative and Depictive Attributes Pick out and label the Resultative or Depictive Attributes in the following clauses. See Section 3.4(iii). For example:

She arrived <u>sick</u>.   Depictive Attribute
He painted the town <u>red</u>.   Resultative Attribute

1. She left town exhausted.   1. ....

2. She planed the edge straight.   2. ....

3. He kissed the cut all better.   3. ....

4. He cooked the onions brown.   4. ....

5. He walked out happy.   5. ....

Exercise 7 Discriminating material, existential and attributive clauses Analyse the following clauses as material, existential or attributive.

1. On the table was a vase of flowers.

2. Immediately there took place a fearful conflagration.

3. The phenomenon occurs every few minutes.

4. Few of the books were on the shelf.

5. There wasn't much rain last year.

6. It happens all the time.

7. Along the stream ran a worn path.

8. The Renaissance began in Italy.

Exercise 8 Discriminating verbal and agentive identifying clauses Analyse the following clauses as verbal or relational identifying, assigning Assigner + Value (+Token) or Sayer roles as appropriate. See Section 3.6(vi) for agentive identifying clauses. For example:

The results confirmed the principle of relativity.
Assigner   Value   identifying
Einstein indicated ‖ that E = mc².
Sayer   locution   verbal

1. She demonstrated that that was the case.

2. She asserted that it was obvious.

3. She proved her point.

4. The map indicates that this is the way.

5. Her actions confirmed their suspicions.

6. He confirmed he'd be there by six.

7. The report proves that the best solution.

8. Their reply shows that to be the point.

9. Their efforts ensured a quick result.

Exercise 9 Circumstantial relational processes Determine the type of circumstantial identifying process in each of the following clauses. Label the participants.

Temperature   affects   humidity.
Token   Process: identifying: causal   Value

1. Night follows day.

2. These voting patterns resulted in a hung Parliament.

3. He faced tremendous opposition.

4. Taking on a new job is related to increased stress.

5. Pressure influences rainfall.

6.   A bronzed skin was associated with health and beauty in their minds.

7.   Spines cover its back.

8.   The earlier figures correlate with our results.

9.   This chapter concerns the rise of imperialism.

10. Jo Chaney resembles a young Marlon Brando.

Exercise 10 Ergativity Analyse the following clauses from both a transitive and ergative perspective.

He	opened	the box	slowly
Actor	Process:material	Goal	Manner
Agent	Process	Medium	Manner

1.   He was shot in the elevator.

2.   They were looking at the dancers.

3.   She'd been waiting every evening for ten nights.

4.   The clothes dried quickly on the line.

5.   The dog chased the bird in a frenzy.

6.   We really enjoyed the concert.

7.   She was very unhappy.

8.   It made her very unhappy.

9.   Don't give Peter any more money, will you?

10. The whole business excited her.

Exercise 11 Ergativity Analyse the following clauses from both a transitive and ergative perspective.

The argument	convinced	her	later that evening.
Phenomenon	Process:mental	Senser	Location
Agent	Process	Medium	Location

1.   The rice lasted them a couple of weeks.

2.   She kept it fresh with daily watering.

3.   According to critics, his dancing reflects tremendous artistry.

4.   This time he asked her the time.

5.   The region boasts a number of attractions for visitors of all ages.

6.   She thought over their proposal without any assistance.

7.   He sang them a moving ballad.

8.   They walked the horses round and round the paddock.

9.   She passed them the contract in light of their request.

10. My daughter proved my harshest critic.

4.3.3 Texts for analysis

Text 1. Description The following text was considered in Chapter 2 from the point of view of Theme choices. Now analyse the transitivity structures.

The trail of the meat
The land was cold and white and savage. Across it there ran a thread of frozen waterway, with dark spruce forest looming on either side. Along this waterway toiled a string of wolfish dogs, hauling a sled of birch-bark. On the sled, along with the camp-outfit, was lashed a long and narrow oblong box. In front of the dogs, on wide snowshoes, toiled a man. Behind the sled came a second man. On the sled in the box lay a third man whose life was at an end – a man whom the Wild had beaten down and conquered. The bodies of the live men were covered with soft fur and leather. Their faces were blurred and shapeless under a coating of crystals from their frozen breath. All around them was a silence which seemed to press upon them as water does upon a diver.

(J. London: *White Fang*. Abridged Edition N. Farr, Pendulum Press 1977.)

Text 2 Historical explanation Identify the participants in the following text as Agent or Medium and write them in the chart below.

How Did the Long March Contribute to the Eventual Communist Victory?
First of all, it established the leadership of Mao Zedong. Although Mao was challenged by the leader of the Fourth Route army, Zhang Guotao, the prestige Mao acquired during the Long March assured his dominance. Mao's leadership also brought an end to the dominance of the Soviet Union in the party and made Chinese Communism more independent.

The Long March forged a tightly knit army that drew strength from its sufferings. The survivors formed the tough nucleus of the New Red Army which developed at Yanan. The policy of going north to fight the Japanese also stimulated high morale in the Red Army and inspired patriots throughout China.

As it passed through twelve provinces the Red Army brought the message of Communism to hundreds of millions of peasants, who would otherwise have never heard of Communism.

(T. Buggy, 1988: *The Long Revolution: A history of modern China*. Sydney: Shakespeare Head Press (Modern History Series), 240.)

Agent	Process	Medium

Text 3 Narrative (excerpt) Analyse the following text for transitivity and/or ergativity and reflect on the world view presented through the narrator's eyes.

The bushes twitched again. Lok steadied by the tree and gazed.

A head and chest faced him, half-hidden. There were white bone things behind the leaves and hair. The man had white bone things above his eyes and under the mouth, so that his face was longer than a face should be. The man turned sideways in the bushes and looked at Lok along his shoulder. A stick rose upright and there was a lump of bone in the middle. Lok peered at the stick and the lump of bone and the small eyes in the bone thing over the face. Suddenly Lok understood that the man was holding the stick out to him but neither he nor Lok could reach across the river . He would have laughed if it were not for the echo of the screaming in his head. The stick began to grow shorter at both ends. Then it shot out to full length again. The dead tree by Lok's ear acquired a voice. 'Clop!' His ears twitched and he turned to the tree. By his face there had grown a twig...

He rushed to the edge of the water and came back. On either side of the open bank the bushes grew thickly in the flood; they waded out until at their farthest some of the leaves were opening under water; and these bushes leaned over...

(Extract from Golding, William 1961: *The Inheritors*. London: Faber, 106–7.)

Text 4 Written Exposition You may have analysed the interpersonal structure of this 'letter to the editor' in Chapter 3. Now add a transitivity analysis.

TV Violence

It is essential for the well-being of the Youth of Australia that we adopt a less tolerant attitude to violence in television. It has been known for some time that young children can be disturbed by the violent scenes presented by the television scene. No apparent effort however has been made by either the producers of children's programmes or the programmers of children's programmes to take this into account: one only has to look at the extraordinary popular cartoon

'Teenage Mutant Ninja Turtles'. At some schools it was necessary to ban the accessories associated with the programme because children were engaging in fights in the playground, emulating their cartoon heroes; this sort of situation is deplorable, this incident also highlights how impressionable young children are. There is a definite danger that children, after years of exposure to violence on television, come to accept that violence is an acceptable solution to conflict. It is of vital importance for the future of Australia that young people realize that violence is not to be condoned, nor applauded. It is also essential that young people do not associate violence with bravery and heroism, which is an inevitable outcome if we persist in allowing our children to be influenced by the garbage that fills our screens every afternoon and evening, and succeeds in passing for entertainment. It is possible that children come to accept violence as an inevitable, but vaguely unpleasant part of the world. If this unfortunate scenario becomes true, we will never combat violence. It is of utmost importance, then, that the television industry assumes a sense of responsibility by carefully regulating the materials that appear in children's programmes.

(Text courtesy of Bill Crowley.)

5 Review and Contextualization

5.1 The clause as experiential construct

When considering the clause from the perspective of the experiential metafunction, the relevant systems are collectively known as TRANSITIVITY and the clause itself is

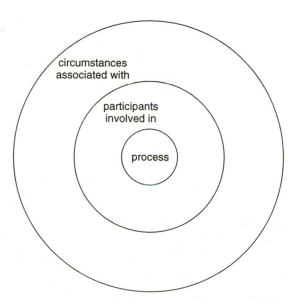

Fig. 4.6 Transitivity structure

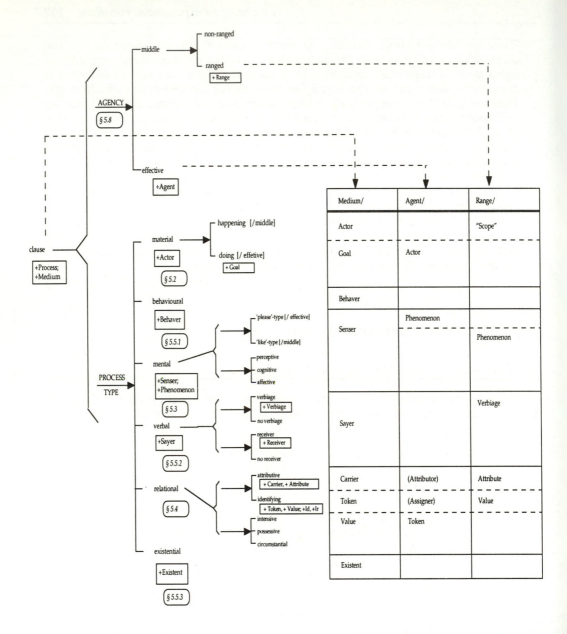

		middle	effective
material	**happening/ doing**	*[happening] The sugar dissolved in the glass.*	*[doing] She dissolved the sugar in the glass.*
behavioural		*She coughed.*	*They criticised IFG.*
mental	**perceptive**	*She saw the kite.*	*The kite caught her attention.*
	cognitive	*She forgot his name.*	*His name escaped her.*

	affective	*She enjoyed the chocolates.*	*The chocolates pleased her.*
verbal		*She told us a story.*	
relational	**intensive**	*She was a leader.*	*She was the leader.*
	possessive	*She had a VW bug.*	*She owned the VW bug.*
	circumstantial	*The trees were around her.*	*The trees surrounded her.*
existential		*There was once a man from Manchuria.*	

Fig. 4.7 Transitivity options and examples

interpreted as a process configuration. Notice in particular the three types of component in this configuration – the process itself, participants involved in the process and circumstances associated with the process. The key to the difference between participants and circumstances lies in the degree of involvement in the process – and it is indeed a matter of degree: participants are actually centrally involved in the process by bringing it about, being affected by it, benefiting from it, and so on; circumstances are much less centrally involved – we say they are associated with (or attendant on) rather than involved in the process. We can diagram these relationships by showing the process as the centre of the transitivity structure of the clause. See Fig. 4.6.

The major options in TRANSITIVITY as they are presented in IFG are summarized in the system network in Fig. 4.7, with references to sections in IFG. (In addition, note also Range, Beneficiary and secondary Agent; circumstances, discussed in IFG Section 5.7, are not shown here.)

5.2 Ergative perspective

In addition to the participant roles associated with each clause type which are shown on the network itself, the table on the right-hand side of Fig. 4.7 shows how these various participant roles can be generalized as Agent, Medium and Range when any clause is viewed from an **ergative** perspective.[15]

Thus, for example:

She	enjoyed	the chocolates	The chocolates	pleased	her.
Senser	Process: mental	Phenomenon	Phenomenon	Process: mental	Senser
Medium		Range	Agent	Medium	

The sugar	dissolved.		It	dissolved	the sugar.
Actor	Process: material		Actor	Process: material	Goal
Medium			Agent		Medium

Viewed from this perspective, the core of the clause is the Process together with the Medium participant. Where the process is something external to this, there will also be an Agent present in the structure. See Fig. 4.9.

---

[15]Note that from an ergative perspective the central core of the configuration is Process + Medium, rather than Process alone.

| | Madam, | you' | ll | look | like a tulip |

Fig. 4.8
Multifunctional analysis of a clause

clause: textual

| | interp. | topical | |
| | Theme | | Rheme |

interpersonal

| Vocative | Mood | Residue |

ideational

| | Carrier | Process | Attribute |

5.3 Relation to other metafunctions

The transitivity structure of the clause maps on to the textual and interpersonal layers described in Chapters 2 and 3. Thus, the example *Madam, you'll look like a tulip*, in addition to its textual and interpersonal meanings, is a representation with

Table 4.18 Correspondences between experiential and interpersonal functions

type of experiential transitivity function:	interpersonal function:	realization:
Process	Finite and Predicator	verbal group
participant functions (Agent, Medium, Beneficiary, Range)	Subject; Complement	nominal group
circumstance functions (Location, Extent, Cause, Contingency, Manner; Accompaniment; Role; Angle, Matter)	Adjunct	adverbial group/ prepositional phrase

Table 4.19 Mapping of participant roles and interpersonal roles:
(i) active clause: *Hermes gave my aunt these flowers out of pity*

participant function:	Subject	Complement	Adjunct
Agent	√ *Hermes*		
Beneficiary		√ *my aunt*	
Medium		√ *these flowers*	
Cause			√ *out of pity*

a process of attribution (*will look*) and two participants, an Attribute (*like a tulip*) and the Carrier of this attribute (*you*). See Fig. 4.8.

This example shows that not every element that enters into a textual or inter-personal structure will be part of the transitivity structure. Here the Vocative *Madam* plays no role in the representation of the process. We can see this easily enough if we probe the clause textually by means of Theme predication: we can get *Madam, it is you who'll look like a tulip* (focus on Carrier), *Madam, it is a tulip that you'll look like* (focus on Attribute), but not *it is Madam that you'll look like a tulip* (attempted focus on Vocative). This difference is explained by the interpretation of the Vocative as a purely interpersonal element.

The general correspondences between the experiential and interpersonal functions are shown in Table 4.18.

The general principle is that participants have the potential for being given the interpersonal status of modal responsibility; thus they serve as Subject (actual modal responsibility) or as Complement (non-actual but potential modal responsibility). For example, all three participants in our earlier example *Hermes gave my aunt these flowers out of pity* can serve as Subject. See Tables 4.19–4.21.

Note that in the passive clauses the Agent does not in fact serve as Complement although it is a participant. We can therefore make a simple yet powerful general-ization about the hierarchy of participants in relation to the interpersonal functions Subject, Complement and Adjunct (see Table 4.22). In the active, unmarked voice, the Agent is Subject and the other participants are Complements; in the passive,

Table 4.20 Mapping of participant roles and interpersonal roles:
(ii) passive clause, 1: *My aunt was given these flowers (by Hermes) out of pity*

participant function:	Subject	Complement	Adjunct
Agent			√ *Hermes*
Beneficiary	√ *my aunt*		
Medium		√ *these flowers*	
Cause			√ *out of pity*

Table 4.21 Mapping of participant roles and interpersonal roles:
(ii) passive clause, 2: *These flowers were given my aunt (by Hermes) out of pity*

participant function:	Subject	Complement	Adjunct
Agent			√ *Hermes*
Beneficiary		√ *my aunt*	
Medium	√ *these flowers*		
Cause			√ *out of pity*

Table 4.22 Hierarchy of participant functions in relation to interpersonal functions

VOICE:	Agent	{Medium, Beneficiary}	{Beneficiary, Medium}
active [unmarked]	**Subject**	Complement	Complement
passive [marked]	Adjunct: *by*	**Subject**	Complement

Table 4.23 Correspondences between transitivity functions and interpersonal functions

experiential transitivity function:		interpersonal	function:
participant functions	**Medium**	Subject; Complement	
	Agent, Beneficiary Range		Adjunct
circumstance functions	Location, Extent, Cause, Contingency, Manner; Accompaniment; Role; Angle, Matter		

marked voice, either of the other participants can be Subject and the one that is not serves as Complement. All of these are simply nominal groups. The passive Agent is marked and its marked status is indicated by the preposition *by*. It serves neither as Subject nor as Complement, but as Adjunct. It has the characteristics of a circumstantial Adjunct: (i) it is realized by a prepositional phrase, not by nominal group; and (ii) it is optional, not obligatory (in fact, the majority of passive clauses have no Agent).

In fact, we can take one step further in our generalization about the relation of participants to interpersonal roles. There is a variant of our three-participant clause where the Beneficiary (but not the Medium) is realized by a prepositional phrase rather than by a nominal group; for example: *Hermes gave these flowers to my aunt*. Here the Beneficiary is an Adjunct rather than a Complement (there is no passive clause *to my aunt was given these flowers (by Hermes)*).

Thus we can now revise the table of correspondences between transitivity functions and interpersonal functions. See Table 4.23. The interesting result is that the participant function we have called the Medium stands out among the participant functions: it is the only one that serves as Subject or Complement but not as Adjunct. Agent, Beneficiary and Range are closer to circumstances in that they can also be mapped onto Adjunct.

This suggests a view of transitivity which has the Medium as a nuclear participant, at the centre of the configuration, as shown in Fig. 4.9.

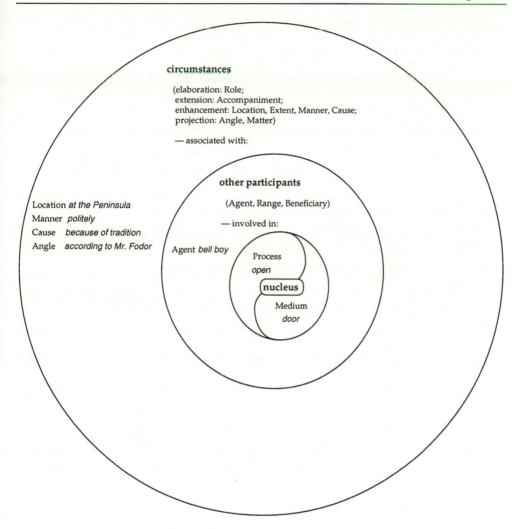

Fig. 4.9 Ergative clause structure

Further reading

Davidse, Kristin 1992: Transitive/ergative: the Janus-headed grammar of actions and events. In M. Davies and Louise Ravelli (eds) *Advances in systemic linguistics*. London: Pinter, 105–35. An intensive study of transitive and ergative motifs in English grammar.

——————— 1996. *Ditransitivity and possession*. In R. Hasan, C. Cloran and D. Butt (eds) *Functional descriptions*. Amsterdam: Benjamins, 85–144.

Fawcett, Robin P. 1987: The semantics of clause and verb for relational processes in English. In M.A.K. Halliday and R.P. Fawcett (eds) *New developments in systemic linguistics v.1: Theory and description*. London: Pinter, 130–183.

Halliday, M.A.K. 1971: Linguistic function and literary style: an enquiry into the language of William Golding's 'The Inheritors'. In Seymor Chatman (ed), *Literary style: a symposium*. New York: Oxford University Press, 362–400. This paper shows how transitivity is used to project different world views in Golding's novel.

_____ 1985: Dimensions of discourse analysis: grammar. In Teun, A. van Dijk (ed), *Handbook of discourse analysis*, Vol. 1. New York: Academic Press, 29–56.

_____ 1992: Some lexicogrammatical features of the Zero Population Growth text. In Sandra Thompson and William Mann (eds), *Discourse description: diverse analyses of a fund-raising text*. Amsterdam: Benjamins, 327–358. For an example of a text analysed in terms of transitivity.

Hasan, Ruqaiya 1987: Lexis as most delicate grammar. In M.A.K. Halliday and R.P. Fawcett (eds) *New developments in systemic linguistics v.1: Theory and description*, London: Pinter, 184–211.

Hasan, Ruqaiya, Cloran, Carmel and Butt, David (eds) 1996: *Functional descriptions*. Amsterdam: Benjamins, 184–211. Includes studies of TRANSITIVITY in English, Dutch, French, Finnish and Pitjantjatjara.

Martin, J.R. 1996a: Metalinguistic diversity: the case from case. In R. Hasan, C. Cloran and D. Butt (eds) *Functional descriptions*. Amsterdam: Benjamins, 323–372. Discusses various theoretical parameters surrounding the study of case relations

_____ 1996b: Transitivity in Tagalog: a functional interpretation of case. In M. Berry, C. Butler, R. Fawcett and G. Huang (eds), *Meaning and Form: systemic-functional interpretations* (Volume 2 in Meaning and Choice in Language: studies for Michael Halliday), Norwood, NJ: Ablex, 229–296. Shows how a transitivity system other than that of English is organized. It introduces another transitivity model alongside the ergative and transitive ones discussed in IFG.

Matthiessen, Christian 1993: The object of study in cognitive science. *Cultural Dynamics* 6, 1–2, 187–242.

_____ 1995: *Lexicogrammatical cartography: English systems*. Chapter 4; experiential resources: Section 2.3.3; metaphor: Section 2.4.2 and Section 7.3.3.3.5; tense and process type: Section 7.5.2.2.4. Tokyo: International Language Sciences Publishers.

McGregor, William B. 1996: Attribution and Identification in Gooniyendi. In M. Berry, C. Butler, R. Fawcett and G. Huang (eds), *Meaning and Form: systemic-functional interpretations* (Volume 2 in Meaning and Choice in Language: studies for Michael Halliday), Norwood, NJ: Ablex, 395–430. Looks at relational processes in an Australian language.

5

The clause complex
above the clause

1 Orientation

1.1 Reading guide to IFG

IFG   Chapter 7 (above the clause)

1.2 Characterization of clause complex

With the study of the clause complex, we move to the **logical** subcomponent of the ideational metafunction and explore the ways in which the highest ranking grammatical unit – the clause – can combine with further clauses. This chapter will not be concerned with the parts of the clause, but with the way the clause as a whole may be related to one or more further clauses to form a **complex** of clauses or a 'clause complex.' For example, having begun with the 'primary' clause *We loved the show ourselves*, the speaker could add a (theoretically) limitless number of further linked clauses, as in: *We loved the show ourselves → so we'll get tickets for Tim and Josie → when they come over next month → to visit her mother... .* The kind of structure created in this way is a 'univariate' one, a series of repetitions of the same grammatical unit (here, a clause), each related to another in various ways.

Traditionally,[1] a series of related clauses of this kind has been seen as making up the higher rank unit of 'sentence'. However, Halliday argues that when clauses combine to form a clause complex, they do not thereby create a new grammatical unit of higher rank. His position is that the sentence is not a unit of grammar, but a unit of English orthography, realizing the grammatical construction clause complex. The two interpretations of the status of 'sentence' are illustrated in Fig. 5.1, with (i) as the traditional view and (ii) as the IFG position.

---

[1]This position has also been taken by e.g. Michael Gregory within systemic linguistics/communication linguistics and Robert Longacre within tagmemic linguistics.

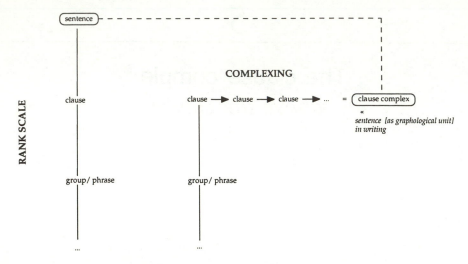

Fig. 5.1   Sentence and clause complex

From a semantic point of view, a clause complex construes a **sequence of process configurations** from the flow of events. Fig. 5.2 shows this construal schematically. The clause complex might be used to group process configurations as constituting one subepisode in an episode, or a subprocedure in a procedure, or a step in reasoning. The following example is taken from a narrative, where one subepisode is construed by 11 clauses related by 'and then' into a clause complex:

> He ran downstairs → splashed into the flood ('Christ!') → hurried into the kitchen → put a kettle on the gas → rummaged for brandy → found a half bottle of whisky → saw a hot water bottle hanging on the back of the door → filled it → made tea → poured in a dollop of whisky → carried them upstairs.

The following examples are from procedural texts; here the clause complexes construe sequences of operations that constitute subprocedures:

> Heat remaining oil in same pan → add salmon → (cook → **until** lightly browned) → remove from pan.

> **If** no successors were generated in (3), ← (**then** label node *no* unsolvable, → and (**if** the unsolvability of *n* makes any of its ancestors unsolvable, ← label these ancestors unsolvable), → and (**if** the start node is labelled unsolvable, ← exit with failure), → and remove from OPEN any nodes with an unsolvable ancestor).

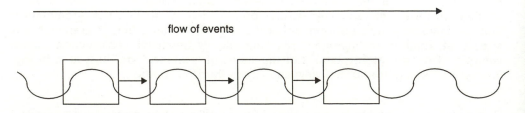

flow of events

Fig. 5.2   Construing the flow of events into a clause complex

As the parentheses indicate, clause complexes may contain subcomplexes such as *if the start node is labelled unsolvable, exit with failure*. In procedures, clause complexes serve to guide the sequence of operations and relate conditions (*if no successors were generated in (3)*; *if you want a more substantial stuffing*) and temporal limits to them (*until it is lightly browned*). Clause complexes are also an important resource in reasoning, as in proofs and explanations.

All the introductory examples so far have been clause complexes where the clauses are related by **expansion**. We will survey the subtypes of expanding relations presently. First we should introduce one other major kind of relation by which clauses may be combined in a clause complex. This relation is **projection**. You have already met it in the context of mental and verbal clauses (see Chapter 4 and IFG Chapter 5), since it usually involves a mental or verbal clause projecting its own content of sensing or saying as a separate clause. For example:

> Calypso *knew* → that her aunt *knew* → she *knew* → how unwelcome Richard would be in Enderby Street.

> "You will have to go to hospital", ← said Dr Smith.

Projection is deployed in narrative to construe the dialogic passages and to represent the characters' processes of consciousness; it is also important in news reporting where it serves to specify the journalists' sources, as with eye-witness reports and comments by 'important people'. Examples:

> Greenpeace's atmosphere and energy campaign co-ordinator Ms Lyn Goldsworthy said → both the tourism and fishing industries at W would be affected by the drilling... 'The world now knows → it has a global warming problem,' ← Ms Goldworthy said. ... A spokeswoman for BHP Petroleum said yesterday → she did not know → when drilling would begin...

The difference and complementarity between expansion and projection can be seen very clearly in the conventions of comic strips. Expansion is represented pictorially by sequences of frames (sometimes with a conjunction added, if the unmarked sequence in time is broken, e.g. *meanwhile*) or by split frames if the expanding relation is one of addition. Projection, on the other hand, cannot be represented simply by the pictures: the content of projection is represented linguistically by text in 'balloons' or 'clouds'.

2 Survey of options

Clauses within a complex are interrelated grammatically in terms of two systems, those of TAXIS and LOGICO-SEMANTIC TYPE.

2.1 TAXIS

TAXIS is concerned with the **interdependency** relations between grammatical units forming a complex, such as groups forming a group complex or clauses forming a clause complex. Some examples of complexes at different ranks are shown in Table 5.1.

Table 5.1 Complexes at different ranks

Type of unit in complex	Example
word (adjective)	The *black and white* kitten
nominal group	*The old man and his dog, Rover...*
nominal gp./prepositional phrase	(I'll take) *the blue shirt, with the button-down collar*
adverbial gp./prepositional phrase	(he threw it) *enthusiastically but without skill*
prepositional phrase	(he drove) *from Sydney to Canberra*
verbal group	(they) *began to sing*

The two options within the system of TAXIS are those of **parataxis** or **hypotaxis**, categories which relate to (but are not identical with) traditional notions of co-ordination and subordination, respectively. If the units in a complex are of equal status, the relation between them is a paratactic one; if the units are of unequal status, the relation is a hypotactic one.

Where two units within a complex are linked in a **paratactic** relation, each unit could stand as an independent functioning whole, and neither is dependent on the other. Here are some examples of paratactic clause complexes:

He looked terrible;	‖ his clothes were crumpled and dirty.
Miriam was somewhat scared by the wind,	‖ but the lads enjoyed it.
He hated her,	‖ for she seemed in some way to make him despise himself.
He replied quickly,	‖ "I can't complain."

This paratactic relation is signalled in the notation by labelling the clauses numerically in sequence. For example:

The rivers overflow, ‖ the streets become rivers ‖ and everything is soaked.
         1   2   3

By contrast, where two units within a complex are linked in a **hypotactic** relation, one unit modifies the other, one clause is a 'principal' or 'dominant' clause and the other is **dependent** upon it. Examples are shown in Table 5.2. A dependent clause may be a non-finite clause, as in the second example in Table 5.2 (*apart from visiting his sister in York once a month*), in which case its dependent status is very obvious.

Table 5.2 Examples of hypotactic clause complexes

dominant (α)	dependent (β)
They spoke to Dr Liu,	*who was an ear, nose and throat specialist*
The man rarely left the village	*apart from visiting his sister in York once a month*
I can do my best things	*when you sit there in your rocking chair*
He explained	*that there was no possibility of a new lease.*

The relation of hypotaxis between a dominant unit and a dependent one is signalled in the notation by labelling the clauses with the Greek alphabet, using an alpha for the dominant, a beta for a clause dependent upon it and a gamma for one dependent on that, and so on. In the following example the notation is written alongside each clause:

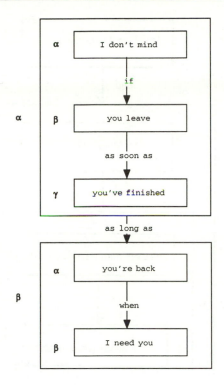

Fig. 5.3 Alternative representation of IFG Fig. 7-2

α   we're going to buy an intercom system
β   so that we can hear Stephen in different parts of the house
γ   whenever he cries.

A hypotactic clause complex will not necessarily have the alpha clause as the initial clause in the sequence, so this notation is sequenced to indicate the dependency relations. For example:

β   As they walked along the dark fen meadow
α   he watched the moon.

Where there are several clauses in the complex, they will not necessarily be linked in a single line of dependency. Fig. 5.3 is an alternative representation of a more complex example diagrammed in IFG, where the first three clauses form a block with the second two clauses dependent upon it.

While they have been exemplified separately here, paratactic and hypotactic relationships may well be combined in a single clause complex. For example:

1   we're going to go to Childworld
2   and we're going to buy some diapers for Stephen and Emily
3α   and we're going to buy an intercom system
  β   so that we can hear Stephen in different parts of the house
  γ   whenever he cries.

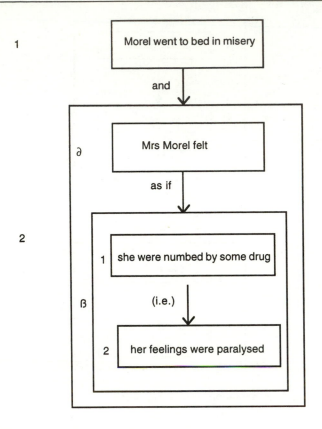

Fig. 5.4   A clause complex, illustrating interdependencies

or:

    1   Morel went to bed in misery,
    2 α   and Mrs Morel felt
      β 1   as if she were numbed by some drug,
        2   as if her feelings were paralysed.

An alternative representation of the last example can also be given (see Fig. 5.4) to show the 'layering' of the structure.

2.2   *Logico-semantic type*

One clause in a clause complex is linked to another not only in terms of TAXIS, but also in terms of a particular logico-semantic relationship. In the most general terms there are two types of such relationship: **expansion** – which includes the meanings realized by conjunctions – and **projection** - which includes direct and indirect speech and thought. Thus for any complex there are simultaneously two sets of choices, as shown in Fig. 5.5.

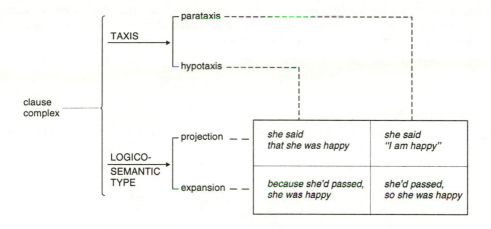

Fig. 5.5 Basic clause complex options

2.2.1 Expansion

The various logico-semantic relations included as expanding relations are of three main kinds: **elaboration**, **extension** and **enhancement**.

2.2.1.1 Elaboration (=)

The elaborating relation is symbolized in the notation with an 'equals' sign. In a paratactic elaborating complex an initial clause is restated, exemplified or further specified by another. There is usually no overt linker between the clauses apart from a colon or semi-colon in a written text:

He looked a fright; ‖ his clothes were damp, dirty and torn.
  1   =2

She didn't like the character she was playing; ‖ she hated her self-confidence.
          1   =2

In a hypotactic elaborating complex, the dependent clause – realized by a 'non-restrictive' relative clause – provides some kind of elaborating description or comment. For example:

They were now in the bare country of stone walls, ‖ which he loved.
The accident left him with two broken front teeth, ‖ which was such a shame.
          α   =β

The dominant and dependent clauses are linked by 'tone concord' in speech (IFG: 228), while in writing a comma or dash can be expected to separate them.[2] The beta

---

[2]An **embedded** clause having the same form, such as *who'd been expelled* in *We spoke to the boy* ⟦*who'd been expelled*⟧, does not have these characteristics.

clause may elaborate just one participant in the alpha clause, in which case it often occurs next to that participant, interrupting or **included** in the alpha clause. Angled brackets are used to enclose the included clause:

> His mother, << who had been watching them all evening>>, made her way over.
> α   <<=β>>

2.2.1.2 Extension (+)

The basic meanings of the extending relation are those of addition (including the adversative relation) or variation. The extending relation combines most frequently with parataxis, being realized most typically by the conjunctions *and*, *nor*, *but* and *or*. For example:

> The beef animal is the buffalo ‖ and its meat is surprisingly tender.
> 1   +2

Note that the Subject of the continuing paratactic clause may be ellipsed:

> The idea of relativity did not originate with Einstein, ‖ but [it] goes back to Newton.
> 1   +2

Extension is less frequently realized in combination with hypotaxis. Typical hypotactic linkers are *whereas*, *instead of*, *except for*, *apart from*, *as well as*, the latter four introducing a non-finite dependent clause. (See IFG: 233 for a summary of the principal markers of extension.)

2.2.1.3 Enhancement (×)

The meanings included as enhancement are those of time, place, manner, cause and condition, which can also be expressed as circumstances within the clause:

manner as circumstance:	They dried their clothes *with the fan*
manner as hypotactic enhancement:	They dried their clothes ‖ *by hanging them on branches in the wind*

In the clause complex, enhancing relations are most frequently found in combination with hypotaxis, although paratactic links with *so* and *and then* are common. IFG: 236 provides a table of paratactic enhancing linkers, while IFG: 237 summarizes the principal markers of hypotactic enhancement.

2.2.2 Projection

Projection typically concerns the relation between a mental or verbal clause and the content which it quotes or reports. A paratactic relation holds when one clause quotes another ('direct speech/thought') , and a hypotactic relation when one clause reports another ('indirect speech/thought'). See Table 5.3.

Projected clauses – i.e. quotes or reports – represent the wording or meaning of the speaker represented in the projecting clause, not the speaker of the clause complex. They are thus **meta**-representations, or **metaphenomena**. The metaphenomenon projected by a verbal clause is a **locution**, symbolized by (") notation, while a mental clause projects an **idea**, notated as (') for example:

Table 5.3 Examples of projection

paratactic projection	They said	'he's hopeless'
(quoting)	They thought	'he's hopeless'
hypotactic projection	They said	(that) he was hopeless
(reporting)	They thought	(that) he was hopeless
	projecting clause	**projected clause**

He told his aunt   that he would write home regularly.
    α   "β (locution)
He decided   that he would take a little time off first.
    α   'β (idea)

All the locutions and ideas illustrated so far have been of information clauses (**propositions**), but it is also possible for commands and offers to be projected. Projected clauses of this latter kind are called **proposals**, and if hypotactic take the form of a modalized declarative or a non-finite clause as shown in Table 5.4.

Table 5.4 Examples of projected proposals

Projecting clause	locution:proposal
His aunt told him	(that) he should write home more regularly
His aunt told him	to write home at least once a month
His aunt told him	not to forget

Projecting clause	idea:proposal
His aunt wishes	that he would write home more regularly
His aunt would have liked	him to write home regularly
His aunt expected	him to forget

2.3 Summary of clause complex relations

See Table 5.5.

3 Troubleshooting

3.1 *Procedure for analysis*

When analysing clause complex relationships in a text, you first identify boundaries between clause complexes. Then identify boundaries between ranking clauses. You may then find it helpful to write out the text with one ranking clause per line so that the analysis – in terms of TAXIS and LOGICO-SEMANTIC TYPE – can be written down the left-hand margin.

Table 5.5 Summary of clause complex relations

	parataxis	hypotaxis
EXPANSION	ELABORATION	
	1 *Jogging on the streets is bad for you;* =2 *it damages your feet.*	α *Jogging stresses your feet,* =β *which can cause serious problems.*
	1 *it was nothing serious;* =2 *it was just a small cut.*	α *I met Granny,* =β *who was looking very well.*
	EXTENSION	
	1 *They cleared the table* +2 *and washed the dishes.*	+β *As well as doing the shopping,* α *they cooked all the meals.*
	1 *Did they complain* +2 *or did they just keep quiet as usual?*	α *They just kept quiet as usual* +β *instead of complaining.*
	ENHANCEMENT	
	1 *She spent all her money on a car,* ×2 *so she couldn't afford to go on holiday.*	α *She couldn't afford to go on holiday* ×β *because she had spent all her money.*
	1 *Heat the mixture to boiling point,* ×2 *then add the milk very slowly.*	×β *When the pudding has cooled,* α *remove carefully from the container.*
PROJECTION	LOCUTION	
	1 *The babysitter said:* "2 *"don't make a noise!"*	α *The babysitter told us* "β *not to make a noise*
	"1 *"That's ridiculous,"* 2 *he snapped.*	α *He said to us* "β *that it was ridiculous.*
	IDEA	
	'1 *'That's funny,'* 2 *he thought.*	α *He thought* 'β *we would enjoy it.*
	'1 *'Don't stop now',* 2 *she thought.*	α *He expected* 'β *everybody to help.*

3.2 Picking out the unit of analysis

When analysing a written text, there is no problem recognizing the boundary of a clause complex since this will be signalled orthographically by a full stop. When working with a transcript of a spoken text, however, there will be occasions when boundaries are less clear cut. This arises when a decision has to be reached as to whether a particular logico-semantic relationship holds between two clauses within a complex or whether it is a cohesive relationship between two clause complexes.

One approach would be to recognize a boundary whenever possible and thus to allow a clause complex relationship only where there is an unambiguous grammat-

Table 5.6 Signals of clause complex boundaries: minimal length principle

Nature of signal	Point where new complex begins
interpersonal	At change of speaker After Moodtag At change of Mood from one clause to next. (An exception can be made for threats such as *Stop or I'll shoot!)* Before a thematic Vocative or after a Vocative in clause final position. Before a thematic comment Adjunct or after a comment Adjunct in clause final position Before *yes, yeah, no*
ideational	Before an apparently extending or enhancing clause which is not introduced by an explicit conjunction Before a β clause preceding its α where the β clause is not linked to the previous one by an explicit conjunction Before a conjunction which can function cohesively (e.g. *and, but, so*) in the following situations: • where there is a pause before the conjunction • where there is a lengthening of the syllable before the conjunction • where there is a change of pitch level on the conjunction and where the conjunction could be substituted in the text by an exclusively cohesive one (e.g. *moreover, however, therefore*)
textual	Before a marked topical Theme (e.g. Angle circumstance) without preceding conjunction At a clause initiating a new move in the generic structure of the text

ical signal of hypotaxis or parataxis. If adopting this '**minimal**' length strategy then the interpersonal, ideational and textual signals of when to recognize the beginning of a new clause complex would be as shown in Table 5.6.

The 'minimal length' approach will allow for a consistency in the analysis, but has the disadvantage that some logico-semantic relations (particularly of elaboration) are likely to be missed. This may not be considered too serious a drawback if the text is also being analysed at the discourse-semantic level, in terms of CONJUNCTION. (See IFG 9.4 and Martin, 1992: Chapter 4.) Alternatively, an opposite, '**maximal**' length approach may be taken whereby a logico-semantic paratactic link is assumed wherever it is possible to argue for one.

In a written text, it is best to allow punctuation to override grammatical expectations concerning clause-complex boundaries. In a similar way, whether a minimal or maximal approach is favoured, intonation should be taken into account to modify the general principles being used. IFG: 306–7 suggests that the unmarked sequence of tones for two clauses in a cohesive relation is tone 1 (falling) followed by tone 1; whereas the unmarked sequence for a paratactic sequence is tone 3 (low rise) followed by tone 1.

Below, some examples will be discussed in terms of the two general approaches (i.e. minimal and maximal).

(i) Paratactic or cohesive elaboration?

Example 1
TEACHER:	...his [=chicken embryo] head tucked up under his wing
CHILD:	He's squashing
TEACHER:	He's squashing
	he's filling up nearly the whole of that shell

A minimal approach will regard the child's *He's squashing* as initiating a fresh complex and the teacher's *He's squashing* as initiating a further complex. A maximal approach might take each clause as a paratactic elaboration of the previous one. Given a tone 1 contour on the first three clauses, there would be additional grounds for favouring the minimal analaysis.

Example 2
CHILD:	What does Daddy do
	when he's sick?
MOTHER:	When he's sick
	he goes to bed
	and lies down
	when you're not very well
	you...etc.

A minimal approach will regard the Mother's β clause *when you're not very well* as initiating a new complex on the grounds that this new βα sequence is not linked to the preceding speech by any explicit conjunction. A maximal approach would see this section as a (paratactic) elaboration by the mother of her sequence beginning *when he's sick*.

(ii) Paratactic or cohesive extension and enhancement?

Example 1
a	...he said
b	he thought
c	he knew
d	where there was one [dog] in a yard
e	so my husband went up
f	and looked over the fence
g	and there was our dog, only about a block away
h	and they also had a male corgi there
i	and the two were running together
j	so he brought ours home
k	and he went back up later...

In this part of an oral recount, clauses e–k might constitute a single complex, or might be taken as several different clause complexes, depending on whether any of the conjunctions are interpreted as cohesive rather than paratactic. We can reason about the boundaries in the following way.

Clause e can be taken as initiating a new complex with a cohesive *So*, on the ideational grounds that it is clearly not part of what is projected by a, b or c; and on the textual grounds that it serves to initiate a new sequence of actions in the story.

Clauses f and g are paratactic links. This is clear from the omission of the Subject in f and the impossibility of substituting an unequivocally cohesive conjunction for *and* at g. It would, however, be feasible to have *Furthermore* at h and/or i and

Consequently at j. It is at these points, then, that phonological considerations will determine the boundaries. A tone 3 + tone 1 sequence for two clauses ambiguously related will suggest that the two form a single complex, whereas a series of tone 1s will indicate a cohesive relation. Other signals of cohesion other than taxis would be a pause before the conjunction and/or a lengthening of the syllable before the conjunction and/or a change of pitch level on the conjunction.

Example 2
   A: Can you do that?
   B: He can
       I can't

In this example there is a contrastive relation signalled by the opposed polarity and the intonation (a tone 4, tone 1 sequence). There is however, no extending conjunction. A minimal clause complex analysis might therefore wish to treat these as lacking any grammatical relation of extension. A maximal analysis will allow for the relation, which can be recognized as paratactic rather than cohesive on the grounds that *but* could more readily be used than *however* between the two clauses.

3.2.1 Boundaries of 'ranking' clauses within a clause complex

There are three possible problems which may arise in determining where clauses begin and end within a complex.

1 Embedded clauses Embedded (i.e. rankshifted or downranked) clauses do not enter into relations of hypotaxis or parataxis with other clauses and should be ignored. It is relations between 'ranking' clauses which are to be analysed. See Section 3.3 below for help in recognizing embedded clauses.

2 Included clauses Sometimes one clause interrupts another clause without being embedded in it. For example:

Sometimes, *when we arrive before 8*, the place is still locked up...
'Mother!', *the girl implored*, 'don't wear that nubbly little bonnet.'
Mary Smith, *who was the teacher's pet*, received a glowing report.
... because, *if we don't*, we'll get busted again...

In each of the above examples the *italicised* clause is 'included' within the other clause without being a part of it. This can be notated using angled brackets:

Sometimes <<when we arrive before 8>> the place is still locked up ||...
... because <<if we don't>> we'll get busted again || ...

or, if displaying the text with one clause per line and the analysis in the left-hand margin:

Sometimes << >> the place is still locked up
<<when we arrive before 8>>

because << >> we'll get busted again
<<if we don't>>

3 Verbal group complex or clause complex? It is important not to confuse an inter-dependency relation between clauses with one between verbal groups at one rank below. See discussion in Chapter 4, Section 3.3. For example, *he started to cry* is one clause with a Process realized by a verbal group complex, *started to cry*, not a combination of a finite clause *he started* and a non-finite clause *to cry*. Among these, the projection cases may be the trickiest – see IFG Section 7A.6 for projection.

4 Separate clause or circumstance within the clause? Note that a semantic relation such as time, cause or manner may be realized as a relation between two clauses or as a circumstance within the clause (see Chapter 4, Section 3.10(iii)):

α They opened it β by twisting the rusty key very firmly   clause complex
They opened it with a firm twist to the rusty key   clause with Manner circ.

(i) Metaphorical realization of logical relation You may be misled into taking a circumstance as a ranking clause where the logico-semantic relation of the clause is **metaphorically realized** as a long nominal group with a nominalization as the Head of the group. For example: *Despite Western suspicions [[that he was behind some of North Korea's most heinous terrorist acts in the past decade]], several Japanese sources paint him as a reasonable, practical man.* Here *Despite Western suspicions that he was behind some of North Korea's most heinous terrorist acts in the past decade* is a circumstance of Contingency within the transitivity structure of the clause; it contains a nominal group whose central element is the nominalization *suspicions*. The congruent (i.e. non-metaphorical) realization would have a clause in a clause complex: *Although the West suspects that he was ... ← several Japanese sources paint him ... .*

(ii) Relational process left implicit You may be misled into taking a dependent clause as a circumstance in cases where the process is omitted (see Section 3.7(ii) below).

Table 5.7 Logico-semantic types in parataxis, hypotaxis and embedding

		clause complex – combining through		Rankshift – clause embedded in other gram unit
		parataxis	hypotaxis	
projection		He thought "I said those words"	He thought (that) he'd said those words	He regretted [the fact] that he'd said those words
expansion	elab.	The boy didn't wait; he ran away	The boy ran away, which surprised us We saw John, who ran away	The boy who ran away returned Whoever ran away returned
	enhancem.	He packed and then he ran away	After he had packed he ran away	The best time would be [the time] after he has packed

(iii) Non-finite verb (as Process) or preposition? (See IFG: 212–13.) It may be diffi-cult to determine whether a unit is a clause or a prepositional phrase where the ambiguous unit has a non-finite verb form such as *including, regarding, concerning, using*. The essential difference is that a prepositional phrase only has a potential for a two-element configuration, Minor process^Minirange, whereas a clause is always expandable and will have some related finite variant. For example:

prepositional phrase (part of clause)
What do you intend to do *regarding Pamela's situation*?
They drank everything in the house, *including the raspberry wine*.

non-finite clause
He laid out his offer, *regarding his opposite number with some hostility*.
Including the entire committee in her criticism, the woman made an emotional speech.

3.3 Complexing versus embedding (downranked clauses)

Table 5.7 sets out the different logico-semantic types that can occur both in the environment of clause complexing (parataxis/hypotaxis) and in the environment of embedding – a clause serving as a constituent part of another unit. See IFG Sections 7.4.5, 7.4.6 (expansion) and 7.5.6, 7.5.7 (projection).

3.3.1 Relative clauses: hypotactic elaboration or embedding?

As shown in Table 5.7, a relative clause like *who ran away* may be embedded within a nominal group[3] (*the boy* [[*who ran away*]]) or may enter a hypotactic relation with another clause (*We saw John, who ran away*). The two structures are readily distin-guishable in speech, since the hypotactic non-embedded clause spoken on a separate tone group maintains tone concord with the main clause. (In writing it is typically preceded by a comma.) In terms of function, the hypotactic clause either elaborates the whole preceding clause or provides further information about a participant within it whose identity (e.g. as *John*) is already fully established. An embedded clause, on the other hand, itself provides the identity of the participant, as in *the boy – which boy? – the boy* [[*who ran away*]] – hence the traditional terminology of 'defining' relative clause. Compare the following two examples:

[hypotactic clause complex]
I spoke to my brother || who works in a bank. (I have only one brother)

[single ranking clause containing a nominal group with embedded clause as Postmodifier]
I spoke to my brother [[who works in a bank]]. (I have several brothers, one of whom works in a bank)

3.3.2 Contexts in which embedded (rankshifted) clauses occur

(i) Within clause Table 5.8 sets out on a continuum the possible ways a participant may be construed in English.

---

[3]As a postmodifying Qualifier. See IFG Chapter 6.

Table 5.8 Realizations of participant function (from Thing to Fact)

Type of realization	Role in clause	Meaning construed	Example
metaphenomenal	None – not participant	(LOCUTION/IDEA)	(separate ranking clause)
	participant (embedded clause)	FACT	*(the fact/proof) [[that he went]] was clear; (the need) [[for him to go]] was clear*
macrophenomenal		ACT	*we saw (the sight of) [[him swimming]]*
		MACROTHING: WH-CLAUSE	*we'll meet (the one) [[who she married]]*
phenomenal	participant (nominal group)	REIFIED PROCESS ETC.	*the long swim; the silly reply*
		CONCRETE THING	*the great white whale*

A participant is most typically realized by a nominal group[4] construing a thing, such as *the great white whale* or *a delectable Chinese meal*. However, a clause can also serve to represent 'things' – *what* -, *whoever, whatever*, etc. – For example [[*what they need*]] *is a nice holiday, you can invite* [[*whoever you like*]], [[*whatever Janey wants*]] *Janey gets*. These types of embedded clauses can occur in various participant roles with various process types.

As well as embedded clauses construing concrete and abstract phenomena, however, there are embedded clauses representing 'macrophenomena' (acts) or 'metaphenomena' (facts) and these only occur in a few different participant roles. The different possibilities are outlined below.

Material clauses Embedded clauses representing acts can occur as Actor.

Act (macro)
[[Cleaning the table with the stain-remover]] damaged its surface
[[Running the marathon]] killed him
[[Crushing him like that]] broke his bones

But embedded fact clauses don't occur:

Fact (meta)
*[[That he ran the marathon]] killed him
*It killed him [[that he ran the marathon]]

(Cf. note in IFG: 249–50, including the interpretation of the example *the fact/knowledge that the experiment had failed destroyed his life*.)

---

[4]See IFG Chapter 6. In general terms a nominal group can be thought of as a noun together with any modifying elements, such as articles, numerals, adjectives preceding the noun and/or an embedded prepositional phrase (or embedded clause) following the noun, as in *the two little boys with red hair* or *that old green Ford [[he used to drive]]*.

Mental clauses Embedded clauses can function as the Phenomenon of a mental clause under certain conditions. Embedded clauses representing acts can occur as the Phenomenon of perception in perceptive clauses.

Act (macro)
The driver didn't see ⟦them crossing the street⟧
He felt ⟦the ant crawling up his leg⟧
I just heard ⟦him come in⟧

Embedded clauses representing facts can occur as the Phenomenon of affective clauses of reaction – metaphenomena: such facts exist independently of the Senser's conscious processing and impinge on his/ her consciousness:

Fact (meta)
I regret (the fact) ⟦that we have been unable to succeed⟧ :
(The fact) ⟦That we have been unable to succeed⟧ annoys me :
It annoys me ⟦*that we have been unable to succeed*⟧ :
The fact annoys me ⟦*that we have been unable to succeed*⟧

As shown, these clauses may function as the postmodifying Qualifier in a nominal group where the Head is a noun such as *fact*, *case*, *news*, *idea* etc. Where there is no such Head noun, the embedded clause itself can be regarded as serving as the Head of the nominal group. See IFG Section 7.5.7.

Cognitive mental clauses usually project ideas. That is, they bring ideas into existence through the cognitive processing (*he thought/believed/guessed/dreamed/ imagined that the earth was flat*); they do not involve pre-existing facts as Phenomenon. However, there are a few examples of facts in a cognitive context – for instance: *he accepted (the fact) that the earth is round.*

Verbal clauses Verbal clauses project locutions in clause complexes but they do not occur with embedded clauses of the act or fact type. There are a couple of exceptions with an embedded clause as Verbiage:

He acknowledged/admitted to the press (the fact) ⟦⟦that he had made a serious mistake⟧⟧

Relational clauses Clauses representing both acts and facts can occur as Carrier in attributive clauses and as Token or Value in identifying ones.

Act (macro)
⟦Leaving early⟧ is better

My preference is ⟦to leave early⟧

Fact (meta)
⟦That he has already left⟧ is unlikely:
It's unlikely ⟦that he has already left⟧

The problem is ⟦that he has already left⟧:
⟦That he has already left⟧ is the problem

(ii) Within groups Downranked clauses only occur within nominal and adverbial groups, not within verbal groups. Within nominal groups, they may serve as Head, which means that the embedded clause functions as participant in the clause. In both nominal and adverbial groups a downranked clause may serve as Postmodifier (see IFG Chapter 6). Table 5.9 provides examples of downranked clauses in nominal groups.

Table 5.9 Downranked clause in nominal group

		embedded clause as Head	embedded clause Postmodifier
projection		*(the problem is) that he is negligent*	*(the problem is) the fact that he is negligent*
expansion	elaboration	*whatever Wren built (was admired)* *frying green tomatoes (can be fun)*	*the gazebo that Wren built (was admired)* *the act of frying green tomatoes (can be fun)*
	extension	*Whose it was (is not the issue)*	*the gazebo whose architect later became famous (was admired)*
	enhancement	*wherever Wren built the gazebo (is now a famous place)*	*the gazebo where they used to meet (was admired); (there were) more flowers than they had expected to find*

Table 5.10 Downranked clause in adverbial group

		embedded clause as Head	embedded clause as Postmodifier
projection		—	—
expansion	elaboration	—	—
	extension	—	—
	enhancement	—	*(he ran) more quickly than a man his age could be expected to*

With adverbial groups, comparative clauses are downranked as standards of comparison, serving as Postmodifier, as shown in Table 5.10.

3.3.3 Distinguishing ranking and embedded clauses

Since difficulties arise within particular logico-semantic types (projection/expansion) we have summarized the analysis of clauses as ranking or as downranked in terms of these types. Contrasting examples are set out in Table 5.11, together with properties that can be used in probes. With those of projection and elaboration in particular, you may have to do some work to decide whether they are ranking clauses or downranked clauses serving within groups.

Table 5.11 Contrast between ranking and downranked clauses

	ranking [hypotactic]	embedded (downranked) in nominal group	in adverbial group
pro-jection	idea: • typically projected by processes of cognition [proposition] and affection: desideration [proposal] • agnate with paratactic projection, i.e. can be quoted (although unlikely) • cannot be the Subject (since it is not a participant) • cannot be the focus of theme predication (since it is not a participant) • can be presumed by substitute *so/not* • cannot follow explicit fact noun as Head/Thing in nominal group *she thought ‖ that she had painted the house : she thought ‖ 'I painted the house' : she thought ‖ so*	fact (as Phenomenon): • typically configured with processes of affection: emotion • not agnate with paratactic projection • can be the Subject in the agnate passive variant of the clause (since it is a participant) • can be the focus of Theme predication (since it is a participant) • cannot be presumed by substitute *so/not*, only by reference item such as *that, it* • can follow explicit fact noun as Head/Thing in nominal gp. *she regretted (the fact) ⟦that she had painted the house⟧ : it was (the fact) ⟦that she had painted the house ⟧ that she regretted : she regretted it*	
elabo-ration	non-defining relative clause: • spoken on separate tone group, with tone concord (IFG p. 238, 306) • written with separating punctuational symbols, usually commas (IFG p. 238) • agnate with paratactic elaboration • range of relative items typically excluding relative *that* and 'contact' relative *Hyde Park,<<which they used to like>>, has been turned into a shopping complex : Hyde Park has been turned into a shopping complex; ‖ they used to like it*	defining relative clause (as Qualifier): • not on separate tone group • not separated by punctuation • not agnate with paratactic elaboration • full range of relative forms, including relative *that* and 'contact' relative (if Complement) *the park ⟦which/that/Ø they used to like⟧ has been turned into a shopping complex*	
exten-sion	*instead of/as well as going fishing, they took a stroll on the beach*	[*]	
enhance-ment	serves as qualifying clause in clause complex • cannot follow explicit circumstantial noun • only certain subtypes can be the focus of Theme predication • is agnate with a paratactic enhancement *they went fishing ‖ just before the sun set : they went fishing ‖ then the sun set*	serves as Qualifier in nominal group: • can follow explicit circumstantial noun as Head/Thing in nominal group • nominal group serves in relational clause • can always be the focus of theme predication • is not agnate with a paratactic enhancement *(the period) ⟦just before the sun sets⟧ is the best time to go fishing*	enhancing clauses down-ranked as Postmodifiers in adverbial groups are only comparative: *than..., as (if)...., (for x) to ...* ['IFG p. 210] *they proceeded more cautiously ⟦than the other team⟧*

[*] Non-defining relative clauses with *whose, of which* can be taken as extending: see IFG: 245.

3.4 Parataxis or hypotaxis?

If you are uncertain as to whether a (non-embedded) clause is hypotactic or parac-
tactic, then you can check for the signals of hypotaxis listed below. (Note, however,
that these criteria do not distinguish hypotactic from embedded clauses.)

(i) A non-finite ranking clause is hypotactic. See italicized clauses in the following examples:

> She entered, *laughing happily*
> She went overseas *to broaden her mind*
> *Having broadened her mind,* she came home.

(ii) A ranking clause is hypotactic if introduced by a relative pronoun: *who,
whose, whom, which.*

(iii) A ranking clause is hypotactic if introduced by a conjunction that 'stays with'
its clause even when that clause is shifted to another place in the complex (see also
Section 3.3.1):

> I didn't hear about the meeting *because I was ill.*
> *Because I was ill*, I didn't hear about the meeting.

(iv) A ranking clause is hypotactic if it is reported (indirect) speech or thought:

> she said *(that) she would come.*
> they believed *(that) the world would end on Saturday at noon.*

3.4.1 Linkers occurring in both hypotactic and paratactic relations

There are a few conjunctions which, while typically constructing a hypotactic link
between clauses, may on occasions be used paratactically (see IFG: 231, 235).
Examples are *when, so that, except that, because* and *though*. Some examples of
paratactic uses are given below.

> He walked to the end of the road ‖ when suddenly he saw the dog.

In this example, the meaning relation between the clauses is of 'and then'. The
paratactic nature of the link is attested by the fact that the *when* clause cannot be
moved to thematic position:

> *when suddenly he saw the dog ‖ he walked to the end of the road.

When *so that* is used paratactically, it creates a meaning of 'result' rather than
'purpose'. For example:

> He worked hard ‖ so that by five o'clock he had finished.

Although, or clause final *though*, may be used paratactically with the meaning of
'however', as in the following examples:

> You could argue that way ‖ although I might have to disagree with you.
> You could argue that way ‖ I might have to disagree with you, though.

In all these cases, thematizing the clause with the conjunction is not possible.

3.5 Identifying the logico-semantic relation

A number of conjunctions can mark different logico-semantic relations, with different senses. These are tabulated in Table 5.12.

Table 5.12 Some common conjunctions and their different logico-semantic senses

conjunction:	TAXIS	elaboration	extension	enhancement
and	paratactic		addition: 'and also' – *also, additionally, furthermore, moreover*	[i] temporal: sequence: 'and then' – *then, subsequently* [ii] causal: reason: 'and so' – *so, therefore, consequently*
but	paratactic		[i] adversative: 'but on the other hand' – *in contrast, on the other hand, and yet, conversely,* [ii] replacive: 'but instead' [with not] – *instead, rather,* [iii] subtractive: 'except' – *except, apart from that*	causal: concessive: 'but nevertheless, and in spite of this' – *and yet, nevertheless, though*
or	paratactic	exposition: 'or in other words' – *in other words, that is*	alternation: 'or alternatively' – *alternatively, either, or*	
yet	paratactic		adversative: 'on the other hand' – *in contrast, on the other hand, conversely*	causal: concessive: 'but nevertheless, and in spite of this' – *nevertheless, though*
since	hypotactic			[i] temporal: later: 'afterwards' – *after, afterwards, then;* [ii] causal: reason: 'because' – *as, because*
while	hypotactic		addition: positive/adversative: 'and'/'and yet' – *whereas, and/and yet, but*	temporal: same time: extent: 'meanwhile' – *meanwhile, as*

You can probe which sense is relevant in a given example by considering what the set of agnate items is: each sense of the item in question will correspond to a different agnation set. When you are trying to identify the sense of a structural conjunction, you can also probe it by checking what a variant with an added cohesive conjunction (a conjunctive Adjunct) would be.

3.5.1 Different meanings for *but*

Perhaps the hardest conjunction to sort out is *but*, because the different senses shade into one another (see Table 5.12).

The **adversative** sense of *but*, relating two points of contrast, is probably the most obvious one. This meaning can be reinforced with a cohesive conjunction such as *in contrast*, *by contrast*, *on the other hand*. For example:

> Now Noah was a good man and this pleased God, **but** [in contrast] all around him, Noah's neighbours were lying and fighting and cheating and stealing [contrast between Noah and his neighbours]

> Then, no sooner do you get started than you have to stop again, **but** [in contrast] with OS/2 you needn't : **whereas** with the OS/2 you needn't. [contrast: other operating systems (from the preceding discourse) – the OS/2]

> If you were one of the people in the book, then time would be the same for everyone in the book; **but** [in contrast] if you were outside the book, it would be different. [contrast: in the book – outside the book]

The **replacive** sense of *but* occurs with negative polarity; here *but* can be reinforced by *instead*, *rather*:

> The idea of relativity did *not* originate with Einstein, **but** [instead] goes back, certainly as a physical principle, to Newton and Galileo. [replacement: originate with Einstein – originate with Newton and Galileo]

> Uniform motion *cannot* be discerned internally **but** [instead] only by reference to an external object. [replacement: internally – externally]

> It *isn't* how sick you are **but** [rather] where you are when you get sick that determines how you're treated by a doctor. [replacement: how sick you are – where you are]

The **subtractive** sense of *but* can also be expressed by *except*:

> They had little choice **but** [except] to turn back.

The **concessive** sense of *but* is used to indicate that a situation does not cause the effect it could be expected to have (a 'frustrated cause'); this can be used internally in the sense of 'I concede p, in spite of this q' or 'you may think p, but in spite of this q'. Here are some examples from *The Concise Columbia Encyclopedia*, illustrating the typical use of concessive *but* in historical accounts to indicate an unexpected situation:

> He continued Roosevelt's policies, i.e., 'trust busting' and, in Latin America, 'dollar diplomacy,' **but** he was more conservative than Roosevelt and antagonized the progressive elements in his party. [concessive: 'and yet, in spite of this' *Although he continued ... , he was more conservative ...*]

> The U.S. long supported and aided the Nationalists, **but** in the 1970s Taiwan's international political position had eroded. [concessive: 'and yet, in spite of this' *Although the US long supported ... , in the 1970s Taiwan's international ...*]

In elections in 1992 the Kuomintang retained control of the assembly, **but** the major opposition party won nearly a third of the seats. [concessive: 'and yet, in spite of this' *Although the KMT retain control ... , the major opposition party...*]

He supported the FRENCH REVOLUTION at first, **but** after the fall of the monarchy fled to England (1792) and then to the U.S. (1794). [concessive: 'and yet, in spite of this' *Although he supported the French Revolution at first ... , after the fall of the monarchy he fled ...*]

A clause complex may contain two *but*s in different senses:

They had not actually completed the crossing **but** [in spite of this] they had little choice **but** [except] to turn back.

Often alternative readings of a *but* are possible, either concessive or adversative; for example:

The Spanish explored the area in 1528, **but** European settlement began only in 1823. [concessive: 'and yet, in spite of this' *Although the Spanish explored ... , European settlement began only ...* OR adversative: 'and in contrast' *The Spanish **explored** the area in 1528; in contrast, European **settlement** began only in 1823.*]

In Buddhist Tantra those rituals opposing the moral precepts of Buddhism have been dropped, but the complex MEDITATION practices have been retained. [concessive: 'and yet, in spite of this' *Although rituals have been dropped... , meditation practices have been retained ...* OR adversative: 'in contrast' *Rituals have been **dropped**; in contrast, meditation practices have been **retained**]*

3.6 How many 'layers' to the clause complex?

The issue here is the notation for analysing multi-clause clause complexes. There are three points to note.

(i) Change of taxis One useful rule of thumb is that you should 'indent' one layer whenever there is a change in taxis, from parataxis to hypotaxis or vice versa. For example: *she never enjoys parties → if her boyfriend's not there → so I won't invite her* will be analysed as follows:

```
  1 α     she never enjoys parties
  ×β      if her boyfriend's not there
×2        so I won't invite her
```

or if the text is not being displayed with one clause per line:

```
she never enjoys parties ‖ if her boyfriend's not there ‖ so I won't invite her
   (1α                        1×β)                             ×2
```

This way of notating indicates for the above example that the paratactic relation holds between the final clause and the previous two taken together.

(ii) Change of logico-semantic relation You should also indent one layer when there is a switch of logico-semantic relation (even if the taxis is of the same kind). Thus:

```
  1       Once I was going up the steps
+2 1      and someone said
  "2      "Don't go up the steps"
```

```
Once I was going up the steps ‖ and someone said ‖ "Don't go up the steps"
   1                              +2 (1                  "2)
```

α   He hoped
'β α   he would be there in good time
  ×β   so that he could get the seat next to Janey

He hoped || he would be there in good time || so that he could get the seat next to Janey
  α   'β(α   ×β)

(iii)Theme marking When a clause complex begins with a dependent hypotactic clause, this has a thematic function, best indicated by regarding it as the outermost 'layer' in the complex, regardless of any continuity in logico-semantic function with following clauses. For example:

×β   When he went away again
α α   the children retired to various places
×β   to weep alone.

3.7 Implicit clause complex relations

(i) Implicit logico-semantic relation Where a non-finite clause is linked to a finite one, the relation will always be one of hypotaxis. However, more often than not, there will be nothing to indicate explicitly which logico-semantic relation is involved. For example: *she skipped downstairs ← whistling happily.* IFG Section 7.4.4 recommends exploring the nearest finite form and using this as a guide to the analysis of the non-finite one. For example:

Hoping to meet somebody famous → she went to the reception.
Because she hoped to meet somebody famous → she went to the reception.

Between finite clauses where there is an explicit paratactic relation signalled by *and*, it may also be possible to infer an enhancing temporal relation which has not been made explicit. For example:

The rivers overflow, the streets beome rivers **and** everything and everybody is soaked.

IFG: 235 argues against interpreting these as enhancing relations.

(ii) Implicit Process in dependent clause A dependent relational clause may have no explicit Process and thus be mistaken for a phrase or group. For example: *With Henry away ← we can really get down to business.* When we probe this, we see that *with Henry away* is not a prepositional phrase, but a clause with an implicit Process, related to *with Henry being away* and *since Henry is away*. Similarly: *When only a young child ← Henry wrote his first short story; An avid angler, ← Henry was very fond of fish.*

(iii) Implicit projection See 3.8.2 below.

3.8 Projection

3.8.1 Notation for analysis of projection

The relationship between projecting and projected clause is notated with single quote (') for an idea and double quote (") for a locution:

| 1 | She thought |
| '2 | 'Don't flatter yourself, chum.' |

| 1 | She said |
| "2 | "That would be wonderful!" |

If the projected clause happens to be the initiating clause in a paratactic complex, the quote symbol is written against the 1 to indicate this:

| '1 | 'Don't flatter yourself, chum' |
| 2 | she thought. |

| "1 | "That would be wonderful!" |
| 2 | she said. |

3.8.2 Locutions without explicit projecting clauses

In a written text, punctuation may signal a locution without there being an explicit projecting process. For example, the underlined complexes in the text excerpt below are within quotation marks, but are not grammatically linked to a verbal process of projection:

Mrs Wilson rejected the compliment ‖ by raising her eyebrow in disdain.
  α   ×β

"It's just a crazy old thing," ‖ she said. ‖‖ "I just slip it on sometimes ‖ when I don't care [[what I look like]]." ‖‖
  "1   2   α   ×β

"But it looks wonderful on you, ‖ if you know what I mean," ‖ pursued Mrs McKee.‖‖
  "1α   ×β   2

"If Chester could only get you in that pose ‖ I think ‖ he could make something of it."
  (×β   α)α   'β

As shown here, the analysis ignores the cohesive effect of the quotation marks and represents only the grammatically explicit projections as part of a clause complex relationship.

3.9 *'Surfacing' from an embedding*

In speech it is not uncommon for a speaker to begin an extended stretch of text with an expression such as *The problem is...* or *My idea was..., What really happened was...* or *The way you do it is...* These openings set up a Value–Token structure, where the Token is an embedded clause or clause complex, as in:

The problem **is** [[that we have no money.]]
My idea **was** [[that we should go to Martha's and wait for the boys there.]]

An issue for analysis arises when the Token turns out to be a substantial monologue. For example:

What you have to do **is** [[make up two teams and get someone from Team A to read a question to team B, who have a set amount of time to answer, and who – if they get it right – go on and roll the dice and go forward that number of squares, but if they can't answer or they get it wrong, the other people on team A get a chance to have a go.]] Then if team A get it right they get to roll the dice and also to receive the next question.

It is as if, having begun with a Value/Theme + Token/News clause structure, the speaker continues by pursuing the typical choreography of spoken language, expanding the initial embedded clause several times. By the time a new clause complex is initiated, there is a sense that it is conjunctively related to the previous 'embedded' clause, as though by then the structure has surfaced from the initial embedding. In such a case it is probably most realistic to let the analysis reflect this 'surfacing' by displaying a 'ranking' clause complex at the initial embedding:

```
              What you have to do is...
  1           make up two teams
 ⁺2  α        and get someone from Team A to read a question to team B,
   ⁼β  1      who have a set amount of time to answer,
     ⁺2  α    and who – <<      >> go on and roll the dice...
       ˣβ     <<if they get it right>>
```

Alternatively, treat the second (or some later clause) within the embedding as linked by taxis with the initial non-embedded part:

```
  1           What you have to do is [[make up two teams
 ⁺2  α        and get someone from Team A to read a question to team B,
   ⁼β         who have a set amount of time to answer,
```

4 Analysis practice

4.1 Phase I

4.1.1 Exercises

Examples taken or adapted from various sources including *The Wentworth Courier*, W. Golding's *Lord of the Flies*, D.H. Lawrence's *Sons and Lovers*, Aldous Huxley's *Antic Hay*, George Orwell's *Animal Farm* and F. Scott Fitzgerald's *The Great Gatsby*.

Exercise 1 Identifying clause boundaries Mark off the clause (||) and clause complex (|||) boundaries in the following pieces of text. For example:

> She complained about the incident to my father || when he returned from work || and was mortified || when he laughed || until the tears rolled down his cheeks. ||| He apologised.

1. Old Mother Hubbard
    Went to the cupboard
    To fetch her poor dog a bone
    When she got there
    The cupboard was bare
    And so the poor dog had none

2. The Randwick mayor said the Council was very enthusiastic about the new bowling centre for the Randwick shopping centre. He said he hoped the AMF company would have the same success as the Manhattan bowling centre at Mascot, which opened last year.

3. His cheeks were ruddy, and his red, moist mouth was noticeable because he laughed so often.

4. The Thai do not kill animals, so the meat butchering is left to the Muslims and Chinese.

Exercise 2 Distinguishing α and β clauses in a hypotactic relation (expansion). Determine which clause in each of the following hypotactic complexes is the (dependent) beta and which is the (dominant) alpha. See Section 2.1. For example:

It was lonely for a day or so ‖ until one morning some man stopped me on the road.
      α   β

1. Mrs Morel was full of information ‖ when she got home from Nottingham.

2. If you want to learn it, ‖ you must begin.

3. Roger remained, ‖ watching the littluns.

4. Seeing Ralph under the palms, ‖ he sat by him.

5. It was a dismal affair, ‖ which might have belonged to Maurice Barres in youth.

6. Whenever I'm having a good time ‖ he wants to go home.

7. I looked back at my cousin, ‖ who began to ask me questions in her low, thrilling voice.

Exercise 3 Distinguishing hypotaxis from parataxis (expansion) Identify (as hypotactic or paratactic) the taxis relation between the following pairs of clauses and notate accordingly. See Sections 2.1, 3.4. For example:

As soon as the skies brightened, Paul drove off in the milkman's heavy float.
      β   α

1. William had just gone away to London, ‖ and his mother missed his money.

2. He sent ten shillings once or twice, ‖ but he had many things to pay for at first.

3. If a quarrel took place, ‖ the whole play was spoilt.

4. In a few minutes she put on her coat, ‖ to walk the two and a half miles to the station.

5. Mrs Morel talked again to Paul, ‖ who was helping her with her housework.

6. He resented Mr Bojanus's negleejay, ‖ he was pained and wounded by the aspersion.

7. Folding him in her arms, ‖ she swayed slightly from side to side with love.

8. Throw it away ‖ or give it to your sister.

9. Whilst Morel was progressing favourably in the hospital, ‖ the family was extraordinarily happy and peaceful.

10. The Thai do not kill animals, ‖ so the meat butchering is left to the Muslims and Chinese.

Exercise 4 Distinguishing α from β clauses in a hypotactic relation (projection) Determine which clause in each of the following hypotactic complexes is the (dependent) beta and which is the (dominant) alpha. See Section 2.2.2. For example:

They say ‖ he's a nephew or a cousin of Kaiser Wilhelm's.
   α   β

1. She had already told him ‖ she could not dance.

2. She knew ‖ that it was not everything.

3. Tell me ‖ where it hurts you.

4. It would all come to an end soon, ‖ she hoped.

5. She never believed ‖ that her life belonged to Paul Morel.

6. She thought ‖ they lived in his own house.

Exercise 5 Distinguishing hypotaxis from parataxis (projection) Indicate the taxis relation between the following pairs of clauses, using 1,2 or α,β notation. For example:

You asked my sister ‖ if there was cancer in the family.
      α   β

"The train gets in at half-past six," ‖ she replied emphatically.
     1   2

1. Sometimes Mrs Morel would say: ‖ "You ought to tell your father."

2. But the Sister says ‖ that it's the pain.

3. The three children realized ‖ that it was very bad for their father.

4. "Now I'll die," ‖ he said, in a detached, dreamy voice.

5. I wish ‖ this boiler was at the bottom of the sea!

6. He felt ‖ his son did not want him.

7. Ask him ‖ if the London train's come.

8. Paul knew ‖ that this girl, Louise Travers, was now Dawes' woman.

9. She wondered ‖ who had been talking to him.

10. "Who has been talking to him?" ‖ she wondered.

Exercise 6 Identifying logico-semantic relations (expansion) Identify the logico-semantic relation between the following pairs of clauses as elaboration (=) or extension (+). Add the appropriate notation to the analysis. For example:

William had just gone away to London, ‖ and his mother missed his money.
          1   +2

1. He didn't offer to help, ‖ but just watched her struggling.
          1   2
2. Mrs Morel talked again to Paul, ‖ who was helping her with her housework.
          α   β
3. It was getting very late; ‖ it was past ten o'clock.
          1   2
4. It matters more than her cleverness, ‖ which, after all, would never get her to
    heaven.
          α   β
5. Take it inside ‖ or put it over there.
          1   2
6   As well as headlining a special meal, ‖ meat composes several Thai delicacies.
          β   α
7. Now he would transform it; ‖ he would add to it its better half.
          1   2
8. He was accompanied by his wife, ‖ whose manner was quite hostile.
          α   β
9. The incident had no serious consequences, ‖ apart from upsetting his cousin.
          α   β
10. He was very clever, very artistic; ‖ he seemed to know all the new things, all
    the interesting people.
          1   2

Exercise 7 Identifying logico-semantic relations (expansion) Identify the logico-semantic relation between the clauses in the following examples as elaboration (=), extension (+) or enhancement (×). Add the appropriate notation to the analysis. For example:

As soon as the skies brightened, Paul drove off in the milkman's heavy float.
   ×β   α

1. If a quarrel took place, ‖ the whole play was spoilt.
   β   α
2. In a few minutes she was gone, ‖ to walk the two and a half miles to Keston Station.
   α   β
3. They drew apart; ‖ they spent less and less time together.
   1   2
4. Whilst Morel was progressing favourably in the hospital, ‖ the family was extraordinarily happy and peaceful.
   β   α
5. She dared not look at him, ‖ but sat with her head bowed.
   1   2
6. To Miriam he more or less condescended, ‖ because she seemed so humble.
   α   β
7. His face quivered ‖ as he looked at his mother.
   α   β
8. The clouds empty their watery load ‖ and are then dispelled by the sun.
   1   2
9. Mrs Morel was not anxious to move into the Bottoms, ‖ which was already 12 years old.
   α   β
10. The women did not spare her, at first; ‖ for she was superior.
   1   2

Exercise 8 Identifying the logico-semantic relation (projection) Go back to Exercise 5 and identify the relation between the clauses as projection of locution (") or projection of idea ('). Add the appropriate notation to the analysis (see Section 2.2.2). For example:

"The train gets in at half-past six," ‖ she replied emphatically.
  "1   2

4.1.2 Texts for analysis

Identify any TAXIS links between clauses in Texts 1 and 2 and consider whether hypotactic or paratactic and whether elaborating, extending or enhancing. What differences do you notice in the way clause complexing resources are used to build information in the two texts?

Text 1 Descriptive report
The numbat
The numbat is an unmistakeable slender marsupial with a pointed muzzle and short erect ears. The body is reddish brown but the rump is much darker and

has about six white bars across it. The eye has a black stripe through it and the long bushy tail is yellowish. The toes are strongly clawed and very effective in digging out termites. The tongue is extremely long, as in all mammalian ant or termite eaters. Unlike most marsupials, the numbat is active during the day. It shelters in hollow logs. It was once relatively common but now lives only in a small area of S.W. South Australia.

(Adapted from *The concise encyclopedia of Australia* 2nd ed. Buderim, Queensland: Bateman, 1984: 459.)

Text 2 Taxonomizing report Note: This text has a number of 'included' clauses. (See 3.2.1(2).) These have been indicated for you with angled brackets << >>. Ellipsed elements have been indicated in round brackets.

There are many species of whales. They are conveniently divided into toothed and baleen categories. The toothed whales are found worldwide in great numbers. The largest is the Sperm whale, which grows to about the size of a boxcar. Other species familiar to Canadians are the Beluga or white whale, the Narwhal with its unicorn-like tusk, the Killer whale or Orca, the Pilot or Pothead whale, <<which is commonly stranded on beaches>>, the Spotted and Spinner Dolphins, <<that create a problem for tuna seiners>>, and the Porpoises which we commonly see along our shores.

There are fewer species of the larger baleen whales, that filter krill and small fish through their baleen plates. The largest is the Blue whale which is seen frequently in the Gulf of St Lawrence. It reaches a length of 100 feet and a weight of 200 tons. The young are 25 feet long at birth and put on about 200 lbs a day on their milk diet. Other species are: the Fins <<which at a length of 75 ft. blow spouts of 20 ft>>, the fast swimming Seis, the Grays, <<(which are) so commonly seen on migrations along our Pacific coast between Baja California and the Bering Sea>>, the Bowheads of Alaskan waters, the Rights, <<(which are) so seriously threatened>>, the Humpbacks <<(which are) enjoyed by tourists in such places as Hawaii and Alaska>>, the smaller Bryde's whales, and the smallest Minke whales, which continue to be abundant worldwide.

(Martin, W.R. 1989: Innovative fisheries management: international whaling. In A.T. Bielak (ed) *Innovative Fisheries Management Initiatives*. Ottawa: Canadian Wildlife Federation, 1–4.)

Text 3 Dialogue in narrative 1. Divide this text into ranking clauses (embedded clauses have been enclosed in square brackets). 2. Identify any expanding links. 3. Classify each projecting relation as paratactic or hypotactic. For example:

	PROJECTION
"What's your interest?" ‖ she asked.	parataxis
"Oh" << I replied breezily,>>	parataxis
I wondered ‖ if it had anything [[to do with the N. Bank robbery]]	hypotaxis

[*Claudia Valentine, detective, is trying to elicit information over the phone from an assistant in a gold shop:*]
"What's your interest?" she asked. "Oh," I replied breezily, "I wondered if it had anything [[to do with the National Bank robbery.]]" She didn't think it did. "You got anything [[to tell us on that score?]]" she asked. I didn't. I cast my line again

into the Chinatown killing. She said as usual no-one had seen anything. Even in reasonably broad daylight. I said I might have. She found that interesting. I asked her if the victim had been wearing a tie. She said no. I asked her if he'd been wearing kung fu shoes. She said what is this, twenty questions? I said no. I told her I'd seen ⟦a man acting suspiciously in the Chinese Gardens⟧. She asked what I'd been doing there but I said it was irrelevant. I said I'd seen the same man later that afternoon in Cabramatta. She asked what I was doing in Cabramatta. I said it was irrelevant. I said it was a long shot and probably had nothing ⟦to do with anything⟧ but it might be worth asking a few discreet questions around the place. Check out the snooker hall. I asked her if she could tell me any more about the victim.

> (Day, Marele 1990: *The case of the Chinese boxes*. Sydney:
> Allen & Unwin, 41–42.)

Text 4 Exposition (High School student answer) We will analyse the clause complexing in this text more fully in Phase II. As a start, consider the following questions.

1. Divide the following text into clauses and check your response with the layout given below. How many clauses per clause complex?
2. Count the paratactic links, then the hypotactic. How do the numbers compare?
3. Are there examples of both projection and expansion?
4. What kind of projection is found? What kind of expansion is most frequent?
5. How does this text contrast with Texts 1 and 2 in its use of clause complexing resources?

Are governments necessary?

I think governments like the Federal Government are necessary because they help to keep our economic system in order and if any problems occur the Federal Government will more or less straighten it out.

   I also think that the State Government isn't necessary because there is the local Government, which is known as a shire or municipality, and so there is hardly any use for the State government because the local governments do all the work.

> (Text courtesy of Geoff Crewes.)

Are governments necessary? [version set out in clauses]
I think
governments like the Federal Government are necessary
because they help to keep our economic system in order
and <<...>> the Federal Government will more or less straighten it out
<<if any problems occur>>.

I also think
that the State Government isn't necessary
because there is the local Government,
which is known as a shire or municipality,
and so there is hardly any use for the State government
because the local governments do all the work.

4.2 Phase II

4.2.1 Exercises

Exercise 1 Identifying clause boundaries (included clauses) Mark off the clause boundaries in the following pieces of text. For example:

The Thai, <<being Buddhist,>> do not kill animals, || so the meat butchering is left to the Muslims and Chinese.

1. They lived, she thought, in his own house.
2. Mrs Blackmore's car, which can't be more than two years old, is already full of rust.
3. Meg and Paul, although they despised the others, remained with the group and took part in their schemes.
4. The older man, who had been sitting in the corner and seemed uninterested, suddenly got up and approached them.
5. Marco Polo journeying through Yunnan in the thirteenth century, after it had been conquered by the Mongols, observed that the people ate their meat raw.

Exercise 2 Identifying both taxis and logico-semantic relations Analyse the taxis and logico-semantic relations between the following pairs of clauses. For example:

They had fetched the money on Friday afternoons, || until they went themselves to work.
   α $^{×}β$

1. So that the children could fetch the money, school closed early on Friday afternoons.

2. Paul always examined the big grass bank, because in it grew tiny pansies.

3. He knew the order of the names – they went according to stall number.

4. If they got half a pound they felt exceedingly happy.

5. Well, there wasn't any blackberries, so we went over Misk Hills.

6. He nodded sympathetically to Miriam, and became gently sarcastic to Beatrice.

7. "Well, you can't be stuck in the house for ever," Annie agreed.

8. Agatha says you're as good as any teacher anywhere.

9. He held her wrists while she wrestled with him.

10. He bent forward to her to light his cigarette at hers.

Exercise 3 Logico-semantic relations and non-finite clauses Determine, by comparison with a finite clause example, the logico-semantic relation in the following clause complexes. See Section 3.7(i). For example:

   She thought him rather wonderful, ‖ never having met anyone like him.
      α   ˣβ
   (She thought him rather wonderful because she had never met anyone like him.)

1.   Hurriedly taking off her bodice, she crouched at the boiler.

2.   The valley was full of corn, brightening in the sun.

3.   Roger remained, watching the littluns.

4.   Mr Pappleworth arrived, chewing a chlorodyne gum, at about twenty to nine.

5.   The Thai <<being Buddhist>> do not kill animals.

6.   On retiring to bed, the father would come into the sickroom.

Exercise 4 Notating taxis and logico-semantic relations in multi-clause complexes
Analyse the following complexes for taxis and logico-semantic relations. Write the analysis on the left as shown in the example:

    1 α   The three children realised
      'β   that it was very bad for their father
  + 2   and the house was silent, anxious.

1.   Paul cleared away,
         put on the kettle,
         and set the table.
2.   Add the pork
         and stir fry
         until it changes colour.
3.   If you're scared of someone
         you hate him
         and you can't stop thinking about him.
4.   They thought
         anything might happen
         if one came from London.
5.   Percival finished his whimper
         and went on playing,
         for the tears had washed the sand away.
6.   "Now I'll die,"
         he said, in a detached, dreamy voice,
         as though he were the dying motion of the swing.
7.   "You know
         that you like them,"
         she said.

8.   Hurriedly taking off her bodice,
            she crouched at the boiler
            while the water ran slowly into her lading-can.

9.   She complained about the incident to my father
            when he returned from work
            and was mortified
            when he laughed
            until the tears rolled down his cheeks.

10.   "I wish
            this boiler was at the bottom of the sea!"
            she exclaimed,
            wriggling the handle impatiently.

11.   The minister glanced several times at his watch,
            so I took him aside
            and asked him
            to wait for a half an hour.

12.   He went to the station in a sort of dream,
            and was at home
            without realizing
            he had moved out of her street.

Exercise 5 Discriminating verbal group complexes from clause complexes See Chapter 4, 3.3; IFG Section 7A.4. Determine the boundaries of ranking clauses in the following clause complexes. For example:

> I liked to walk up 5th Avenue ‖ when I was in New York.
> I'd like ‖ you to walk up 5th Avenue ‖ when we are in New York.

1. Soon the larvae begin to hatch and the queen must feed them.
2. He hopes to make this a particularly boring campaign.
3. She had decided, ineptly, that everything was very very sad.
4. He tried frantically to escape but it was no use.
5. Maybe he means it's some sort of ghost.
6. Why couldn't you say there wasn't a beast?
7. He wanted to crush her onto his breast to ease the ache there.
8. "Why on earth don't you let him stop?" he exclaimed.
9. The heat seemed to increase until it became a threatening weight.
10. I had expected that he would be a florid and corpulent person in his middle years.
11. He began to poke about in the water, while the brilliant fish flicked away.
12. "You must make him come back," he insisted.
13. She told him not to hurry; there was plenty of time.
14. "I didn't mean to interrupt your lunch," I said.
15. He would dearly have liked the children to talk to him, but they could not.

Exercise 6 Discriminating ranking clauses from embeddings (defining and non-defining relative clauses) Determine which of the relative clauses below are embedded and which are elaborating β clauses. See Section 3.3.1. For example:

> They gave it to the one [[who scored the most goals]].
> My daughter <<who has just turned four>> must now pay for a ticket on the bus.

1. I was one of the few guests who had actually been invited.
2. I'm the first man who ever made a stable out of a garage.
3. Next year she will be issued with a school bus pass which will save us a lot of money.
4. We all looked in silence at Mrs Wilson, who removed a strand of hair from over her eyes and looked back at us with a brilliant smile.
5. I wanted somebody who wouldn't gossip.
6. I glanced at Daisy, who was staring between Gatsby and her husband.
7. He was a photographer and had made the dim enlargement of Mrs Wilson's mother which hovered like an ectoplasm on the wall.
8. Those littluns who had climbed back on the twister fell off again.
9. They spoke to the gardener, whose wheezy cough interrupted every question.
10. Japan had a major earthquake in Hokkaido a year ago, which shook the island with a magnitude of 7.9 on the Richter scale.

Exercise 7 Discriminating ranking clauses from embeddings (acts) Determine the boundaries of ranking clauses in the following examples and mark any embedded clauses. See Section 3.3.2.

> She saw the sunshine going out of him, and she resented it.
> She saw [[the sunshine going out of him]], || and she resented it.

1. I could have sworn I heard the owl-eyed man break into ghostly laughter.
2. When Mrs Morel entered, she saw him almost running through the door to the stairs.
3. They heard their father throw down his boots and tramp upstairs in his stockinged feet.
4. I can remember that Tautina O'Brien coming there at least once.
5. Playing the piano in the evening had always calmed her but now she could not play.
6. I thought that it was a fire and tried to get out.
7. Sometimes they watched the three or four lamps growing tinier and tinier swaying down the fields in the darkness.

Exercise 8 Distinguishing types of *but*: extending versus enhancing Identify the relation signalled by *but* in the following clause complexes as extending or enhancing. See Section 3.5.1.

> Uniform motion cannot be discerned internally || but only by reference to an external
> object
> extending
>
> We supported the French Revolution at first, || but after the fall of the monarchy fled to
> England.
> enhancing

1. They don't emphasize rote learning of facts ||
   but try to encourage problem-solving techniques.   1. ....
2. I tried very hard to die, || but I seemed to bear
   an enchanted life.   2. ....
3. He half expected || her to wander into one of his
   parties, some night || but she never did.   3. ....

4. I tried to go then, || but they wouldn't hear of it.   4. ....
5. They worked as fast as they could || but couldn't
    meet the deadline.   5. ....
6. The pigs did not actually work || but directed
    and supervised the others.   6. ....
7. The indigenous population was wiped out in the
    nineteenth century || but a few thousand
    mixed-race descendants survive.   7. ....
8. By the mid-1830s it was fighting for reforms
    for the common people || but increasingly   8. ....
    controlled by the privileged classes.
9. She was honest in her way || but the rest of the   9. ....
    family were quite untrustworthy.
10. He didn't run, but loped along awkwardly.   10. ....

4.2.2 Texts for analysis

Text 1 Parent-child conversation Analyse the clause complex relations in this text
in the left-hand margin. Note how this contributes to the meaning of the text already
considered in earlier chapters.

C: How could birds die?
M: ...Like the one in the garden, are you thinking of?
     Well, sometimes birds die
     when they get very old,
     or maybe they get sick
     because they got some disease,
     or maybe a cat got it.
     Baby birds sometimes die
     when they fall out the nest,
     or, in the winter – <<   >> – birds might die
     <<if you were in a cold place>>
     because they can't get enough food.
C: Yeah, but what happens
     if one bird falls out
     and then – and when it's just about at the ground
     it flies?
M: Yes, well if it's big enough to fly
     it'll be all right.

Text 2 Recount This text is a written version of a spoken text where the speaker is
recalling a period from his youth. Divide the following text into clauses and analyse
the clause complex relations.

If I would be too late in the morning the station owner would pour cold water
over me. Sometimes I would watch the cattle while they had their lunch or got
ready in the morning, and if a calf would walk away he would yell out from the
camp "Hey, what do you think, don't you want that calf, eh?" I wouldn't know,
because I was looking in another direction. He would come up and say. "You've
got to start watching those cattle." I couldn't talk back to him because I was too

small. That bloke always did that to me, and he would give me a good beating with a whip. When I was working there I really had a terrible life with that man. And if I didn't do my job, he would starve me for two days and just give me dry damper. And if I didn't do my job well, he would next time just give me a piece of meat.

(Adapted from Paddy Patrick Jangala 1985: *Stories from Lajamanu*. Darwin NT: Department of Education.)

Text 3 Children's story (opening) Divide the text into clauses and analyse the clause complex relations.

My name's Laura and this is my place. I turned ten last week. Our house is the one with the flag on the window. Tony says it shows we're on Aboriginal land, but I think it means the colour of the earth, back home. Mum and Dad live here too, and Terry and Lorraine, and Aunty Bev, and Tony and Diane and their baby Dean. He's my nephew and he's so cute! We come from Bourke, but Dad thought there'd be more jobs in the city. This [picture] is me and Gully. I have to keep her on a lead because she chases cars. She comes from Bourke too. I guess she thinks they're sheep. This is a map of my place. We've got a McDonalds right on the corner! In the McDonald's yard, there's this big tree, and whenever I sit in it, it always makes me feel good. There's a canal down the bottom of the street, and Mum says it must have been a creek once. It's too dirty to swim in, but Tony made me a tin canoe and now some of the other kids are making them too. If you tip over and go in, the water tastes yucky and your parents go wild. For my birthday, Mum said we could have tea at McDonalds! We sat in the outside bit, under the tree, and it felt just like home!

(From Wheatley, N. 1989: *My place*. Blackburn: Collins Dove.)

Text 4 Written exposition Here we return to a text from Phase I. This time notate the clause complex relations in the left-hand margin.

I think
governments like the Federal Government are necessary
because they help to keep our economic system in order
and <<...>> the Federal Government will more or less straighten it out
<<if any problems occur>>.
I also think
that the State Government isn't necessary
because there is the local Government,
which is known as a shire or municipality,
and so there is hardly any use for the State government
because the local governments do all the work.

4.3 Phase III

4.3.1 Exercises

Exercise 1 Identifying embedded clauses (acts and facts) Enclose in square brackets any embedded clauses in the following examples:

It is important to understand the strategy adopted by the developers.
It is important [[to understand the strategy adopted by the developers.]]

1. It infuriated him that she could not give him an answer.
2. It is instructive to recall the invitation for expressions of interest.
3. That its likely market value had diminished had certainly occurred to him.
4. It is good to be seen as the great reformer.
5. It wasn't true that he had seen her.
6. To understand the natural order is a good thing.

Exercise 2 Discriminating ranking clauses from embeddings (wh- clauses) Determine the boundaries of ranking clauses in the following examples and mark any embedded clauses. See Section 3.3.3 and Chapter 4, 3.5(iv). For example:

She asked ‖ what she should do next.
She appreciated [[what they had done]].

1. Whatever she sees, she wants.
2. They didn't like what she was saying.
3. Tell me what to do next.
4. She asked if he was going by car.
5. She asked where he was going.
6. I don't understand why you won't come out frankly and tell me.
7. They didn't explain how to mix the colours.
8. I hate how he always interrupts you with petty little queries and details.
9. He doesn't know where they go on holiday.

Exercise 3 Discriminating ranking clauses from embeddings (facts) Determine the boundaries of ranking clauses in the following examples and mark any embedded clauses.

He decided ‖ that there was no other course of action possible.
They remain convinced [[that the political winds are blowing in their direction]].
Buckingham Palace expressed relief [[that the Bodyline cricket series was over]].

1. The common factor is the belief that New Zealand has gone too far along the monetarist-free market path.
2. Our understanding was that they would accept the money as final payment.
3. Police believe the fire was lit on a pile of carpet in the stairwell.
4. I see I have given the impression that the events of three nights several weeks apart were all that absorbed me.
5. He noted that civic leaders did not greet him wearing jacket and tie.
6. I read somewhere that the sun's getting hotter every year.
7. I would have accepted without question the information that Gatsby sprang from the swamps of Louisiana.
8. They were convinced that it was theirs for a few words in the right key.
9. She implied that a dozen chefs awaited her orders there.
10. That's because your mother wanted to show you off.
11. You kid yourself he's all right really.
12. One suspects they will have the same problem.
13. NASA's satellite had discovered landmark evidence that the universe did in fact begin with the 'Big Bang'.
14. One prediction that comes out of the theory of inflation is that the mix of big and small spots in the early universe should follow a characteristic pattern.

Exercise 4 Distinguishing circumstances from clauses with implicit process Decide whether the underlined unit in the examples below is a circumstance or a β clause whose (relational) process is not explicit. For example:

> They waited at the cinema <u>with their cousins</u>.   circumstance
> <u>With John right beside me</u>, I couldn't say any more at the time.   clause

1. They made way for him silently, <u>all of them conscious of his grim mood</u>.   1. ....
2. <u>With all hope of a quick resolution gone</u>, they settled in for a long night.   2. ....
3. <u>With her two dalmatians</u>, she stood waiting at the kerb.   3. ....
4. They were in the bare country of stone walls which, <u>though only ten miles from home</u>, seemed so foreign to Miriam.   4. ....
5. We didn't like to take any major decisions <u>with you away</u>.   5. ....

Exercise 5 Distinguishing hypotaxis from parataxis (typically 'hypotactic' conjunctions) See Section 3.4.1. In the following examples, determine whether the relationship between the clauses is hypotactic or paratactic.

1. They scrambled up the slope as fast as they could so that they might warn the others.
2. A sudden breeze shook the fringe of palm trees, so that the fronds tossed.
3. He was chattering away to his mother on the phone when he heard a tremendous crash in the yard.
4. We wanted to ask him along, except that we were too shy.
5. They did not speak of it when they were alone together once more.
6. They used to meet in secret because her father disapproved of their friendship.

4.3.2 Texts for analysis

Text 1 Conversational narrative In the transcription of this originally spoken text clause complex boundaries have already been determined. Now divide the text into ranking clauses and analyse the clause complex relations.

> There's lots of things that happen that you just take for granted really. When we first moved down here from Orange we lost one of our bitches, the first day. And we advertised and put little notes all around to try and get her back. Anyway about a week later a man came down and asked had we lost a dog. And he said he thought he knew where there was one in a yard. So my husband went up and looked over the fence and there was our dog, only about a block away. And they also had a male corgi there, and the two were running together. So he brought ours home and he went back up later to let the people know that we had her, that he'd brought her home, and offered to pay the food that she'd eaten for the week. Anyway, the people were very good. I don't think they'd tried to steal her or anything like that. But anyway, about two days after that, two big boys came down – they were about seventeen – to let us know that Mummy said not to be worried that the bitch would have puppies because even though they ran in her

yard all day she locked them up separately at night. Our bitch wasn't even in season so they obviously didn't take her for gain. They didn't know enough.

(From Plum, Guenter 1988: *Textual and contextual conditioning in spoken English: a genre based approach*. PhD thesis. Dept. of Linguistics, University of Sydney.)

Text 2 Expository Divide the following text into ranking clauses and analyse the clause complex relations.

...Advice such as this (i.e. be wary of approaching children before they are 'ready' to learn mathematics) has produced teachers who are likely to be wary about interference into children's play in case they are not 'ready' or they spoil something spontaneous which is going on, and when they do so interfere they expect that they will have to provide children with experiences which will lead them to make the appropriate discriminations, which they will not expect the children already to have mastered. The framework for the interpretation of errors is therefore given by the pedagogy: that is, that children will fail because they are not 'ready' for that kind of learning, which will in turn lead the teacher to feel implicitly at fault because (by implication) she was also not sensitive enough. This provides one aspect of a 'regime of meaning', a regime of 'truth' in which the teacher herself is positioned. This creates her insertion as subject into the practice and provides both the basis of her readings and the aspect of the regulation to which she is subjected. The regime is not one which is provided by the teacher, but which itself produces her consciousness of what teaching means: thus it produces not only her assessment of the children but is bound up with her assessment of herself. The teacher can in no way be judged as standing outside the practices in which she as teacher is positioned and which delimit, define, and evaluate her work.

(Walkerdine, V. 1988: *The Mastery of Reason: cognitive development and the production of rationality*. London: Routledge (Critical Psychology).)

Text 3 Teaser Try puzzling out the clause complex relations here (no key provided).

Jack thinks
     he does not know
   what he thinks
      Jill thinks
      he does not know
But Jill thinks Jack does know it.
So Jill does not know
     she does not know
   that Jack does not know
   that Jill thinks
   that Jack does know
and Jack does not know he does not know
   that Jill does not know she does not know
   that Jack does not know
     that Jill thinks Jack knows
what Jack thinks he does not know
Jack doesn't know he knows
and he doesn't know
   Jill does not know.

Jill doesn't know she doesn't know,
     and doesn't know
          that Jack doesn't know Jill does not know.
They have no problems.

('Knots' by R.D. Laing, quoted in H.H. Clark 1992: *Arenas of Language*.
Chicago and Stanford: University of Chicago Press and
Center for the Study of Language and Information, 9.)

5 Review and Contextualization

In chapters of IFG and this workbook concerned with 'Clause as message', 'Clause as exchange' and 'Clause as representation', you have seen how the three metafunctions come together to define the clause as a plurifunctional grammatical unit; it is internally organized according to the textual (thematic), interpersonal (modal) and ideational: experiential (transitivity) metafunctions. See Fig. 5.6.

		Madam, you'	ll	look	like	a tulip.

clause	textual	interp.	topical		
		Theme		Rheme	
	interpersonal	Voca-tive	Mood	Residue	
			Subj	Fin	Predicator	Complement
	ideational: experiential		Carrier	Process	Attribute

Fig. 5.6   The clause as a plurifunctional unit

In this chapter we have been concerned with how any clause can be combined with another to form a clause complex, using the resources of the logical metafunction. These resources also serve to combine smaller grammatical units such as words, groups and phrases into complexes. When clauses are combined, no higher grammatical unit with constituent parts is created. A clause complex is just a complex of units – clauses; it is not itself a new kind of higher-ranking grammatical unit.

A clause complex would arise if, after having said *Madam, you'll look like a tulip*, the speaker decides to expand this clause by another clause; and this option of expansion could then be selected again:

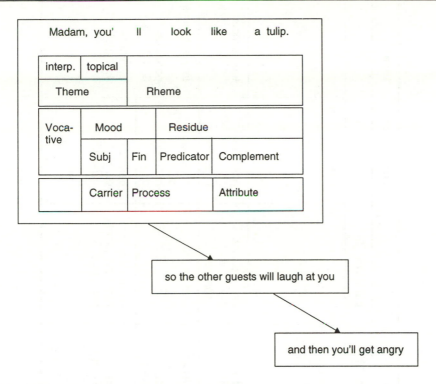

Fig. 5.7 Expansion of clause into clause complex

Madam, you'll look like a tulip
Madam, you'll look like a tulip → **so** the other guests will laugh at you
Madam, you'll look like a tulip → **so** the other guests will laugh at you → **and then** you'll get angry

This expansion is shown diagrammatically in Fig. 5.7. In fact, there is no theoretical limit to the number of times a clause complex can be expanded by another clause. The reason is that the structure of the clause complex is **serial**: one clause is related or linked to another step by step. A clause complex is thus like a chain – it can be expanded indefinitely. Compare TV serials like *Days of our Lives*, *Coronation Street* or *Neighbours* that just go on and on. A clause complex is thus structurally quite different from a simple clause. A simple clause is, as we have seen, an organic whole. Just like other organic wholes such as biological organisms or atoms, it has a fixed number of component parts with particular values relative to the whole: Theme + Rheme (textual), Mood + Residue [+ Moodtag + Vocative] (interpersonal), and Participants + Process + Circumstances (experiential). That is, the organization of the clause is configurational rather than serial or relational.

5.1 Relations between clauses

The serial structure of the clause complex can be described in terms of the two systems of TAXIS (interdependency relations) and LOGICO-SEMANTIC TYPE. Table

Table 5.13 TAXIS and LOGICO-SEMANTIC TYPE

		'initiating':	'continuing': hypotaxis (β)	'continuing': parataxis (2)	punctuation	tone
projection	locution "	verbal clause (without Verbiage)	that, whether; wh-; non-finite: perfective		parataxis " " , " " : " " : . . . -	
	idea '	mental clause (without Phenomenon)				
expansion	elaboration =		wh-; non-finite: imperfective/ neutral	i.e., e.g., viz., that is, for example, ...	parataxis : ; - hypotaxis ,	tone concord
	extension +		besides, instead of, as well as, rather than, while, whereas,	and, or, but	parataxis ø ; ; hypotaxis ø ,	tone sequence parataxis 3, 1
	enhancement ×		while, when, before, after, since, until, by, because, if, although, in spite of	(and) then, for, (and) so, (and) yet, but...	parataxis ø ; ; hypotaxis ø ,	hypotaxis 4, 1 (βα)

5.13 summarizes these, showing how the five general logico-semantic relations – two of the projecting type and three of the expanding type – are realized in combination with either parataxis or hypotaxis.

Further reading

Martin, J.R. 1981: CONJUNCTION and CONTINUITY in Tagalog. In M.A.K. Halliday and J.R. Martin (eds) *Readings in Systemic Linguistics*. London: Batsford, 310–36.

_____1983: Participant identification in English, Tagalog and Kâte. *Australian Journal of Linguistics* 3.1, 45–74. The discourse function of clause complexing in languages other than English is discussed here and in Martin 1981, 1995.

_____1988: Hypotactic recursive systems in English: toward a functional interpretation. In J.D. Benson and W.S. Greaves (eds) *Systemic functional approaches to discourse*. Norwood, NJ: Albex 240–70.

_____1992: *English text: system and structure*. Amsterdam: Benjamins, Chapter 4. The semantic resources of conjunctive relations are discussed here, with the clause complex as one type of realization

_____1995: Logical meaning, interdependency and the linking particle *{-ng/na}* in Tagalog. *Functions of Language* 2.2, 189–228. Discusses logical meaning across ranks in Tagalog.

Matthiessen, Christian 1995: *Lexicogrammatical cartography*. Tokyo: International Language Sciences Publishers. Chapter 3; rhetorical-relational organization of text: Section 1.7.2; logical resources: Section 2.3.4.

Matthiessen, Christian and Thompson, Sandra A. 1989: The structure of discourse and 'subordination'. In J. Haiman and S.A. Thompson (eds) *Clause combining in grammar and discourse*. Amsterdam: Benjamins, 275–331. Also as ISI/RS-87-183.

Nesbitt, C.F. and Plum, G. 1988: Probabilities in a systemic grammar: the clause complex in English. In A. Fawcett and D. Young (eds) *New developments in systemic linguistics vol. 2: theory and application*. London: Pinter 6–38.

Key to Chapter 2: Theme

Phase I Key to exercises

Exercise 1
1. <u>He</u>'s out.
2. <u>You</u>'re just in time for a little smackerel of something.
3. <u>One</u> mustn't complain.
4. <u>That</u>'s a very good idea...
5. <u>Christopher Robin</u> had spent the morning indoors...
6. <u>The wind</u> had dropped...
7. <u>My mind</u>'s full of junk, isn't it?
8. <u>This room</u> does not need air.
9. <u>A peaceful smile</u> came over his face...
10. <u>His argument</u> just crumbled.

Exercise 2
1. <u>Kanga's house</u> was nearest...   U
2. <u>For at least two hours</u> the boy loved him...   M
3. <u>Nobody</u> sits out there at this time of year.   U
4. <u>After a long munching noise</u>, he said...   M
5. <u>The Extract of Malt</u> had gone   U
6. <u>For students</u> they don't half come out with some rubbish.   M
7. <u>The nearest house</u> was Owl's...   U
8. <u>To Owl's house</u> he made his way.   M
9. <u>For a little while</u> he couldn't think of anything more...   M
10. <u>Of its type</u> it's quite interesting.   M

Exercise 3

	Theme		Rheme
	textual	**topical**	
1.	And	Christopher Robin	has a house...
2.	Anyway,	this tutor	came up to me...
3.	Because	I	care for you...
4.	Well	any analogy	will break down eventually.
5.	Afterwards	he	had an idea.
6.	...but	one line	is hardly an essay.
7.	If	he	'd been warned of the consequences...
8.	...but	two thousand people	had seen me...

Phase I Key to text analysis

Key: Topical Theme underlined, textual Theme in italics. Ellipsed elements in square brackets.

Text 1 Descriptive report

The numbat is an unmistakeable slender marsupial with a pointed muzzle and short erect ears. || The body is reddish brown || *but* the rump is much darker || *and* (it)* has about six white bars across it. || The eye has a black stripe through it || *and* the long bushy tail is yellowish. || The toes are strongly clawed and very effective in digging out termites. || The tongue is extremely long, as in all mammalian ant or termite eaters. || Unlike most marsupials, the numbat is active during the day. || It shelters in hollow logs. || It was once relatively common || *but* (it) now lives only in a small area of S.W. S.A. ||

*The ellipsed Subject is unmarked topical Theme. See Section 3.2.2.

The method of development is displayed in Table K2.1 over the page.

Comment The function of the text as a brief information report on numbats is reflected in the Theme choices. There are no interpersonal Themes, contributing to the impersonal information-giving character of the text. The text moves from a classification of the numbat (as a marsupial) to a description of its appearance to a mention of its habits and location. The method of development provided by the topical Themes is thus from the numbat as a class through various parts of the body and back to the numbat as a class. (The classification and description itself is provided in the Rheme as New information.)

The single marked Theme serves to signal the return from 'parts of the body' to 'the numbat' as Theme, by differentiating the class from other marsupials. Textual Themes are of the structural type providing local links of addition or contrast.

Table K2.1 Method of development for Text 1

		Themes	
textual	marked topical	unmarked	topical
		(class of animal)	(body part)
		the numbat	
			the body
but		the rump	
and		it (= the rump)	
			the eye
and			the long bushy tail
			the toes
			the tongue
	Unlike most marsupials		
		it (= the numbat)	
		it (= the numbat)	
but		it (= the numbat)	

Text 2 Explanation

<u>After flash floods</u>, desert streams from upland areas carry heavy loads of silt, sand and rock fragments. || *As* <u>they</u> reach the flatter area of desert basins || <u>they</u> slow down || *and* <u>their waters</u> may soak quickly into the basin floor.|| *Then* <u>the streams</u> drop their loads; || *first* <u>they</u> drop the heaviest material – the stones, || *then* (<u>they</u> drop)* the sand || *and finally* (<u>they</u> drop) the silt. || *Soon* <u>these short lived streams</u> become choked by their own deposits || *and* <u>they</u> spread their load in all directions.|| <u>After some time</u>, fan or cone-shaped deposits of gravel, sand, silt and clay are formed around each valley or canyon outlet. || <u>These</u> are called alluvial fans.||

*The ellipsed Subject is unmarked topical Theme. See 3.2.2.

See Table K2.2.

Comment Ten of the eleven unmarked topical Themes show continuity in choice, being versions of 'desert streams', while the New information in the Rhemes describes what the streams do. The text is organized in terms of temporal sequence, quite a different method of development from Text 1. Two marked topical Themes provide a temporal point of departure for the beginning and end stages in the sequence, while Textual Themes provide further temporal links between one event and the next. The final clause is distinct in having an unmarked Theme different from all the preceding ones. This Theme provides a conclusion to the text by taking the lengthy New information of the previous clause as its point of departure (and providing a technical name in the Rheme as the final New).

Table K2.2 Method of development in Text 2: Explanation

| | Themes | |
textual	marked Topical	unmarked topical
	after flash floods	
as		they (= desert streams)
		they (= desert streams)
and		their (= desert streams') waters
then		the streams
first		they (= streams)
then		they (= streams)
and finally		they (= streams)
soon		these short lived streams
and		they (= short lived streams)
	After some time	
		These (fan or cone-shaped deposits of gravel, sand, silt and clay formed around each valley or canyon outlet)

While Texts 1 and 2 are alike in their lack of interpersonal Themes, and in their use of textual and both marked and unmarked topical Themes, they differ in their methods of development. Text 1 is topically organized, in terms of the whole and its various parts, using unmarked Themes to achieve this and one marked Theme to provide a reorientation from parts back to whole. Text 2 is sequentially organized using marked topical Themes together with textual Themes to make the steps in the sequence the consistent point of departure. The breaking of the consistent pattern of unmarked Theme choice in the final clause and the relation between final Theme and previous Rheme helps construct the final clause as a conclusion of a sort not found in Text 1.

Phase II Key to exercises

Exercise 1

| | Theme | | Rheme |
	interpersonal	topical	
1.	Perhaps	he	won't notice you, Piglet.
2.	Frank,	it	was fantastic.
3.	For God's sake,	you	had me worried.
4.	Honest to God	I	stood up...
5.	Sometimes[1]	I	wonder...

[1]'Usuality' realized by *sometimes, always* etc. is an interpersonal system. See Chapter 3.

Exercise 2

	Theme		Rheme
	interpersonal	topical	
1.	Can	you	hop on your hind legs?
2.	Aren't	you	clever?
3.	Were	you	a famous poet?
4.	Did	I	ever say that?
5.	Is	that	all?

Exercise 3

	Theme		Rheme
	interpersonal	topical	
1.	Wh...	...at	's the matter, Eeyore?
2.	Wh...	...o	lives there?
3.	Wh...	...at	shall we do?
4.	Wh...	...y	are they at the station instead of in town?
5.	H...	...ow old	are you?

Exercise 4

	Theme		Rheme
	interpersonal	topical	
1.		Come	on.
2.	Oh	go	away, Frank.
3.	Don't	be	soft.
4.		Listen	to me.
5.		Let's	visit Kanga and Roo and Tigger.

Exercise 5

	Theme			Rheme
	textual	interpersonal	topical	
1.	But	sometimes	I	hate them.
2.	Then	wh...	...y	did it try to bite me?
3.	But	surely	you	can see the difference...?
4.	But	don't	you	realize...?
5.	In fact,	Christopher Robin,	it	's Cold.
6.			We	really should talk about you and Denny, my dear.

Exercise 6

	Theme				Rheme
	textual	inter-personal	marked topical	unmarked topical	
1.	And then			we	'll go out, Piglet...
2.	So		after breakfast		they went round...
3.			In criticism		sentiment has no place.
4.	...because		halfway through that book		I couldn't go on reading it.
5.				A crowd of us	stuck together all week.
6.		Frank,		it	was fantastic.
7.	Well,			look	in my cupboard...
8.	And		in a little while		they felt much warmer...
9.	...and		on the way		they told him of the...
10.	...until suddenly		a hundred miles above him		a lark began to sing.

Phase II Key to text analysis

Text 1 Procedure Key: Textual Theme in italics, interpersonal Themes dotted underlined, topical Themes underlined.

Paprika-Garlic Roast Chicken

1 medium whole frying chicken (2½–2¾ pounds)
1½ teaspoons garlic powder
1½ teaspoons paprika
3 tablespoons salad oil
salt and pepper

Preheat oven to 325°.

Remove giblets from inside chicken *and* save for chicken stew or soup. Wash chicken inside and outside. (Don't use soap!)

Rub chicken inside and out with garlic powder. __ Using a pastry brush or paper towel*, coat chicken with oil *and* sprinkle with paprika to give a nice red tint. Salt and pepper lightly.

Place chicken in a deep oven pan, breast down, *and* cover tightly with aluminium foil. The juices will seep into the breast *and* __ keep the chicken moist.

Roast in oven for 40 minutes. At the end of this time, turn chicken breast up *and* cover again with foil. Return to oven for another 30 minutes. *Then* remove foil *and* continue roasting for 20–30 minutes more, *or until* chicken is fork tender and golden brown. Serve with Brown Rice or Bulgar Wheat.

*A subjectless non-finite clause such as this has no Theme. The entire clause, however, could be taken as Theme of the clause complex (see 3.7).

Comment The first part of the text consists of minor clauses without any Theme-Rheme structure (see 3.1). (This whole section – list of ingredients – could be regarded as the point of departure for the second part of the text – the method of preparation. See 2.5 for brief discussion of extending the Thematic principle to whole texts.)

All but one of the topical Themes is an unmarked imperative Theme, organizing the text as a series of actions. The most frequent textual Theme is *and* since readers can be expected to infer the sequential temporal relation between the processes. Towards the end of the text, when timing becomes an important aspect of the activity, there are temporal conjunctions as textual Themes (*Then*, *until*) and a temporal circumstance as a marked topical Theme (*At the end of this time*). Only occasionally does the dish being prepared become thematic (*the juices*, *chicken*), since the text is not concerned with information about a thing (chicken) but with the activity of cooking it.

Text 2 Parent-child conversation Key: Textual Theme in italics, interpersonal Themes dotted underlined, topical Themes underlined.

C: <u>How</u> could birds die?
M: ...<u>like the one in the garden</u>, are you thinking of?
Well, sometimes <u>birds</u> die
just when <u>they</u> get very old,
or maybe <u>they</u> got sick
because <u>they</u> got some disease;
or maybe <u>a cat</u> got it.
<u>Baby birds</u> sometimes die
when <u>they</u> fall out the nest,
or, <u>in the winter</u> –
if <u>you</u> were in a cold place
   ... <u>birds</u> might die
because <u>they</u> can't get enough food
C: *Yeah, but* <u>what</u> happens
if <u>one bird</u> falls out
and then – *and when* <u>it</u>'s just about at the ground
<u>it</u> flies?
M: *Yes, well if* <u>it</u>'s big enough to fly
<u>it</u>'ll be all right.
And sometimes <u>birds</u> fall out the nest
but <u>they</u> don't die...

Comment Textual (conjunctive) Themes show the movement of reasoning within a speaker's turn (e.g. deploying condition (*if*) and alternation (*or*), as a variety of possibilities are explored). Textual (continuative) Themes link one speaker's turn to another, acknowledging either the question posed or the information given by the addressee.

Interpersonal Themes from M show that an assessment of probability or usuality is her frequent starting point for the information she is providing.

Interpersonal Themes from the child make the demand for information his starting point.

Topical Themes from both speakers display a consistency of choice. Almost all concern birds, a topic introduced in the child's opening Rheme and picked up as a marked Theme in M's response, where the child's general question is related to shared personal experience (*Like the one in the garden*). Following this, all but one of the topical Themes are unmarked as the bird motif is pursued (*baby birds*, ...*they*; *one bird...it*). There is some variation when the child initiates a question, i.e. the manner of the process is initially thematic (*how*) and later the process itself in *what happens?*

Text 3b Exposition (rewritten)

	Theme			Rheme
	textual	marked topical	unmarked topical	
a	Although		the United States	participated heavily in World War I,
b			the nature of that participation	was fundamentally different from [[what it became in World War II.]]
c			The earlier conflict	was a one-ocean war for the Navy and a one-theatre war for the Army;
d			the latter	was a two-ocean war for the Navy and one of five major theatres for the Army.
e			A vital responsibility of the Navy	was escort-of-convoy and anti-submarine work in both wars,
f	but		it	never clashed with the enemy on the surface in the 1917–1918 conflict;
g	whilst		it	fought some twenty major and countless minor engagements with the Japanese Navy between 1941 and 1945.
h			American soldiers [[who engaged in World War I]]	were taken overseas in transports
i	and		"	landed on docks or in protected harbours;
j			the art of amphibious warfare	had to be revived and developed in World War II,
k	since		assault troops	were forced to fight their way ashore
l			Airpower	was still inchoate and almost negligible in the earlier conflict;
m			it	was a determining factor in the latter.
n			The battleship	still reigned queen of the sea in World War I,
o	as		she	had in changing forms, since the age of Drake.
p	and		Battle Line	fought with tactics [[inherited from the age of sail]];
q	but		the capital naval force	was the air-craft carrier taskgroup in World War II,
r	wh...		...ich[2]	completely new tactics had to be devised for.

[2]Relative pronouns function as conflations of textual and topical Theme.

Comment The two versions of this text contrast in their deployment of topical Theme. In 3a, it is the pattern of marked Themes which constructs the text's method of development. The writer, Morison, explores a piece of US naval history by contrasting the different roles played by the navy in WW1 and WWII. This difference is explicitly announced in the first two clauses of the text and then exemplified five times. The opposition of one great war to the other is constructed thematically for each example except the fourth and many of the textual Themes also involve relations of contrast (*although*, *but*, *whilst*, *but*). In the rewritten (b) version, the textual Themes remain the same, but there are no marked Themes at all. The contrast between the two wars announced at the beginning does not thereafter organize the text in the same way. Instead it is the various forms of warfare that constitute the method of development (the navy, soldiers, amphibious warfare, airpower, the battleship).

Phase III Key to exercises

Exercise 1

1. <u>The Zoroastrian at the gate</u> would not let me in...
2. <u>The nature of that participation</u> was fundamentally different...
3. <u>The paint on the window frames</u> had chipped...
4. <u>The current interest in iconicity and related themes</u> points to this issue as a palpitating one.
5. <u>The history of American linguistics over the past 50 years</u> is awash with acrimonious name-calling...

Exercise 2

1. <u>Future historians, philologists, and lexicographers</u> might find their labours lightened by being enabled to appeal to such a standard.
2. <u>STC, with more than $200 million in annual sales,</u> is only the seventh Korean enterprise to sell foreigners bonds that can be converted into shares.
3. <u>Basilosaurus, an early whale,</u> grew as long as 70 feet.
4. <u>The bored, lazy and unruly</u> are not the only kind of problem students that teachers have to tackle.
5. <u>Matter, in all its forms,</u> is endowed by the figurative genius of every language with the functions which pertain to intellect.
6. <u>'Fault', 'responsibility', and 'cause'</u> are explicit references to causation.
7. <u>Relative genericness, non-specificity, and emptiness</u> is commonplace in noun phrases.
8. <u>Mesoamerica, with its rich genetic and typological diversity,</u> deserves attention...

Exercise 3

1. <u>What I've been thinking</u> is this.
2. <u>What people see on the screen</u> is me.
3. <u>What he did for a living</u> was the best he could.
4. <u>What you see</u> is what you get.

5. <u>What I am proposing about compounding</u> is, rather conservatively, that there are a number of compounding rules.

Exercise 4

1. <u>Squeezing the spots</u> may damage the skin permanently.
2. <u>Rocking baby</u> may help her to sleep.
3. <u>To see him all by himself like that</u> really upset them.
4. <u>To have requested leave just now</u> would have been a bit unreasonable.
5. <u>Eating an occasional Mars bar</u> won't do you any harm.

Exercise 5

1. <u>It</u> is good to understand the natural order.
2. <u>It</u> astonished me that you should even suggest such a thing.
3. <u>It is the parasitic mode of life</u> that makes mites and ticks of economic importance.
4. <u>It</u> is probable that Mrs Kelly would have endured the strain of a divided family.
5. Naturally <u>it is not the PSG's money</u> that is at risk in this proposal.
6. <u>It</u> had occurred to him that this might be the result.
7. <u>It is only recently</u> that reasonable proposals for using and saving the wharves have come to the public's attention.
8. <u>It</u> excited him, too, that many men had already loved Daisy.
9. In fact, <u>it was the husband and not the wife</u> who got custody in that case.
10. <u>It</u> happened that we were there at the same time.

Phase III Key to text analysis

Text 1 Biographical recount Key: Textual Theme in italics, topical Themes underlined.

<u>George Bernard Shaw</u> was born in Dublin, Ireland, on July 26, 1856. <u>He</u> attended four different schools *but* <u>his real education</u> came from a thorough grounding in music and painting, *<u>which</u>* he obtained at home. <u>In 1871</u>, he was apprenticed to a Dublin estate agent, *and later* <u>he</u> worked as a cashier. <u>In 1876</u>, Shaw joined his mother and sister in London, *<u>where</u>* he spent the next nine years in unrecognized struggle and genteel poverty.

<u>From 1885 to 1898</u>, he wrote for newspapers and magazines as critic of art, literature, music and drama. *But* <u>his main interest at this time</u> was political propaganda, *and*, <u>in 1884</u>, he joined the Fabian Society. <u>From 1893 to 1939</u>, <u>the most active period of his career</u>, Shaw wrote 47 plays. <u>By 1915</u>, his international fame was firmly established *and* <u>productions of 'Candida', 'Man and Superman', 'Arms and the Man', 'The Devil's Disciple',</u> were being played in many countries of the world, from Britain to Japan. <u>In 1925</u>, the playwright was awarded the Nobel Prize for Literature. <u>Between the ages of fifty-seven and sixty-seven</u>, Shaw wrote such dramas as 'Heartbreak House', 'Back to Methuselah', 'Androcles and the Lion', 'St. Joan'. <u>During his lifetime</u> he was besieged by offers to film his plays, *but* <u>he</u> accepted only a few, <u>the most notable</u> being 'Pygmalion', *<u>which</u>* was adapted (after his death) as the basis for the musical 'My Fair Lady'. <u>He</u> died at the age of ninety-four at Ayot St. Lawrence, England, on November 2, 1950.

Comment This text is a biographical recount – in this case a highly synoptic account of Shaw's life. Naturally, a number of Themes refer to the author; but more striking is the recurrent selection of circumstance of location in time as marked Theme. The effect of these selections is to scaffold the text through (re)setting in time (as opposed to sequence in time which would be handled by conjunctions). This method of managing time is typical of texts which deal with longer spans of time that cannot be handled in detail – of history, as opposed to narration.

Text 2 Topographic procedure Key: Textual Theme in italics, interpersonal Themes dotted underlined, topical Themes underlined.

Singapore's city centre straddles the Singapore River *and* __ runs parallel to the waterfront along Raffles Quay, Shenton Way, Robinson Rd and Cecil St. The Singapore River was once one of the most picturesque areas of Singapore ‖ with old shops and houses ['being'] along the river *and* soaring office buildings ['being'] right behind them.

Sadly, it doesn't look like the old places will be around much longer. All the bustling activity along this stretch of river – the loading and unloading of sampans and bumboats – has ceased. The cranes are gone and the yelling, sweating labourers, ['are gone'] too. All boats have been kicked out of the area *and* __ relocated to the Pasir Panjang wharves away from the city centre. You can still sit in the hawkers' centres by the river, *but rather than* watch all the activity you can bet on *which building* will be next under the wrecking ball.

On the Empress Place side of the river a statue of Sir Stamford Raffles stands imperiously by the water. It's in the approximate place where he first set foot on Singapore island. There is a second statue of Raffles in front of the clock tower by Empress Place. Nearby is the Supreme Court and City Hall, *across from which* is the open green of the Padang, site for cricket, hockey, football and rugby matches. There are also memorials to civilians ⟦*who* died as a result of the Japanese occupation⟧ and to Lim Bo Seng, a resistance leader ⟦killed by the Japanese⟧.

If you continue up Coleman St from the Padang, you pass the Armenian Church *and* __ come to Fort Canning Hill, a good viewpoint over Singapore. Once known as 'Forbidden Hill', the hill is now topped by the old Christian cemetery which has many gravestones with their poignant tales of hopeful settlers ⟦*who* died young⟧. There too is the tomb of Sultan Iskander Shah, the last ruler of the ancient kingdom of Singapura. At the mouth of the river, or at least what used to be the mouth before the most recent bout of land reclamation, stands Singapore's symbol, the Merlion.

Change Alley, Singapore's most famous place for bargains, has survived or rather adapted to modernization. It still cuts through from Collyer Quay to Raffles Place, *but* __ has become a pedestrian bridge *and* __ is known as 'Aerial Change Alley'. It's still lined with shops and money-changers *although* now it's air-conditioned! The older alley runs below.

Further along the waterfront you'll find large office blocks, airline offices and more shops. Here too is the popular Telok Ayer Transit Food Centre by the waterfront. Singapore's disappearing Chinatown is inland from this modern city centre.

Comment This text is intended as a part of the blueprint for a walking tour of Singapore, and so its unmarked Themes refer to the tourist (you) and the places of interest on the tour. Of particular interest are the circumstances of location in space which function as marked Themes (contrast the temporal marked Themes in Text

1 above). These scaffold the journey as a progression from one landmark to the next as the text unfolds from one space to another.

Text 3 Advertisement Key: Textual Theme in italics, topical Themes underlined.

<u>Be</u> seen in all the right places.

<u>From New York to Los Angeles to Atlanta to Dallas/Ft. Worth</u>, the Delta system flies to all the top business centres in America. <u>That</u>'s over 4200 flights a day to more than 260 cities around the U.S. and around the world. *So* <u>next time business takes you to the States</u>, book Delta. <u>We</u>'ll make sure <u>you</u>'re seen in all the right places. At all the right times.

Delta Air Lines.

<u>We</u> love to fly *and* <u>it</u> shows.

Comment This is an example of a text whose texture needs ultimately to be addressed in conjunction with the images it accompanies. The main motif foregrounded in its Themes is interpersonal, rather than ideational – as the text engages 'you' (the customer) to fly with 'we' (Delta Airlines).

Text 4 Description within narrative

Textual Theme	Marked topical Theme	Unmarked topical Theme	Rheme
		The land	was cold and white and savage.
	Across it (=land)		there ran a thread of frozen waterway,
with		dark spruce forest	looming on either side.
	Along this waterway		toiled a string of wolfish dogs, ‖
			hauling a sled of birch bark.
	On the sled, along with the camp-outfit,		was lashed a long and narrow oblong box.
	In front of the dogs, on wide snowshoes,		toiled a man.
	Behind the sled		came a second man.
	On the sled in the box		lay a third man, ⟦whose life was at an end⟧ – a man ⟦whom the Wild had beaten down and conquered⟧.
		The bodies of the live men	were covered with soft fur and leather.
		Their faces	were blurred and shapeless under a coating of crystals from their frozen breath.
	All around them		was a silence ⟦which seemed to press down upon them as water does upon a diver⟧.

Comment In this opening paragraph of the novel *the land* is the orienting unmarked Theme symbolizing its important role in the story. Seven marked Themes take the reader in from the wider vista to the sled party and back out to the surrounding landscape. Objects and persons in the story (participants) are introduced in Rhemes and then picked up in a later Theme, mainly as reference points for introducing a further participant: For example: [Rheme:] *a string of wolfish dogs - - - - - >* [Theme:] *In front of the dogs;* [Rheme:] *a sled of birch bark - - - - ->* [Theme:] *On the sled,* [Theme:] *Behind the sled.*

Text 5 Casual conversation Key: Textual Themes in italics, interpersonal Themes dotted underlined, topical Themes underlined. Ellipsed elements in square brackets.

> B: Do you think it's worth going to see The Godfather?

Or we can take it as an interpersonal metaphor, 'in your opinion' (see discussion below) and analyse as follows:

> B: Do you think it's worth going to see The Godfather?
> C: Yes. [it's worth going to see] The Godfather Two, yes.
> B: Darling, Murder on the Orient Express is now at the ABC Shaftesbury Avenue. [It's] on with The Godfather.
> A: [It would] be a pretty good double bill, that, actually. We'd be out of the house all night, wouldn't we?
> B: *But* you can't see both of them, can you?
> A: *Well, if* it's the same price,...
> B: I mean there are two screens at the ABC Shaftesbury Avenue.
> C: *Oh sorry, yes, no no no no* you're right. *Yes, yes* they are...
> B: Les Enfants du Paradis, what about that?
> D: *Oh,* that's nice.
> C: That's a real classic. I do want to see that *cos* I never saw it ever, *even when* I was a student. [:m] The Pasolini Arabian Nights apparently[3] are rather fun.
> B: Erotic Inferno and Hot Acts of Love, I don't think they're quite down our street.
> A: That must be in the Tottenham Court Road...
> B: They love sex and lusty laughs. What rubbish! [i.e. What rubbish it is!]
> A: What is that lovely cinema in Victoria? Have you ever been to it, the Biograph?

Note on interpersonal metaphor as Theme Modality may be expressed by means of an interpersonal Adjunct, such as *probably*. Alternatively, this meaning could be constructed as a clause, such as *I think, I reckon* or, in interrogative forms, *do you think?*, *do you reckon?* When it comes to a Theme analysis, there are alternative possibilities. One approach would be to analyse them at 'face value' as two clauses:

> Do you think ‖ it's worth going to see the Godfather?

Alternatively the clause realizing the modality could be treated as equivalent to an interpersonal Adjunct initiating the second clause – as a metaphor for a modality element (see Chapter 3, Section 2.5.2 and IFG: 58):

---

[3]Note that the modal Adjunct *apparently* is not an interpersonal Theme here, since it does not precede the topical Theme.

<u>*Do you think*</u> it's worth going to see the Godfather?
Interpersonal   Top
Theme   Rheme

Comment Themes in this text foreground deixis – with several exophoric references to the interlocutors (*I*, *you*, *we*) and anaphoric references to the immediately preceding text (*it*, *they*, *that*). In addition there are a number of interpersonal Themes, scaffolding the text as interaction (*Darling*, *what*, *do*, *have*) and textual Themes scaffolding the text as repartee (*but*, *well*, *oh*).

Text 6 Exposition Key: Textual Themes in italics, interpersonal Themes dotted underlined, topical Themes underlined. Ellipsed elements in square brackets.

> ... <u>The claims for the educational value of Show and Tell and Morning News sessions</u> are at best rather questionable, however, for several reasons. *In the first place*, <u>the commitment to promoting oral language as something independent of other areas of language development</u> is itself very dubious. <u>The notion of language development</u> must involve development both in speech and in literacy, *and* <u>no very useful distinction</u> can be drawn between the two. <u>They</u> are necessarily very closely related.
>
> *Furthermore*, <u>even the children who are successful in Showing and Telling or Newsgiving</u> will benefit from being given opportunities to use spoken language in other ways in schools. <u>The particular activity and genre</u> are not uniquely suitable for the development of oral language abilities.
>
> *On the contrary, since*<u> the particular genre used at any time</u> is itself dependent upon the activity concerned, <u>it</u> should be clear that the need is to generate a range of differing activities in schools, to enable children to master the associated range of genre types. <u>Regrettably</u>, <u>Morning News and Show and Tell sessions</u> frequently feature as the only concessions made to the development of oral language in daily school programs. *Where* <u>this is the case</u>, <u>the language program</u> is impoverished indeed. <u>In a good language program</u> children move easily through many learning activities of a kind designed to stimulate and extend abilities to speak, to read and to write....

Comment It is useful to contrast this text where the topical Themes are complex nominal groups with Text 5 above where they are mainly pronouns. This reflects the abstract nature of Text 6, which makes use of nominalizations (*claims, commitment, notion, distinction*) and a good deal of embedding (*even the children who are successful in Showing and Telling or Newsgiving; the particular genre used at any time*) in order to construct a theoretical critique of the morning news genre. This critique involves argument, which is scaffolded by rhetorically oriented textual Themes (the cohesive conjunctions *in the first place, furthermore, on the contrary*).

Text 7 Taxonomizing report Key: Topical Theme in bold face; marked Themes underlined; conductors, insulators and semiconductors dotted underlined when News. The thematic structure of Text 7 is shown below (Table K2.3). The text is a taxonomizing report, presenting a classification of conducting substances. Note however that conductors, insulators and semiconductors tend to be realized last in the text's clauses, as what Halliday calls New; they are not woven systematically through Theme to constitute the method of development.

Table K2.3 Distribution of information in Text 7

THEME	(minimal) NEW
<u>If we connect a battery across a body,</u>	
there	towards the positive end
This movement of electrons	an electric current
All materials	into three groups
how readily	to flow
These (= three groups)	conductors, insulators and semiconductors
<u>In the first category</u>	substances
which	an easy path for an electric current
All metals	conductors
some metals	do not conduct well
Manganin	a poor conductor
Copper	a good conductor
it (= copper)	for cables
A non-metal which conducts well	carbon
Salt water	an example of a liquid conductor
A material...	an insulator
Rubber, nylon, porcelain	insulators
There	no perfect insulators
All insulators	some flow of electrons,
however this	can usually be ignored
the flow they permit	so small
Semiconductors	midway between conductors and insulators
<u>Under certain conditions</u>	easily
under others	as insulators
Germanium and silicon	semiconductors
Mixtures of certain metallic oxides	as semiconductors
These	as thermistors
The resistance of thermistors	rapidly
their temperature	rises
They	in temperature-sensing devices

Title

Conductors, Insulators and Semiconductors

Introduction

<u>**If we connect a battery across a body**</u>, **there** is a movement of free electrons towards the positive end. **This movement of electrons** is an electric current. **All materials** can be classified into three groups according to **how readily** they permit an electric current to flow. **These** are: conductors, insulators and semiconductors.

Topic sentence 1 (and following text)

<u>In the first category</u> are substances which provide an easy path for an electric current.

All metals are <u>conductors,</u> however **some metals** do <u>not conduct well.</u> **Manganin**, for example, is <u>a poor conductor</u>. **Copper** is <u>a good conductor</u>, therefore **it** is widely used for cables. **A non-metal which conducts well** is carbon. **Salt water** is an example of <u>a liquid conductor.</u>

Topic sentence 2 (and following text)

A material which does not easily release electrons is called <u>an insulator</u>.

Rubber, nylon, porcelain are all <u>insulators</u>. **There** are <u>no perfect insulators</u>. **All insulators** will allow some flow of electrons, however **this** can usually be ignored because **the flow they permit** is so small.

Topic sentence 3 (and following text)

Semiconductors are <u>midway between conductors and insulators</u>.

<u>Under certain conditions</u> they allow a current to flow easily but **under others** they behave <u>as insulators</u>. **Germanium and silicon** are <u>semiconductors.</u> **Mixtures of certain metallic oxides** also act as <u>semiconductors.</u> **These** are known as thermistors. **The resistance of thermistors** falls rapidly as **their temperature** rises. **They** are therefore used in temperature-sensing devices.

Comment The distribution of information as Theme and minimal New in Text 7 is outlined in detail in Table K2.3. The minimal domain of New in each clause has been specified, assuming that TONICITY is unmarked throughout the text; in other words assuming that the text will be read with the Tonic falling on the last salient syllable of each information unit. (Unmarked TONALITY has been assumed, with the information unit corresponding to a single clause.)

It is clear from Table K2.3 that text 7 systematically maps conductors, insulators and semiconductors onto New. This makes good sense in the text's introduction and its topic sentences where these categories are being introduced and established as the text's anticipated method of development. Elsewhere, however, it results in a recurrent association of new information with clause initial position (where it has not been predicted) and old information with final position (where the reader expects news). It thus inverts the unmarked distribution of given and new information in the English clause and in this respect it is not surprising that students find the reading and comprehension exercise a difficult one. The text poses a set of puzzling questions as to how the author of these materials managed so systematically to invert the natural textual periodicity of information-giving texts of this kind.

Key to Chapter 3: Mood

Phase I Key to exercises

Exercise 1

1. <u>You</u> heard me, didn't <u>you</u>?
2. <u>That</u>'s shocking, isn't <u>it</u>?
3. <u>No one</u> said anything, did <u>they</u>?
4. <u>We</u> could have done something about it, couldn't <u>we</u>?
5. <u>There</u>'s no need to be getting snotty, is <u>there</u>?
6. <u>Jimmy</u>'s the one that should be getting snotty, isn't <u>he</u>?
7. <u>Linda</u>'s hitting me, isn't <u>she</u>?
8. <u>Your mammy and Sharon and me</u> are having a chat, aren't <u>we</u>?
9. <u>The hot shower</u> refreshed them, didn't <u>it</u>?
10. <u>Those two little kittens</u> were chasing the ball, weren't <u>they</u>?

Exercise 2

1. Now get out, won't <u>you</u>?
2. Don't start that, will <u>you</u>?
3. Ah Veronica, stop that, won't <u>you</u>?
4. Mind yourself against that table there, won't <u>you</u>?
5. Just tell us, will <u>you</u>?

Exercise 3

1. You went in by yourself.
    Go in by yourself.
2. Does the old girl drive it?
    Drive it.
3. You will tell them soon.
    Tell them soon.
4. Will you come for a drink, Sharon?
    You will come for a drink, Sharon.
5. I'll bring home a few chips.
    Bring home a few chips.

Exercise 4

Sample answer	Possible alternatives
1. Did that girl get there on the train?	Did that girl get there somehow/easily...
That girl got there on the train.	That girl got there somehow/easily...
2. Do you mean you're shocked, Veronica?	Do you mean something/that it's late...
You mean you're shocked, Veronica.	You mean something/that it's late...
3. Will all those people say it's shocking?	Will all those people say something...
All those people will say it's shocking.	All those people'll say something...
4. Is it due in March?	Is it due soon/now/next week...
It's due in March.	It's due soon/now/next week..
5. Did the wretched man go to the pub?	Did the wretched man go somewhere...
Go to the pub.	Go somewhere/to the office...

Exercise 5

	Possible alternatives
1. – Can I?	I can?, Yes/maybe I can, No I can't etc.
2. – She can of course.	Yes, she can/No, she can't/Perhaps she can, etc.
3. – It is of course.	Yes, it is/No, it isn't, it isn't really, etc.
4. – Yes I do.	No, I don't/Of course I do etc.
5. – She did of course.	She didn't/Did she?/Yes, she did etc.

Exercise 6

1. Can   Tracy   watch?   – She   can   of course.
    Finite   Subject   Subject   Finite

2. Abortion   's   murder.   – It   is   of course.
    Subject   Finite   Subject   Finite

3. You   don't   care about that.   – Yes,   I   do.
    Subject   Finite   Subject Finite

4. Dawn has   had   her baby for Paddy Bell.   – She   has   of course.
    Subject Finite   Subject   Finite

5. Will   all our friends be there?   – They   will   be.
    Finite   Subject   Subject   Finite

6. Your little brother   isn't going to like it.   – Isn't   he?
    Subject   Finite   Finite   Subject

Exercise 7

1. Can   Tracy   watch?   – She   can   of course.
    Finite   Subject   Subject   Finite
    Mood   **Residue**   **Mood**

2. Abortion   's   murder.   – It   is   of course.
    Subject   Finite   Subject   Finite
    Mood   **Residue**   **Mood**

3. You   don't   care about that.   – Yes, I   do.
    Subject   Finite   Subject   Finite
    Mood   **Residue**   **Mood**

4. Dawn has   had   her baby for Paddy Bell.   – She   has   of course.
    Subject Finite   Subject Finite
    Mood   **/Residue**   **Mood**

5. Will   all our friends be there?   – They will   be.
    Finite Subject   Subject Finite
    Mood   **Residue**   **Mood**   **Residue**

6. Your little brother   isn't going to like it.   – Isn't he?
    Subject   Finite   Finite Subject
    Mood   **Residue**   **Mood**

Exercise 8

1. He <u>might</u> already know.   1....probability......
2. Excuse me a moment, I <u>ought</u> to say hello to someone   2....obligation.......
    over there.   3....obligation.......
3. You <u>shouldn't</u> speak to your mother like that.   4....tense...............
4. <u>Are</u> you looking for someone?
5. Well, he certainly <u>must</u> have strained himself to get this   5....probability......
    menagerie together.   6....tense...............
6. He <u>hasn't</u> begun yet.   7....tense...............
7. <u>Didn't</u> he explain?   8....obligation.......
8. You <u>mustn't</u> drink so much, darling.   9....probability......
9. It <u>couldn't</u> be him driving.   10...tense...............
10. They <u>don't</u> know the answer to that one.

Exercise 9

1. I   'm   not   telling.
    Mood   **Residue**
    Su   Finite   Adjunct:polarity

2. She   certainly   wasn't   kidding.
    Mood   **Residue**
    Su   Adjunct:probability   Finite

3. She   'd   always   been like that.
    Mood   **Residue**
    Su   Finite   Adjunct:usuality

4. Your mind   's   probably   made up.
    Mood   **Residue**
    Subject   Finite   Adjunct:probability

5. They   might   have told me before this.
    Mood   **Residue**
    Su   Finite

6. He   must   necessarily   be dismissed for the theft.
    Mood   **Residue**
    Su   Finite   Adjunct:obligation

7.	You	're	definitely		not		going to tell us.
	Mood						Residue
	Su	Finite	Adj:probability		Adj:polarity		

8.	Would	the lads	sometimes		go out?
	Mood				Residue
	Finite	Subject	Adjunct:usuality		

9.	Maybe		it	's	a bad idea.
	Mood				Residue
	Adjunct:probability		Su	Finite	

10.	I	'll	gladly		do it.
	Mood				Residue
	Su	Finite	Adjunct:readiness		

Phase I Key to text analysis

Text 1 Explanation (for young children)

1.	Do **you** enjoy making sounds?	interrog:yes/no
2.	What sounds do **these things** make ‖ if **you** bang them?	interrog:wh-
3.	What different sounds can **you** make with your body...	interrog:wh-
4.	(**you**) Put your fingers on your throat ‖ as **you** talk ‖ or [as **you**] sing.	imperative
5.	What can **you** feel?	interrog:wh-
6.	(**you**) Hold a ruler on the edge of a table.	imperative
7.	(**you**) Press down the end ‖ and (**you**) let go.	imperative (×2)
8.	Can **you** hear a sound?	interrog:yes/no
9.	What do **you** see?	interrog:wh-
10.	Whenever **you** hear a sound ‖ **there** is something moving.	declarative
11.	**This movement** is called a vibration.	declarative
12.	(**you**) Try this with a rubber band ‖ and (**you**) see.	imperative (×2)
13.	**You** can make musical sounds with rubber bands... ‖ or if **you** pluck the strings of a guitar.	declarative
14.	(**you**) Strike a triangle with a beater.	imperative
15.	(**you**) Touch the triangle ‖ while **it** is ringing.	imperative
16.	What can **you** feel?	interrog:wh-
17.	When **something** stops vibrating ‖ **the sound** stops.	declarative
18.	How does **someone's voice** reach you?	interrog:wh-
19.	**The sound** travels through the air as sound waves.	declarative
20.	(**you**) Throw a stone in a pool of water.	imperative
21.	(**you**) Watch [[the waves spreading out]].	imperative
22.	**Sound waves** move through the air in a similar way.	declarative

Comment The writer uses information-giving declaratives on relatively few occasions, instead placing the child reader in a number of (responding) roles. The reader must do things (in response to imperatives) and then give information (in response to wh- interrogatives). After two such cycles, the author gives a piece of information at 11 and then again at 17, 19, 22 – each time after further imperative(s) +/or interrogative moves. Thus, despite being the non-expert, the child reader is placed several times in the role of information-giver and, despite the book's status as an 'information book', much of the text concerns exchange of action rather than information. The view of learning implied would seem to be a version of 'discovery learning' which prizes learning by doing rather than telling. Correspondingly, the most frequent Subject choice is *you*, and it is only in a minority of clauses that information is negotiated in terms of some aspect of the topic of sound as Subject.

Text 2 Parent–child conversation Key: Modality elements in italics. Subject in bold, Finite underlined. (Only part of the word is underlined where the verb realises both Finite and Predicator functions.)

C:	How *could* **birds** die?	C:	low prob
M:	Like the one in the garden, <u>are</u> **you** thinking of?		
	Well, *sometimes* **birds** <u>di</u>e	M:	low usuality
	when **they** <u>ge</u>t very old,		
	or *maybe* **they** <u>ge</u>t sick		low prob
	because **they**<u>'ve</u> got some disease,		
	or *maybe* **a cat** <u>go</u>t it		low prob
	Baby birds *sometimes* <u>di</u>e		low usuality
	when **they** <u>fa</u>ll out the nest,		
	or, in the winter –		
	<<if **you** <u>were</u> in a cold place>>–		
	birds *<u>might</u>* die		low prob
	because **they** <u>can't</u> get enough food.		low ability
C:	Yeah, but **what** <u>happ</u>ens		
	if **one bird** <u>fa</u>lls out		
	and then – and when **it**<u>'s</u> just about at the ground		
	it <u>fl</u>ies?		
M:	Yes, well if **it**<u>'s</u> big enough ⟦to fly⟧		
	it'<u>*ll*</u> be all right.		median prob
	And *sometimes* **birds** <u>fa</u>ll out the nest		low usuality
	but **they** <u>don't</u> die...		
	But **that** <u>didn't</u> look like a baby bird;		
	maybe **there** <u>was</u> something wrong with it;		low prob
	maybe **a cat** <u>ki</u>lled it –		low prob
	(hastily) **I** <u>don't</u> think		low prob*
	it <u>was</u> our cat.		
C:	*Perhaps* **it** <u>was</u> on the ground	C:	low prob
	and then **a cat** <u>go</u>t it.		
M:	Yeah, **it** <u>was</u> *probably* pecking something	M:	median prob
	on the ground...		
	maybe **it** <u>was</u> just a very old bird.		low prob
	...		
C:	(referring to dead bird in garden)		
	But **it** <u>look</u>s as if it's alive.		
M:	Yeah, **it** <u>does</u>, <u>doesn't</u> **it**?		
C:	*Perhaps* **its eye** <u>go</u>t blind	C:	low prob
M:	*<u>Could</u>* have been,	M:	low prob
	but **it** *definitely* <u>wasn't</u> alive.		high prob

*The whole clause *I don't think* stands for low probability. (See Section 2.5.2.)

Comment The text is striking for the repeated selection of low modality choices by both parties. Thus the hypothetical nature of the talk – that there are a range of equally possible answers to the question – is foregrounded. This contrasts with Text 1 where the only modal choices relate to the ability of the child reader-experimenter, and information-giving is unmodalized.

The distribution of mood choices differs also from Text 1. Here the child learner uses wh- interrogatives and most of the information-giving is carried out by the adult. The child does contribute information himself through declarative choices (*Perhaps it was on the ground and then a cat got it; perhaps its eye got blind*) but these are not in reponse to the teacher-like questions of Text 1. Instead they reformulate or build on M's earlier propositions (*maybe a cat got it, maybe a cat killed it, maybe there was something wrong with it*).

Again, unlike Text 1, Subject choices (with one exception) are consistently third person, with information negotiated in terms of *birds, a bird, the bird*. Finite choices are occasionally modal but otherwise construe present tense for generalizations and past tense for propositions about shared experience (e.g. *a cat got it*).

Phase II Key to exercises

Exercise 1

1. Darling, would you carry this for me?
   Vocative   Su
2. All of you,   get out of here.
   Vocative
3. Bruce   was inspecting the lab.
   Subject
4. Robin,   let's go.
   Vocative   Su
5. You really ought to leave straight away.
   Su
6. Chase   had a thing for black rubber.
   Subject
7. Mr Eliot disagreed.
   Subject
8. You   had better get ready   Alfred.
   Subject   Vocative
9. Don't, Riddler,   even think about it.
          Vocative
10. Look at you.

Exercise 2

1. She'd have been walloped.
2. Why won't we be told?
3. Jimmy shut the door.
4. His tea got squirted back into the cup.
5. The arguments had won her over.
6. Will a few chips be brought home for you?
   Will you be brought home a few chips?
7. Pregnancy may heighten my perceptions.

Exercise 3

1. | Can | Tracy | watch? |
    |---|---|---|
    | Finite | Subject | Predicator |
    | Mood | | Residue |

– She	can	of course.
Subject	Finite	
Mood		

2. | Abortion | 's | murder. |
    |---|---|---|
    | Subject | Finite | Complement |
    | Mood | | Residue |

– It	is	of course.
Subject	Finite	
Mood		

3. | You | don't | care | about that |
    |---|---|---|---|
    | Subject | Finite | Predicator | Adjunct |
    | Mood | | Residue | |

– Yes,	I	do.
	Subject	Finite
	Mood	

4. | Dawn | has | had | her baby | for Paddy Bell. |
    |---|---|---|---|---|
    | Subject | Finite | Pred. | Complement | Adjunct |
    | Mood | | | Residue | |

– She	has	of course.
Subject	Finite	
Mood		

5. | Will | all our friends | be | there? |
    |---|---|---|---|
    | Finite | Subject | Predicator | Adjunct |
    | Mood | | Residue | |

– They	will	be.
Subject	Finite	Pred.
Mood		Res.

6. | Your little brother | isn't | going to like | it. |
    |---|---|---|---|
    | Subject | Finite | Predicator | Comp. |
    | Mood | | Residue | |

– Isn't	he?
Finite	Subject
Mood	

Exercise 4

1. | They | are | going to sell | the house as soon as possible. |
    |---|---|---|---|
    | Su | Fi | Predicator | |

2. | I | was | expecting to see* | you earlier. |
    |---|---|---|---|
    | Su | Fi | Predicator | |

3. | He | seemed to be* | perfectly cheerful. |
    |---|---|---|
    | Su | Fi/Predicator | |

4. | He | was | beginning to get* | into the car. |
    |---|---|---|---|
    | Su | Fi | Predicator | |

5. | Couldn't | they | have done | something about it? |
    |---|---|---|---|
    | Finite | Su | Predicator | |

6. | She | might | have stopped listening.* |
    |---|---|---|
    | Su | Fi | Predicator |

7. | Didn't | they | try to understand* | you? |
    |---|---|---|---|
    | Finite | Su | Predicator | |

8. | They | started to listen.* |
    |---|---|
    | Su | Fi/Predicator |

Exercise 5

1. | Stop | that. |
    |---|---|
    | Predicator | Complement |

2. | How | did | it | happen? |
    |---|---|---|---|
    | Wh/Adjunct | Finite | Subject | Predicator |

*These examples have a 'verbal group complex' (a combination of verbal groups) realizing the Predicator function. See further Chapter 4, 3.3.

3. Don't   start   that.
   Finite   Predicator   Complement
4. Why   won't you   tell   us?
   Wh/Adjunct   Finite Subject Predicator   Complement
5. What   do   you   mean?
   Wh/Complement   Finite Subject   Predicator
6. When   's   it   due?
   Wh/Adjunct   Finite Subject   Complement
7. What a house   this   is!
   Wh/Complement   Subject   Finite

Exercise 6

1. She   was   usually   seen by someone.
   Subject Finite   mood Adjunct
2. Frankly,   she   'd   hardly   been anywhere.
   comment Adjunct   Subject Finite mood Adjunct
3. She   'd   already   visited some of the sights.
   Subject Finite   mood Adjunct
4. Apparently   she   'd   barely   seen any of the sights...
   comment Adjunct   Subject Finite mood Adjunct
5. In general   she   shopped   in the fashionable streets.
   comment Adjunct   Subject Finite/Predicator
6. Surprisingly,   she   probably   didn't see anyone any more.
   comment Adjunct   Subject mood Adjunct   Finite
7. Provisionally,   we   might   plan for a whole day then.
   comment Adjunct   Subject Finite

Exercise 7

1. Lay   off,   Veronica
   Predicator   Adjunct   Vocative
   Residue
2. I   'll   sort   this fella   out.
   Subject Finite   Predicator Complement   Adjunct
   Mood   Residue
3. They   won   her   over.
   Subject Finite/Predicator   Complement   Adjunct
   Mood   Residue
4. They   put   her   up to it.
   Subject Finite/Predicator   Complement   Adjunct
   Mood   Residue
5. She   saw   through their plan.
   Subject Finite/Predicator   Adjunct
   Mood   Residue
6. He   watched   over the baby.
   Subject Finite/Predicator   Adjunct
   Mood   Residue
7. She   chewed   out   the opposition.
   Subject Finite/Predicator   Adjunct   Complement
   Mood   Residue

Exercise 8

1. It stood there,   <u>rattling,</u>
                             Predicator
                             <u>its paws   slipping   on the formica.</u>
                             Subject   Predicator   Adjunct

2. Tracy came back in   <u>with the pup clinging   to the front of her jumper</u>.
                           Subject   Predicator   Adjunct

3. <u>Drawn   by only two horses,</u> the coach moved clowly down the road.
   Predicator   Adjunct

4. Jummy Sr wished   <u>for Sharon   to go out   in the hall   first</u>.
                      Subject   Pred.   Adj   Adjunct   Adjunct

5. He quickly took the King's part, <u>wielding   his flail   against the attackers.</u>
                                 Predicator   Comp.   Adjunct

6. <u>Given my aunt by the Duke</u> the teapot remained a family heirloom...
  Pred.   Comp.   Adjunct

7. He would attempt to repay him <u>by showing him through the royal apartments</u>.
                                   Pred.   Comp. Adjunct

8. <u>To give him   cause for rejoicing,</u> he granted him sole possession of the farm.
  Pred.   Comp.   Complement

Exercise 9

1. <u>The points that you made there</u> surprised me.
2. <u>Your mammy and Sharon and I</u> are having a chat.
3. What chance gave, <u>chance</u> took away.
4. <u>The increase of empirical knowledge, and more exact modes of thought,</u> made...
5. ...<u>the increasingly complex machinery of the State</u> necessitated...
6. <u>The inner unity of human nature</u> was severed too.
7. <u>The near identity of these two criticisms of the governmental state</u> can of course...

Exercise 10

1. Gosh, I   forgot.
   xxxx   Mood   ...Residue
2. Tracy,   go up to your room.
   xxxx   Residue
3. I don't   think so,   Veronica.
   Mood   Residue   xxxxxxx
4. Finally, they all   left.
   xxxxxx   Mood   Residue
5. I didn't meet anyone   though.
   Mood   Residue   xxxxx
6. Personally, I don't   like him.
   Mood   Residue
7. Frankly, my dear, I don't   give a damn.
   Mo...   xxxxxx   ...od   Residue
8 They don't, as a rule, arrive before six.
   Mood   Residue
9. They lost,   surprisingly.
   Mo...   ...Residue   ...od

Phase II Key to text analysis

Text 1 Classroom talk (1)

1. Teacher: minor clause   Alright,
2. Teacher: minor clause   a quick summary of what we have just seen.
    (teacher writes heading 'Summary' on the board.)
3. Teacher: minor clause   Quick.
4. Andrew   minor clause   Lever.[1]
5. Teacher: imperative

Hold	on
Predicator	Adjunct
Residue	

6. Daniel: minor clause   Seesaw.
7. Teacher: minor clause   Right.
8. imperative

Just	wait
mood Adjunct	Predicator
Mood	Residue

9. declarative

till	we	are	all	here.
	Subject	Finite	Adjunct	Adjunct
	Mood		Residue	

10. yes/no ('polar') interrogative

Have	you	got	enough scrap paper	on your desk	please?
Finite	Subject	Pred.	Complement	Adjunct	Adjunct
Mood		Residue			

11. declarative

You	'll	probably	only	need	two or three pieces.
Subject	Finite	mood Adjunct	mood Adjunct	Predicator	Complement
Mood				Residue	

---

[1]Following IFG 4.6.2 *Lever* (see also 6, 22, 24, 26, 28, 29, 39 etc.) can be treated as the minor clause function Absolute (i.e. might be either Subject or Complement were the minor clause expanded into a major one).

12. declarative

Right,	you	may	have to use	the stand.
conjunctive Adjunct	Subject	Finite	Predicator	Complement
	Mood		Residue	

(the teacher is waiting for the class to settle before he begins)

13. declarative (reminding the boys to take their hats off inside)

Steven and Brad,	the sun	is	shining	inside.
Vocative	Subject	Finite	Predicator	Adjunct
	Mood		Residue	

14. minor clause   Alright, thankyou.

15. yes/no interrogative (ellipsis of Subject and Finite 'have you')

Solved	your problem?
Predicator	Complement
Residue	

16. declarative

You	'll	probably	need to see	that film	tomorrow,	as an extra,
Subject	Finite	mood Adjunct	Predicator	Comp	Adjunct	Adjunct
Mood			Residue			

17. non-finite clause

to get	your ideas	...sorted	out.
Pred...	Complement	...icator	Adjunct
Residue			

18. minor clause   Right.

19. imperative

Let's	have a summary of what was the film basically about.
Subject	Pred. Complement
Mood	Residue

20. declarative

They	seem to mention		two basic machines.
Subject	Finite	Predicator	Complement
Mood		Residue	

21. minor clause

Um, Andrew?
Vocative

22. Andrew: minor clause Levers.
(pronounces the work with an American accent as in the film)

23. Teacher: declarative

It	has	an Australian pronunciation.
Subject	Finite	Complement
Mood		Residue

24. Simon: minor clause Levers.

25. Teacher: imperative (said as a joke and the class laughs)

Yeah,	leave	her	alone.
conjunctive Adjunct	Pred.	Complement	Adjunct
	Residue		

26. minor clause Lever (writes on the board)

27.   and...(pause)

28. Brad: minor clause An inclined plane.

29. Teacher: minor clause An (pause) inclined plane.

30. imperative

Hold	on,
Predicator	Adjunct
Residue	

31. imperative

hold	on,

32. declarative

now	they		extended	these two basic machines,	into five separate machines.
conjunctive Adjunct	Subject	Finite	Predicator	Complement	Adjunct
	Mood		Residue		

33. declarative

In that movie	they		extended	them	out,
Adjunct	Subject	Finite	Predicator	Complement	Adjunct
Res-	Mood		-idue		

34.   declarative

they	extended		out	some of the machines.
Subject	Finite	Predicator	Adjunct	Complement
Mood		Residue		

35.   declarative

They	used		the lever.
Subject	Finite	Predicator	Complement
Mood		Residue	

36.   imperative

Hold	on,
Predicator	Adjunct
Residue	

37.   imperative   Hold on. (a child is calling out)

38.   Teacher: minor clause

Joanne
Vocative

39.   Joanne: minor clause   Lever.

40.   Teacher: declarative

No,	we	've	done	a lever.
conjunctive Adjunct	Subject	Finite	Predicator	Complement
	Mood	Residue		

41.   Brad: minor clause   Baseball bat.

42.   Teacher: minor clause   Baseball bat.
      (pause)

43.   minor clause   Any bat really.

44.   Joanne: minor clause   Flying fox.
      (said very quietly)

45.   Teacher: minor clause   Pardon, flying fox?
      (writes on the board)

46.   Kane: minor clause   Clothesline.

47.   Teacher: minor clause   And what with it?

48.   Kane: minor clause   A wheel.

49.   Teacher: minor clause   A wheel.
      (repeats out loud to the class and writes on the board)

50. declarative

Yeah, no	you	're	right.
conjunctive Adjunct	Subject	Finite	Complement
	Mood		Residue

51. minor clause   Clotheslines.

52. (interrupted)

That	was	a...
Subject	Finite	Complement
Mood		Residue

53. wh- interrogative

what	did	she	use	on the clothesline?
Wh-/Complement	Finite	Subject	Predicator	Adjunct
Res-	Mood		idue	

54. Several: elliptical declarative (ellipsis of she used)

Pulley.
Complement
Residue

55. Teacher: minor clause A pulley,

56. declarative

which	is	a type of lever.
Subject	Finite	Complement
Mood		Residue

57. declarative

Except	of course,	you	've	got	also	a what	with it?
	mood Adjunct	Subject	Finite	Pred.	Adjunct	Comp.	Comp.
	Mood			Resi...		...due	

58. elliptical declarative: (ellipsis of you've also got)

A (pause) wind (prompting children) lass
Complement
Residue

59.   elliptical interrogative (ellipsis of 'is there')

Anything else that wasn't mentioned that possibly uses the principles of a lever.
Complement
Residue

60.   Steven: elliptical declarative

Door handle.
Complement
Residue

61.   Teacher: elliptical derivative
      A door handle,

62.   minor clause   Good one, hey.

63.   Teacher: minor clause   Yep.
(writes on board)

64.   minor clause (or textual continuative to clause 65)   Righto,

65.   imperative

let's	have	a look	at an inclined plane one
Subject	Predicator	Complement	Adjunct
Mood	Residue		

66.   declarative

well	actually	that	is	a type of tool which you have seen in action,
conjunctive adjunct	mood Adjunct	Subject	Finite	Complement
	Mood			Residue

67.   elliptical declarative

come to think   of it.

Fi/Predicator	Adjunct

68.   declarative

Maybe	we	can	get	six uses of an inclined plane.
mood Adjunct	Subject	Finite	Pred.	Complement
Mood			Residue	

69.   minor clause

Um Aranthi?
Vocative

70.   Aranthi: minor clause   Stairs.
71.   Teacher: minor clause Stairs,
72.   minor clause   Right.
73.   minor clause   Great answer. (writes on board)

Table K3.1 Selected SPEECH FUNCTION choices and their realization in MOOD in text

Teacher's commands	MOOD	Notes
2? 21, 38, 69	minor	Andrew in 4 seems to take 2 as a command. Vocatives function as commands to take a turn
5, 8, 30, 31, 36, 37, 65	imperatives	Congruent grammatical choice
10	interrogative	Use of *please* shows proposal not proposition
11, 12, 16?	modalized declaratives	Following commands, all could be read as negotiating action rather than information
13	declarative	Satisfactory response is action not acknowledgement of information
15	elliptical interrogative	Satisfactory response is quiet and attention not provision of information
Teacher's questions		
19	imperative	A demand for information
53	interrogative wh-	Congruent grammatical choice
59	elliptical interrogative: yes/no	A demand for specific information (rather than yes or no)
23, 32–34, 57, 68	declarative	Specific answer sought not just acknowledgement of information
47	minor	

Comment The teacher is very much in control of the discourse in this extract, essentially giving commands, asking questions and acknowledging answers. He uses some modality and considerable mood metaphor (see Table K3.1) to exert control while keeping a friendly tenor.

The children's familiarity with the sequence of Teacher Question + Student Response + Teacher Evaluation (e.g. 53–56) enables them to participate appropriately even though only one question is congruently coded as a full interrogative clause. The children take on a responding role throughout, modifying their behaviour and providing information, through minor clauses (and two elliptical declaratives). They use no imperatives or interrogatives and no modality.

Given the strong element of control, it is not surprising that *you* is the most prominent Subject choice (12 instances), although the inclusive *we/us* also features five times. In addition, persons in the film (*they, she*) are in the Subject role seven times, with elements in the taxonomy being built up occurring as Subject only three times.

Text 2 Classroom talk (2)

1. c: declarative

Ok,	we	are	doing	this one.
conjunctive Adjunct	Subject	Finite	Predicator	Complement
	Mood		Residue	

2. A: declarative

So	we		need		that.
	Subject	Finite	Predicator		Complement
	Mood		Residue		

3. c: minor   OK.

4. K: declarative

Hey,	I		got	it.
conjunctive Adjunct	Subject	Finite	Predicator	Complement
	Mood		Residue	

5. c: minor   Oh, excellent.

6. Y: declarative (Subject Ellipsis)

Looks		good.	
Finite	Predicator	Complement	
Mood	Residue		

7. c: declarative

We		need	a heavy nut.
Subject	Finite	Predicator	Complement
Mood		Residue	

8. K: declarative

There	is	one	off the um...
Subject	Finite	Complement	Adjunct
Mood		Residue	

9. N: declarative

We		need (interrupted)	
Subject	Finite	Predicator	
Mood		Residue	

10. c: minor   Yeah, yeah.

11. N: imperative

Go ask	Bill
Predicator	Complement
Residue	

12. A: declarative

We		need		a thin saw blade.
Subject	Finite	Predicator		Complement
Mood		Residue		

13. C: imperative

Use	this.
Predicator	Complement
Residue	

14. N: minor   Oh yeah.

15. A: yes/no interrogative

Do	you	have	a matchbox	anywhere?
Finite	Subject	Predicator	Complement	Adjunct
Mood		Residue		

16. N: yes/no interrogative

Do	you	want	me	to ask	Mr Kelly?
Finite	Subject	Predicator	Subject	Predicator	Complement
Mood		Residue	Mood	Residue	

17. A: elliptical imperative ?   Empty one.

18. K: declarative

We		got		a heavy nut.
Subject	Finite	Predicator		Complement
Mood		Residue		

19. K: declarative

We		need to tie		some string.
Subject	Finite	Predicator		Complement
Mood		Residue		

20. A: declarative

Now	we		need		another matchbox.
conjunctive Adjunct	Subject	Finite	Predicator		Complement
	Mood		Residue		

21. N: declarative

It	doesn't,
Subject	Finite
Mood	

22.   declarative

it	doesn't	need	a matchbox,	does	it?
Subject	Finite	Predicator	Complement	Finite	Subject
Mood		Residue		Moodtag	

23. A: minor   Yeah.

24. K: declarative

Now	we		need	one string,
conjunctive Adjunct	Subject	Finite	Predicator	Complement
	Mood		Residue	

25.   declarative

we	've	got	that.
Subject	Finite	Predicator	Complement
Mood		Residue	

26.   declarative

We	've	got	this.
Subject	Finite	Predicator	Complement
Mood		Residue	

27. A: declarative

OK,	we		need	a cork.
conjunctive Adjunct	Subject	Finite	Predicator	Complement
	Mood		Residue	

28. K: Wh-interrogative

Where	are	we	going to get	some of those?
Wh-/Adjunct	Finite	Subject	Predicator	Complement
Residue...	Mood		...Residue	

29. C: declarative

What we need	is	wire and a cork.
Subject	Finite	Complement
Mood		Residue

30. A: polar-interrogative

OK,	could	you	ask	for one cork and one wire.
conjunctive Adjunct	Finite	Subject	Predicator	Adjunct
	Mood		Residue	

Comment In contrast to Text 1, only five of the 30 utterances by the children take the form of minor clauses; between them they contribute 18 declaratives, four interrogatives and two to three imperatives. Y speaks only once but the others take on a range of speech roles. The offer expressed in (16) can be interpreted as involving explicitly subjective modulation (see Section 2.5) and the final interrogative, functioning as a command, is modalized, otherwise MOOD choices are congruent with SPEECH FUNCTION and Finites consistently construe present tense as the speakers focus on the ongoing task.

Thirteen out of 22 Subject choices are realized as *we*, symbolizing the collaborative nature of the task in which the talk is embedded. *You* as Subject features five times, *I* twice and *it* (referring to their model) twice. Overall, then, the negotiation of information, as well as goods and services, centres on the interactants themselves. By contrast the pieces of equipment with which they are concerned (as well as persons not in their group) appear in the Complement role.

Phase III Key to exercises

Exercise 1

1. It ___ would be ___ difficult ___ to enjoy it.
   Sub... ___ Finite Predicator ___ Complement ___ ...ject

2. It ___ 's ___ surprising ___ (that) they said that.
   Sub... Finite ___ Complement ___ ...ject

3. It ___ 's ___ a relief ___ (that) they've left.
   Sub... Finite ___ Complement ___ ...ject

4. It ___ 's ___ often ___ said ___ (by people) (that) no good will come of it.
   Sub... Finite ___ Adjunct Predicator ___ Adjunct ___ ...ject

5. It ___ irritates ___ me ___ (that) they didn't apologize.
   Sub... Finite/Predicator ___ Complement ___ ...ject

6. It ___ 's ___ true ___ (that) they don't often come here.
   Sub... Finite ___ Complement ___ ...ject

Exercise 2

1. There ___ was ___ one particularly repulsive specimen in spotted blue.
   Subject ___ Finite ___ Complement

2. On another wall there ___ was ___ a smaller shelf holding an assortment of china cats.
   Adjunct ___ Subject Finite ___ Complement

3. There ___ was ___ a record player in a corner.
   Subject ___ Finite ___ Complement

4. And ___ beside it ___ was ___ a greetings card.
   ___ Adjunct ___ Finite Complement

5. There ___ was ___ a large number of cushions of all sizes and colours.
   Subject ___ Finite ___ Complement

6. Along the stream ___ ran ___ a worn path.
   Adjunct ___ Finite/Predicator ___ Complement

7. On the table ___ was ___ a vase, a book and a greeting card.
   Adjunct ___ Finite ___ Complement

Exercise 3

1. Riddler was **absolutely** beside himself.
2. **Obviously** he was smitten.
3. Robin had **not even** become his partner.
4. His parents were **already** dead.
5. **By all means** see it.
6. He **readily** agreed to join the firm.
7. **In fact**, he **just** hated it.
8. I **scarcely** think about it any more.
9. He **mainly** did it for fun, **of course**.
10. **Possibly** they just haven't **yet** arrived.

1. degree
2. obviousness
3. polarity, intensity
4. time
5. obligation
6. readiness
7. intensity, intensity
8. degree
9. typicality, obviousness
10. probability, time

Exercise 4

1. obligation
2. probability
3. ability
4. usuality
5. obligation
6. probability
7. obligation
8. obligation
9. inclination (do you insist...?) obligation (is it necessary...?)
10. probability

Exercise 5

1. I suppose (so) — probability
2. He thinks (he'll leave). — not metaphorical
3. You're sure now (he's not married?) — probability
4. I promise (I'll go). — readiness: inclination
5. I don't think (so). — probability
6. I'd love (you to do it). — obligation
7. Do you reckon (he'll come)? – I doubt it. — probability
8. I demand (you leave). — obligation
9. She said (she was pregnant) — not metaphorical
10. I still think (you should tell us who the dad is.) — two readings: first speaker is construing probability, whereas second speaker responds to it as not metaphorical.

Phase III Key to text analysis

Text 1 Dialogue in narrative

instance:	MODALITY	TYPE		
	explicitly subjective	**implicitly subjective**	**implicitly objective**	**explicitly objective**
W: I have no doubt that	high prob			
W: perfectly self-evident				high prob
W: I should be obliged to you if	median oblig			
W: you would		median incl		
H: not very obscure				high prob
H: the same elementary class				high prob
H: I should		high prob		
W: I don't admit that...	high prob			
H: you would probably		median prob	median prob	
H: they would certainly		median prob	high prob	
H: it is clear that				high prob
H: it is equally clear that				high prob
W: that is very evident				high prob
H: absurdly commonplace				high prob
H: equally childish				high prob
H: you are in the habit of				median usual
H: not your usual method of				median usual
H: it is unlikely that				median prob
H: absurd, is it not				high prob

Comment This typical example of repartee between Holmes and Watson illustrates a full range of modality selections, both congruent and metaphorical – reflecting one aspect of the interpersonal meaning potential available to mature middle-class English 'gentlemen' of their period. Of particular interest is the range of explicitly objective selections through which Holmes asserts the indisputability of his deductions. Most of these are clearly agnate to alternative selections:

> Therefore it is clear that you sat at the side. [explicitly objective]
> Therefore you certainly sat at the side. [implicitly objective]
> Therefore you must have sat at the side. [implicitly subjective]
> Therefore I'm convinced you sat at the side. [explicitly subjective]

and fit snugly into a canonical explicitly objective frame:

Therefore it is **perfectly self-evident** that you sat at the side.
Therefore it is **not very obscure** that you sat at the side.
Therefore it is **clear** that you sat at the side.
Therefore it is **equally clear** that you sat at the side.
Therefore it is **very evident** that you sat at the side.
Therefore it is **unlikely** that you sat at the side.

Out of context, there are others which seem more ideational in meaning, perhaps just beyond the bounds of modality proper – even when our conception of modality is broadened to include the co-option of ideational resources to realize modality 'metaphorically':

the same **elementary** class of deduction
equally childish
absurd

Note, however, that the text itself seems to be instructing us to include these selections as modal ones:

'...Therefore it is **clear** that you sat at the side. Therefore it is **equally clear** that you had a companion.'
'That is **very evident**.'
'**Absurdly commonplace**, is it not?'
'But the boots and the bath.'
'**Equally childish**....'

In this passage, as the text unfolds, Holmes is in the process of amplifying the certainty of his deductions. In the process of doing so he expands the meaning potential normally associated with modality. This is a typical example of the (textual) instance expanding the meaning potential of the (language) system. Holmes has bequeathed at least one of these expansions to the system proper: '**Elementary**, my dear Watson.'

Text 2 Written exposition Note: embedded clauses are analysed separately below, following the initial analysis.

TV Violence

It	is	essential for the well-being of the Youth of Australia	that we adopt a less
S..	Fi	Complement	...Subject.................................
Mood...		Residue_____	...Mood _____

tolerant attitude to violence in television.
....
_____

It has	been known for some time	that young children can be disturbed by the
S.. Fi	Predicator Adjunct	..Subject...
Mood..	Residue_____	..Mood_____

violent scenes presented by the television scene.   No apparent effort however
....   Subject...................................
_____   Mood_____

has	been made	by either the producers of children's programmes or the
Fi	Predicator	Adjunct..
___	Residue_____	

programmers of children's programmes to take this into account: one only has to look at
....Subject (cont)..........................   Su   Adj.   Fi   Pred   Ad
_____   ..Mood_____   Mood_____   Residue

the extraordinary popular cartoon 'Teenage Mutant Ninja Turtles'. At some schools it
...junct...,,,,...............   Adjunct   S..
Residue_____   Residue_____   M..

was necessary to ban the accessories associated with the programme because children
Fi   Comp.   ..Subject...   Subject
...o..   Resid.   ..od_____   Mood-

were engaging in fights in the playground, emulating their cartoon heroes; this sort of
Fi   Pred.   Adjunct   Adjunct   Predic   Complement   Subject...........
___   Residue_____   Residue_____   Mood.............

situation is deplorable, this incident also highlights how impressionable young chn are.
.................Fi Comp.   Subject   Fi/Pred.   Complement..
_____   Residue   Mood_____   Residue_____

There is a definite danger that children, after years of exposure to violence on television,
Su   Fi   Complement...
Mood____   Residue_____

come to accept that violence is an acceptable solution to conflict. It   is   of vital
....   S..   Fi   Adjunct
_____   Mood...   Residue-

importance for the future of Australia that young people realize that violence is not to
....Subject...
_____   ..Mood_____

be condoned, nor applauded. It   is   also essential that young people do not associate
....   S..   Fi   Comp.   ..Subject.................................
_____   Mood..   Residue   ..Mood_____

violence with bravery and heroism, which is an inevitable outcome if we persist in
....   Su   Fi Complement   Su   Fi/Pred...............
_____   Mood   Residue_____   Mood   Residue-

allowing our children to be influenced by the garbage that fills our screens every
....   Comp.   ..Pred...........................   Adjunct...

afternoon and evening, and succeeds in passing for entertainment. It is possible that
....   S.. Fi   Comp   ..S
_____   Mood.. Res.   Mo..

children come to accept violence as an inevitable, but vaguely unpleasant part of the
....
..od_____

world. If this unfortunate scenario becomes true, we will never combat violence.
....   Subject...........................   Fi/Pred   Comp Su Fi   Adj   Pred   Comp.
_____   Mood_____   Residue____   Mood_____   Residue_____

It is   of utmost importance, then, that the television industry assumes a sense of
S.. Fi   Adjunct   ..Subject...
Mood   Residue_____   ..Mood_____

responsibility by carefully regulating the materials that appear in children's programmes.
....

Table K3.2 Modality in Text 2

	MODALITY	TYPE
instance:	**congruent**	**metaphorical: explicitly objective**
It is essential that		high oblig
(young children) can	low prob	
(one only) has to (look)	high oblig	
it was necessary		high oblig
(a) definite (danger)		high prob
It is also essential that		high oblig
(an) inevitable (outcome)		high prob
It is possible that		low prob
(an) inevitable (part ...)		high prob
never	high usuality	

Comment We can see the young writer making every effort to produce an objective sounding argument overall, repeatedly using the split Subject structure to avoid personalizing attitude (*it is of vital/utmost importance that...*) or subjective modal assessment (*it is possible that....*). For the same reason nominal forms of assessment are favoured (*a **definite** danger*). Modal choices are either probability/usuality (assessing what is the case) or obligation (exhorting action), with high value realizations in the majority, in an attempt at greater persuasiveness. See Table K3.2.

Many of the Subjects in the text – the pegs on which the propositions rest – are 'facts', packaged as embedded clauses. The embedded clauses themselves mainly have the meaning 'children/young people' as Subject.

Embedded clauses analysed

that we adopt a less tolerant attitude to violence in television.
    Su Fi/Pred Complement

that young children can be disturbed by the violent scenes presented by the tv scene.
      Subject   Fi   Predicator   Adjunct

presented by the television scene
Predicator   Adjunct

to take this   into account
Pred   Comp   Adjunct

to ban the accessories associated with the programme
Pred   Complement

associated with the programme
Pred   Adjunct

how impressionable young children   are.
Complement   Subject   Fi

that children come to accept that violence is an acceptable solution to conflict
    Subject   Fi/Predicator   Complement

violence is an acceptable solution to conflict.
Subject   Fi Complement

that young people realize ‖ that violence is not to be condoned, ‖ nor applauded.
    Subject   Fi/Pred   Subject   Fi Adj Predicator   Predicator

that young people do not associate violence with bravery and heroism
    Subject   Fi Adj Predic   Comp   Adjunct

fills our screens every afternoon and evening ‖ and succeeds in passing for entertainment
Fi/P Comp   Adjunct   Fi/Pred.........   Adjunct

that the television industry assumes a sense of responsibility
    Subject   Fi/Pred   Complement

by carefully regulating the materials [[that appear in children's programmes]].
   Adjunct   Predicator Complement   Su   Fi/P   Adjunct

Text 3 Dramatic dialogue

Speaker	Turn	Kate	Deeley
Kate	(Reflectively) [**She was**] Dark.	major: finite: indic: declar: non-exclamative: untagged	
Deeley	[**Was she**] Fat or thin?		major: finite: indic: interrog: yes/no
Kate	[**She was**] Fuller than me, **I think**.	major: finite: indic: declar: non-exclamative: untagged	
Deeley	**She was** [fuller than you] then.		major: finite: indic: declar: non-exclamative: untagged
Kate	**I think** so [she was fuller than me then].	major: finite: indic: declar: non-exclamative: untagged	
Deeley	**She may not** be [fuller than you] now.		major: finite: indic: declar: non-exclamative: untagged
	Was she your best friend?		major: finite: indic: interrog: yes/no
Kate	Oh, what **does that** mean?	major: finite: indic: interrog: wh: non-subject-wh: complement-wh	
Deeley	[What **does**] **What** [mean]?		major: finite: indic: interrog: wh: non-subject-wh: complement-wh
Kate	[What **does**] **The word friend** [mean] ...	major: finite: indic: interrog: wh: non-subject-wh: complement-wh	

	when **you** *look* back ... all that time	major: finite: indic: declar: non-exclamative: untagged	
Deeley	**Can't you** remember what you felt?		major: finite: indic: interrog: yes/no
Kate	**It is** a very long time.	major: finite: indic: declar: non-exclamative: untagged	
Deeley	But **you remember** her.		major: finite: indic: declar: non-exclamative: untagged
	She remembers you.		major: finite: indic: declar: non-exclamative: untagged
	Or why **would she** be coming here tonight?		major: finite: indic: interrog: wh: non-subject-wh: adjunct-wh

Comment The MOOD selections in this passage reflect the interrogation genre, which we recognize from courtroom drama, police prodecures and detective fiction. Deeley grills and Kate replies. Thus all of Kate's clauses are declarative, giving information which has been requested, except for two wh- clauses that try to clarify what Deeley has asked. Over half of Deeley's clauses on the other hand are interrogative, soliciting information (including one negative interrogative *Can't you remember...* which implies that Kate should have been able to answer a question she has just avoided). Deeley's declarative clauses are presumptuous (about Kate rather than Deeley), either extrapolating from Kate's replies, or offering comments about Kate and her friend which Deeley has surmised must be true.

Key to Chapter 4: Transitivity
clause as representation

Phase I Key to exercises

Exercise 1
1. He has a sceptre in his hand.
2. The young king is calming the crowds.
3. The lad is James V of Scotland.
4. His father is falling in battle.
5. James wants his uncle's sword.
6. Only his closest attendants know his identity.
7. The farmer sees the battle on the bridge.
8. He says that his name is 'The Goodman of Ballengiech'.

Exercise 2
1. What had the farmer been doing to the corn?
2. What did they immediately do with the bondsman?
3. What did James do to Willie through the palace?
4. What did he do to his hat?
5. What did he do with the farm?
6. What did feuding do to the country?
7. What did the ruffians do to the king?
8. What did he do with the water?

Exercise 3
1. He answered that his name was Willie.
2. James saw that he was a good man.
3. James knew it was not just a dream.
4. The king replied, 'My name is The Goodman of Ballengiech'.
5. 'You'll get what you wish', the king smiled to himself.
6. James assured him he was welcome.

Exercise 4
1. material
2. material
3. mental
4. mental
5. material
6. mental
7. mental
8. material
9. mental
10. mental

Exercise 5
1. mental
2. verbal
3. verbal
4. mental
5. verbal
6. mental
7. mental
8. verbal
9. mental
10. verbal

Exercise 6
1. relational
2. material
3. relational
4. relational
5. material
6. relational
7. relational
8. material
9. material
10. relational

Exercise 7
1. The sight of their king calmed   the crowds.
   participant   process   participant

2. This lad   was   James V of Scotland.
   participant   process   participant

3. Shortly after his birth his father   had fallen   in battle.
   circumstance   participant   process   circumstance

4. Disorder   spread   throughout the kingdom.
   participant   process   circumstance

5. In the hall,   Mum   took off   his boots.
   circumstance   participant   process   participant

6. One day   he   was attacked   by a band of ruffians.
    circumstance   participant process   participant

7. He   retreated   to a nearby bridge.
    participant process   circumstance

8. Jamie   put on   his thickest jersey.
    participant process   participant

9. The farmer had been threshing   corn   in his barn.
    participant process   participant   circumstance

10. He   travelled   with the king.
    participant process   circumstance

Exercise 8
1. relational
2. material
3. verbal
4. relational
5. mental
6. relational
7. material
8. mental
9. relational
10. mental
11. verbal
12. material
13. material
14. mental

Exercise 9
1. relational
2. existential
3. existential
4. relational
5. relational
6. existential
7. existential
8. relational
9. existential
10. relational

Exercise 10
1. Role: product
2. Location: place
3. Accompaniment
4. Manner: quality
5. Extent: frequency
6. Extent: duration
7. Manner: quality
8. Location: time

9. Extent: distance
10. Matter
11. Role: guise
12. Location: place
13. Cause: behalf
14. Cause: purpose
15. Manner: means
16. Cause: purpose
17. Angle
18. Contingency: concession
19. Angle
20. Role: guise

Exercise 11
1. However no one followed him <u>into the valley</u>.
2. We hurried || but did not arrive <u>until the evening</u>.
3. While they were taking the boxes <u>into the yard</u> || they were singing <u>loudly</u>.
4. They were probably working <u>the whole week</u>.
5. They just came <u>with their friends</u> || although they were uninvited.
6. The men often travelled <u>away from home</u>.
7. Next they opened the presents <u>with great excitement</u>.
8. <u>During the long drought</u>, he lost much of his crop.
9. Although she disliked him || she <u>quickly</u> offered him a drink.
10. Perhaps he will be noticed <u>at the hunt</u> by some of the others.

Phase I Key to text analysis

Text 1 Descriptive report

	Process type	Circumstantiation
1.	relational	
2.	relational	
3.	relational	
4.	relational:possessive	Location: place
5.	relational:possessive	Location: place
6.	relational	
7.	relational	
8.	relational	Manner: comparison
9.	relational	Manner: comparison Location: time
10.	material	Location: place
11.	relational	Location: time
12.	material	Location: place

Text 2 Explanation

	Process type	Circumstantiation
1.	material	Location: time
2.	material	
3.	material	
4.	material	Manner:quality Location: place
5.	material	
6.	material	
7.	material	
8.	material	
9.	material	
10.	material	Location: place
11.	material	Location: time Location: place
12.	relational	

Comment These two informational texts contrast in the process types they include. The encyclopedia entry (a type of text often known as a 'descriptive report') functions to document key information about a class of animal, focusing on classification and description, using relational clauses to do so. Text 2, on the other hand, does not describe the appearance of a static phenomenon but explains the sequence of material events that gave rise to it. It thus consists almost entirely of material process clauses, concluding with a relational clause that provides a technical name for the final stage in the sequence. Both texts have circumstances of Time, Place and Manner, but (as seen in Chapter 2), Text 2 uses temporal Location thematically to help organize the information as a sequence of events.

Text 3 Taxonomizing report

Key
<u>material</u>   = underlined
<small>MENTAL</small>   = small caps
relational = bold
existential = bold italics

There ***are*** many species of whales. They <u>are</u> conveniently <u>divided</u> into toothed and baleen categories. The toothed whales <u>are found</u> worldwide in great numbers. The largest **is** the Sperm whale, which <u>grows</u> to about the size of a boxcar. Other species familiar to Canadians **are** the Beluga or white whale, the

Narwhal with its unicorn-like tusk, the Killer whale or Orca, the Pilot or Pothead whale, which <u>is</u> commonly <u>stranded</u> on beaches, the Spotted and Spinner Dolphins that <u>create</u> a problem for tuna seiners, and the Porpoises which we commonly SEE along our shores.

There *are* fewer species of the larger baleen whales, that <u>filter</u> krill and small fish through their baleen plates. The largest **is** the Blue whale which IS SEEN frequently in the Gulf of St Lawrence. It **reaches** a length of 100 feet and a weight of 200 tons, equivalent to about 30 African elephants. The young **are** 25 feet long at birth and <u>put on</u> about 200 lbs a day on their milk diet. Other species **are**: the Fins which at a length of 75 ft <u>blow</u> spouts of 20 ft, the fast swimming Seis, the Grays so commonly SEEN on migrations along our Pacific coast between Baja California and the Bering Sea, the Bowheads of Alaskan waters, the Rights, so seriously <u>threatened</u>, the Humpbacks, ENJOYED by tourists in such places as Hawaii and Alaska, the smaller Bryde's whales, and the smallest Minke whales, which **continue to be** abundant worldwide.

As with the growing interest in birding, increasing numbers of whale watchers now NOTICE the differences between the various species of whales.

Comment The text opens with an existential clause which announces what the text is to be about. The second paragraph also opens with an existential clause alerting the reader to what will be elaborated on in that paragraph. There are also, as with Text 1, a number of relational clauses doing the work of classifying and describing, though in this case the focus is not on a single class (as in Text 1) but on a number of subclasses.

A number of doings are also represented in the text as material processes. The first two of these describe the action of scientists, who are however not explicitly mentioned: (*They <u>are</u> conveniently <u>divided</u>* [*by scientists*], *The toothed whales <u>are</u> found* [*by scientists*]). The other doing processes mainly describe the typical behaviour of whales (*which <u>grows</u>, that <u>create</u>, that <u>filter</u>* etc.).

Somewhat unusually for a scientific report (and unlike Text 1), this text also includes a number of mental processes. These are included to relate different whale species to the first hand experience of readers. In a sense they help bridge between the technical classification of whales and the more common sense understandings of non-scientists. For example: *which we commonly SEE along our shores, which IS SEEN, {which ARE} so commonly seen, {which are} enjoyed.*

Text 4 Magazine feature (excerpt)

material	verbal	mental	relational
can reform	say	believe	's
works	notes	understand	's
have ended	adds	know, know	are
	are telling	like	are
		want	're
		believe	appear

Phase II Key to exercises

Exercise 1

1. The ruffians **robbed** him.
   Actor _____ Goal

2. The king **retreated** to a nearby bridge.
   Actor

3. The farmer **saw** the battle.
   Senser _____ Phenomenon

4. The farmer **wanted** a farm of his own.
   Senser _____ Phenomenon

5. Kinsmen **performed** the service for 300 years.
   Actor _____ Goal

6. The king **was amused** by his wonder and comment.
   Senser _____ Phenomenon

7. Nothing **could please** me more.
   Phenomenon _____ Senser

8. ...whenever the king **should pass** over the land.
   Actor

9. How **will** I **recognize** the king?
   Senser _____ Phenomenon

10. Willie suddenly **realized** the true rank of the man.
    Senser _____ Phenomenon

Exercise 2

1. James **wanted** his uncle's sword.
   Senser _____ Phenomenon

2. Willie eagerly **agreed**.
   Sayer

3. James **asked** a question.
   Sayer _____ Verbiage

4. James **decided on** peace.
   Senser _____ Phenomenon

5. Willie **answered** slowly.
   Sayer

6. James **heard** things about the feuding chieftains.
   Senser _____ Phenomenon

7. He **liked** the simple pleasures.
   Senser _____ Phenomenon

8. "Easily", **replied** his companion.
   _____ Sayer

9. Willie suddenly **realized**   the true rank of the man.
   Senser   Phenomenon

10. "His hat", **repeated**   his escort.
                                Sayer

Exercise 3
1. He granted Willie sole possession of the farm.   participant (Recipient)
2.   circumstance
3.   circumstance
4. He poured her a glass of milk.   participant (Client)
5.   circumstance
6. She made her a good dinner.   participant (Client)
7.   circumstance
8.   circumstance
9. She sang her sister a song.   participant (Client)
10. He sent his friend some money.   participant (Recipient)
11.   circumstance

Exercise 4
1. The regent was his mother.   identifying
2. Courage is represented by the lion. identifying
3.   attributive
4.   attributive
5.   attributive
6. Willie was his name.   identifying
7.   attributive
8. You are who?   identifying
9. You or I must be the king.   identifying
10.   attributive

Exercise 5
1. In his hand there was <u>a royal sceptre</u>.
2. There will be <u>a continuing struggle.</u>
3. In the townships, there had been <u>a riot</u>.
4. There was <u>a rose</u> in the vase.
5. On the table lay <u>some tattered books</u>.

Exercise 6
1. They didn't **explain** <u>to us</u> that we needed to pay in advance.
   <u>The rules</u> didn't **explain** that we needed to pay in advance.   1. verbal
2. We always **hope** for a quick response.   2. mental
3. Please **consider** all the options carefully.   3. mental
4. They **suggested** <u>to us</u> that there were alternative flights.
   <u>The timetable</u> **suggested** there were alternative flights.   4. verbal
5. They **promised** <u>us</u> that there would be a short interval.
   <u>The programme</u> promised that there would be short interval.   5. verbal
6. We **believe** it's the best idea.   6. mental
7. They **understand** that they won't be able to stay.   7. mental
8. They **insisted** <u>to me</u> that portable computers would not be covered.
   <u>The policy</u> **insisted** that portable computers would not be insured. 8. verbal

Exercise 7

		Unmarked present?	Can report?	Process type
1.	*The baby was watching me.*	present in present	no	behavioural
2.	*No one will notice.*	present	yes	mental
3.	*She suddenly heard movements.*	present	yes	mental
4.	*He pondered the situation.*	present in present	no	behavioural
5.	*Jamie hadn't remembered.*	present	yes	mental
6.	*Listen to this.*	present in present	no	behavioural
7.	*They all looked round.*	present in present	no	behavioural
8.	*Jamie could smell the holly and the ivy.*	present	yes	mental

Exercise 8
1. They all talked at once.
2. They were singing at the top of their lungs.
3. Jamie agreed (that it was so).
4. The barometer says rain/(that rain is coming).
5. The baby was screaming.
6. Everyone praised him.
7. They stated their beliefs/(that they believed in God).
8. She spoke loudly and firmly.

1. behavioural
2. behavioural
3. verbal
4. verbal
5. behavioural
6. behavioural
7. verbal
8. behavioural

Exercise 9
1. She   took   a bow.
    Behaver   Range
2. He   insulted   his audience.
    Behaver   Target
3. He   did   a poo.
    Behaver   Range
4. She   drove   the car.
    Behaver   Range
5. They   scaled   the wall.
    Behaver   Range
6. He   slandered   his rival.
    Behaver   Target
7. She   blamed   the judges.
    Behaver   Target
8. She   gave   a speech.
    Behaver   Range
9. He   smiled   a most compelling smile.
    Behaver   Range
10. He   pondered   the problem.
    Behaver   Range

Exercise 10
1. mental
2. mental
3. relational attributive
4. mental
5. relational attributive
6. mental
7. mental
8. relational attributive
9. relational attributive

Exercise 11
1. material
2. relational attributive
3. relational attributive
4. material
5. material
6. relational attributive
7. relational attributive
8. material

Exercise 12

1. We're doing 'The Coventry Carol'.	Range
2. I'll have to find a place to rest.	Goal
3. I will sing you beautiful songs.	Range
4. He pulled his little broken wing along.	Goal
5. Why would they do that to such a little bird?	Range
6. He made a nest.	Goal
7. He smelled that smell in every nook and cranny.	Range
8. They had a game of catch.	Range
9. They licked their fingers.	Goal
10. I can taste prunes.	Range
11. The Sergeant kicked another cannon ball.	Goal
12. They climbed the wall.	Range
13. He had the best dinner ever.	Range

Exercise 13

1. What was   the last item on the program?
   Token   Value

2. The student's response   is   a site for surveillance.
   Token   Value

3. Now   was   the time for everyone to join in.
   Token   Value

4. The basic mechanism   is   one where the teacher surveils the student.
   Value   Token

5. It   's   his fault.
   Token   Value

6. The view of English that I have developed   represents   a minority position.
   Token   Value

7. It   was   the best concert ever.
   Token   Value

8. One of the results   is   that real differences are obscured.
   Value   Token

9. What is immediately striking   is   the manner in which it works.
   Value   Token

10. The exercise   doesn't involve   composing a written response.
    Token   Value

11. My birthday   is   today.
    Value   Token

Exercise 14

1. He   was   in the phone booth.   circumstantial
   Carrier   Attribute

2. It   was   a tracksuit.   intensive
   Carrier   Attribute

3. He   grew   thoughtful.   intensive
   Carrier   Attribute

4. Has   he   got   a plan?   possessive
         Carrier   Attribute

5. The fare   seems   exorbitant.   intensive
   Carrier   Attribute

6. That   's   easy.   intensive
   Carrier   Attribute

7. He   had   a sore head.   possessive
   Carrier   Attribute

8. Where 's   our lunch?   circumstantial
   Attribute   Carrier

9. Here   are   his paw marks.   circumstantial
   Attribute   Carrier

Exercise 15

1. They   love ice-cream.
   Senser   Phenomenon

2. They   don't like   ⟦us   doing   this.⟧
   Senser   Phenomenon: act
                       Actor   Range

3. I   want   ‖   you   to have   it.
   Senser   idea
                     Carrier   Attribute

4. She   repeated   the answer.
   Sayer   Verbiage

5. I   wish   ‖   there   was   someone to talk to.
   Senser   idea
                                                Existent

6. Are   you   quite sure   ⟦I   'm not dreaming?⟧
            Carrier   Attribute   Matter:fact
                                        Behaver

7. We   've all been wondering   where   you   disappeared   to.
   Senser   idea
                                       Loc...   Actor   ...ation:place

8. "But   we   'll get   cold,"   said   Rachel.
   locution   Sayer
               Carrier   Attribute

9. I   told   everyone   ‖   to leave.
   Sayer   Receiver   locution

10. The toy   amused   her.
    Phenomenon   Senser

11. I   don't even know ‖   if   her family   has   gifts   at Christmas.
    Senser   idea
                                  Behaver   Range   Location:time

12. It   was   wonderful   ⟦to be wrapped   in paper with pictures on it.⟧
    Car...   Attribute   ...rier
                                                Manner

Exercise 16

1. On Christmas eve,   he   crept   out   to his woolshed.
   Location:time   Actor   Location:place   Location:place

2. He   ran   away   out of fear.
   Actor   Location:place   Cause:reason

3. He   had   a surprise   for them all.
   Carrier   Attribute   Cause:behalf

4. The sledge   began moving, ‖   because   the ground   sloped   down.
   Actor   Actor   Location:place

5. They   saw   some toys   in the sack.
   Senser   Phenomenon   Location:place

6. In no time at all,   he   made   a top.
   Extent:duration   Actor   Goal

7. They   ate   the icing on the cake.
   Actor   Goal

8. They   ate   the icing   off the cake.
   Actor   Goal   Location:place

9. What   did   the youngsters   say   on your arrival?
   Verbiage   Sayer   Location:time

10. Can   I   see   the presents you got from Santa?
        Senser   Phenomenon

Phase II Key to text analysis

Text 1 Explanation (for young children) Processes in **bold**, circumstances underlined.

1. **Do**   you   **enjoy**   ⟦making sounds?⟧
   Behaver   Process:behavioural:affective   Phenomenon

2. What sounds **do**   these things   **make** ‖ if   you   **bang**   them?
   Range   Actor   Process:material   Actor   Process:material   Goal

3. What different sounds **can** you   **make**   with your body and your voice?
   Range   Actor Process:material   Manner:means

4. **Put**   your fingers   on your throat ‖ as you   **talk** ‖ or [as   you]**sing**.
   Pro:material Goal   Location   Beh. Pro:behavioural:verbal Beh. Pro:behav:verbal

5. What **can**   you   **feel**?
   Phenom   Senser   Process:mental:perception

6. **Hold**   a ruler   on the edge of a table.
   Process:material Goal   Location:place

7. **Press down**   the end ‖ and **let go**.
   Process:material Goal   Process:material

8. **Can**   you   **hear**   a sound?
        Senser Process:mental:perception   Phenomenon

9. What **do** you   **see**?
   Phenom.   Senser   Process:mental: perception

10. Whenever you   **hear**   a sound ‖ there **is**   ⟦something moving⟧.
      Senser Pro:mental: perception Phenom.   Pro:existential Existent

11. This movement **is called**   a vibration.
   Value   Process:identifying Token

12. **Try**   this   with a rubber band ‖ and **see**.
   Process:material Goal   Manner: means   Process:mental: perception

13. You **can make**   musical sounds with rubber bands of different sizes‖
   Actor Process:material   Range   Manner:means

   or by **plucking**   the strings of a guitar.
        Process:material Goal

14. **Strike**   a triangle with a beater.
   Process:material Goal   Manner: means

15. **Touch**   the triangle ‖ while it   **is ringing**.
   Process:material Goal   Actor Process:material

16. What   **can**   you   **feel**?
    Phenom.   Senser   Process:mental:perception

17. When something **stops vibrating** ‖ the sound **stops**.
                    Actor   Process:material   Actor   Material

18. <u>How</u>   **does**   someone's voice   **reach**   you?
    Manner   Actor   Process:material   Range

19. The sound **travels**   <u>through the air</u>   <u>as sound waves</u>.
    Actor   Process:material   Location:place   Role:guise

20. **Throw**   a stone   <u>in a pool of water</u>.
    Process:material   Goal   Location:place

21. **Watch**   ⟦the waves spreading out⟧.
    Process:behavioural:perception   Phenomenon

22. Sound waves **move**   <u>through the air</u>   <u>in a similar way</u>.
    Actor   Process:material   Location:place   Manner:comparison

Comment As shown in Table K4.1, this text spends considerably more time representing the actions and perceptions of the reader than representing what sound is
or does.

   The choice of process type is linked to the mood choices. The child reader is
commanded to undertake material processes (e.g. 4, 6–7, 14–15) and after each one,
or each series, the reader is interrogated via mental processes regarding his/her
perceptions (e.g. 5, 8–9, 16). The reader is then informed (via declaratives) by means
of existential, relational or material processes (with sound as Actor) as to what
relevant information can be drawn from these perceptions. Note that *talk* and *sing*
in Line 4 concern verbal activity as a physical rather than a symbolic process and
are therefore behavioural. The identifying clause of 11 provides a technical term
(*vibration*) for a physical observable action.

   Circumstances play quite an important role. Those of Manner:means and
Location:place specify how the child is to carry out the commanded actions.
Location circumstances also describe the movement of sound. In (19) a technical

Table K4.1 Transitivity in Text 1

Processes	participant meanings	no. of instances
material	objects as Actor	3
material	sound as Actor	4
material	reader as Actor	12
behavioural:verbal	reader as Behaver	2
behavioural:affect	reader as Behaver	1
behavioural:perception	reader as Behaver	1
mental:perception	reader as Senser	6
relational:identifying	technical term as Token	1
existential	(Actor^Material) as Existent	1

term is introduced through the Role circumstance and in (22) Manner:comparison is used to relate the new term to what the child can perceive.

Text 2 Children's story (opening)

[Value:] My name [Process:identifying:] 's [Token:] Laura ‖ and [Token:] this [Process:ident:] is [Value:] my place. [Carrier:] I [Process:attributive:] turned [Attribute:] ten [Location: time:] last week. [Value:] Our house [Process:identifying:] is [Token:] the one with the flag on the window. [Sayer:] Tony [Process:verbal:] says ‖ [Sayer:] it [Process:verbal:] shows ‖ [Carrier:] we [Process:attributive:] 're [Location:place:] on Aboriginal land, ‖ but [Senser:] I [Process:mental:] think ‖ [Token:] it [Process:identifying:] means [Value:] the colour of the earth, back home. [Actor:] Mum and Dad [Process:material:] live [Location:] here too, ‖ and [Actor:] Terry and Lorraine, and Aunty Bev, and Tony and Diane and their baby Dean. [Carrier:] He [Process:attributive:] 's [Attribute:] my nephew ‖ and [Carrier:] he [Process:attributive:] 's [Attribute:] so cute! [Carrier:] We [Process:attributive:] come [Attribute/Location:place:] from Bourke, ‖ but [Senser:] Dad [Process:mental:cognition:] thought ‖ there [Process:existential:]'d be [Existent:] more jobs [Location: place:] in the city. [Token:] This (=picture) [Process:identifying:] is [Value:] me and Gully. [Attributor:] I [Process:attributive:] have to keep [Carrier:] her [Location:] on a lead ‖ because [Actor:] she [Process:material:] chases [Goal:] cars. [Carrier:] She [Process:attributive:] comes [Attribute/Location:place:] from Bourke too. [Senser:] I [Process:mental:] guess ‖ [Senser:] she [Process:mental:] thinks ‖ [Carrier:] they [Process:attributive:] 're [Attribute:] sheep. [Carrier:] This [Process:attributive:] is [Attribute:] a map of my place. [Carrier/Possessor:] We [Process: attributive/ possessive:] 've got [Attribute/Possessed:] a McDonalds [Location: place:] right on the corner!

Notes *We come from Bourke* is taken here as a relational clause, agnate to *we are from Bourke*. The relational drift of the whole passage suggests this interpretation as does the tense choice of simple present (*we have come* or *we came* would be more likely for a material clause). Similarly, *I have to keep her on a lead* has been taken as causative relational clause (see Section 2.7, 3.4(iii)), agnate to *I have to keep her cool, I have to make her be on a lead/cool*. An alternative analysis is to see it as a material clause, agnate to *I have to hold her on a lead*. The analysis would then be [Actor:] *I* [Process:material:] *have to keep* [Goal:] *her* [Manner:] *on a lead*. *He's my nephew* has been read as 'he's a nephew of mine', and so attributive.

Processes Relational 14   (identifying 5, attributive 9); Existential 1; Verbal 2; Mental 4; Material 4.

(Value role: *my name, my place, my house, the colour of the earth back home, me and Gully*)

Circumstances
    Location:time – *1988; Last week*
    Location:place – *on Aboriginal land; here; from Bourke; in the city; from Bourke; right on the corner, on a lead*

Comment This orienting paragraph is concerned with building a picture of the narrator and her relation to 'her place'. This is achieved through relational processes which describe qualities and circumstances (*I turned ten; we're on Aboriginal land; we come from Bourke*) or which identify (*My name is Laura, our house is the one with the flag, it means the colour of the earth back home*). Mental and verbal processes contribute by suggesting attitudes and circumstances of the narrator's family through the child's reporting of what they say and think. In fact, other family members appear individually as Actor, Senser, Sayer and Carrier in Theme position, as well as collectively with the narrator as *we*, suggesting the Aboriginal child's embeddedness in the family context. In general, the ideas of identity and location which are a concern of the book emerge from the start through the prominence of identifying clauses and also the foregrounding of Location circumstances, often as a participant in an attributive clause.

Text 3 Parent-child conversation (Elements without analysis have solely textual or interpersonal function.)

C: How   could birds die?
   Manner   Process: Actor   ....material

M: ...[One] Like the one in the garden, are you thinking of?
         Phenomenon   Pro ... Beh. ...cess:behavioural:cognition

Well, sometimes birds die   ‖ when they get   very old,
        Actor Process:material   Carrier Process:rel. Attribute

or maybe they get sick ‖   because they got   some disease,
      Carrier Pro:relational   Attribute Carrier Pro:rel. Attribute

or maybe a cat got   it. Baby birds sometimes die ‖
     Actor Process:material Goal Actor   Process:material

when they fall   out the nest, ‖ or, in the winter –
   Actor Process:material Location:place   Location:time

<<if you   were   in a cold place>>
    Carrier Pro:relational Attribute/Location:time

    –birds might die ‖   because they can't get   enough food.
    Actor   Process:material   Actor Process:material Goal

C: Yeah, but what happens ‖ if one bird falls   out ‖
        Actor Process   Actor   Material   Location:place

and then – and when it   's   just about at the ground ‖ it   flies?
              Carrier Pro:rel. Attribute/Location:place   Actor Pro:mat.

M: Yes, well if it   's   big enough ⟦to fly⟧ ‖ it   'll be all right.
      Carrier Pro:relational Attribute   Carrier Pro:rel. Attribute

And sometimes birds fall   out the nest ‖ but they don't die...
       Actor Pro:material Location:place   Actor Pro:material

But that   didn't look like a baby bird;   ‖
    Carrier Pro:relational Attribute/Manner:comparison

maybe there was   something wrong with it; ‖ maybe a cat killed   it –
    Pro:exist. Existent   Actor Pro:mat. Goal

(hastily) I   don't think ‖ it   was   our cat.
      Senser Pro:mental   Value Pro:relational   Token

C: Perhaps it   was   on the ground ‖ and then a cat got   it.
      Carrier Pro:relational Att/Location:place   Actor Pro:material Goal

M: Yeah, it   was   probably pecking something on the ground...
      Actor Process: ...material Goal

Maybe it   was   just a very old bird.
      Carrier   Pro:relational   Attribute

C: (referring to dead bird in garden) But it   looks   as if it's alive.
                                          Carrier Pro:relational Attrib/Manner:comp

M: Yeah, it   does [ ],   doesn't it?
         Carrier   Pro(:relational)

C: Perhaps its eye got   blind.
            Carrier   Pro:relational Attribute

M: Could have been [ ], ‖ but it   definitely   wasn't   alive.
    Pro:relational   Carrier   Pro:relational Attribute

Comment Two types of process are strongly represented here: Material and Relational: attributive. The Actor in the material clauses and the Carrier in the relational ones shifts between a construal of birds in general, a non-specific hypothetical bird and a specific bird of shared memory. Occasionally too a non-specific cat is construed as Actor in clauses where the bird is Goal. The bird itself is Actor in a transitive clause only twice and on the first occasion the clause is modalized in terms of negative ability (*they can't get enough food*). In general then the bird (whether generic or specific) acts in a location rather than on another participant – it is construed as being, moving and dying, and the target of action, but not as impinging much onto other things.

Note that the attributive clauses are often of the circumstantial type as the location or manner of the bird functions as the Attribute being explored.

Text 4 Magazine feature

[Senser:] Women ⟦who form relationships with prisoners⟧ often [Process:mental: cognition:] believe ‖ [Senser:] they alone [Process:mental:cognition:] understand [Phenomenon:] the men, ‖ and [Process:material:] can reform [Goal:] them. [Sayer:] 'They [Process:verbal:] say, ‖ [Senser:] "I [Process:mental:cognition:] *know* [Phenomenon:] this guy;‖ [Senser:] I [Process:mental:cognition:] *know* ‖ [Carrier:] he [Process:attributive:] 's [Attribute:] good". [Carrier:] It [Process:attributive:]'s partly [Attribute:] a nurturing instinct, ‖ but [Carrier:] some prisoners [Process: attributive:] are also [Attribute:] very physically attractive and charming,' ‖ [Process:verbal:] notes [Sayer:] Sister Janet Glass, ‖ [Actor:] who [Process:material:] works [Accompaniment:] with a Catholic chaplaincy team [Location:] at Sydney's Long Bay jail.

'Often, [Carrier:] these women [Process:attributive:[1]] are [Attribute:] attracted to prisoners ‖ because [Actor:] they [Process:material:] have just ended [Goal:] a relationship,' ‖ [Sayer:] Glass [Process:verbal:] adds. [Carrier:] 'They [Process: attributive:] 're [Attribute:] empty, ‖ and [Process:mental:affect:] want [Phenomenon:] some sort of emotional fillip. [Behaver:] The prisoners are probably [Process:behavioural:verbal:[2]] lying [Receiver:] to them, ‖ but [Carrier:] they [Process:attributive:] appear [Attribute:] gallant and masculine ‖ and [Senser:] women [Process:mental:] believe [Phenomenon:] them.'

[Token:] Prison Fellowship ([Process:mental:perception:] see [Phenomenon:] main story) [Process:identifying:[3]] is [Value:] an interdenominational organization with its own programs and volunteers. Although [Process:mental:perception:] seen

[Role:guise:] as independent, [Actor:⁴] PF [Process:material:] has received [Goal:] financial support [Location:] from the Baptist Church ‖ and [Carrier:] its director, Ross Coleman, [Process:attributive:] was [Attribute:] a welfare worker with Baptist Community Services. [Sayer:] Coleman [Process:verbal:] says ‖ [Actor:] PF volunteers [Process:material:] must provide [Goal:] character references ‖ and [Process:material:] undergo [Range:] a training program ‖ before [Process:material:] starting [Goal:] the work. [Actor:] Volunteers [Process:material:] use [Goal:] pseudonyms [Location:place:] in letters ‖ and [Goal:] prisoners' replies [Process:material:] are sent [Location:] to PF headquarters ‖ and then [Process:material:] redirected. [Verbiage:] The forming of emotional attachments with prisoners [Process:verbal:⁵] is forbidden.

[Sayer:] Coleman [Process:verbal:] admits ‖ that [Phenomenon:] volunteers ⟦who transgress⟧ [Process:mental:cognition:] 'would only be detected ‖ if [Sayer:] they [Process:verbal:] told [Receiver:] us, ‖ so sometimes [Actor:] that [Process:material] could happen ‖ and [Carrier:] we [Process:attributive:] were [Attribute] oblivious to it, ‖ [Carrier:] which [Process:attributive:] is always [Attribute:] a risk...' [Sayer:] He [Process:verbal:] says ‖ [Carrier:] PF [Process:attributive:] is [Process:attributive:⁶] 'particularly concerned' ⟦with Christian prisoners, or prisoners ⟦who have found Christ whilst in prison.⟧⟧

Not unexpectedly, [Behaver:] mainstream churches often [Process:behavioural: verbal] criticise [Range:] the influence of pentecostal or charismatic Christian groups within the penal system. [Actor:] 'Some PF volunteers [Process:material:] want to baptise⁷ [Goal:] prisoners [Location:] after one week,' [Process:verbal:] says [Sayer:] Sister Glass. [Actor:] 'Some pentecostal types [Process:material:] raise [Goal:] emotional levels [Manner:] to an extraordinary degree, ‖ then [Process:mat-] leave [Actor:] prisoners [-erial:causative] to deal with [Goal:] the realities of prison life, ‖ [Carrier:] which [Process:attributive:] can be [Attribute:] dangerous,' ‖ [Process:verbal:] says [Sayer:] Sister Glass. [Senser:]'Born again prisoners [Process:mental:cognition:] believe ‖ [Actor:] they [Process:material:] can wipe out [Goal:] all memory of their crimes, ‖ because [Sayer:] Jesus [Process:verbal:] has forgiven [Target:] them.'

Notes

1. *These women are attracted to prisoners* has been taken as relational, agnate to *These women are susceptible to prisoners*. Had it been *These women are attracted by prisoners* it would have been a material process with *prisoners* as Actor.

2. In Phase 1, this was edited to read *telling lies*, a Verbal+Verbiage structure. Here, in the original version, we have *lying*, which is a behavioural clause (since *lie* cannot report another clause).

3. This has been analysed as an Identifying clause, defining Prison Fellowship, but it is difficult to determine the attributive/identifying distinction here.

4. Grammatically PF is the Actor not the Beneficiary.

5. This has been analysed as a passive. Since *forbid* can occur with a Receiver and can project a proposal (command) as in *They forbid you to go*, it has been classed as a Verbal process. The alternative analysis would see it as an Attributive, analysed as [Carrier:] *Forming relationships* [Process:attributive] *is* [Attribute:] *forbidden/undesirable*.

6. Here the presence of *particularly* suggests a relational interpretation (see Section 3.5 (iii)).

7. *Want to baptise* is analysed here as a verbal group complex realizing a single Process. The alternative analysis would be to have two clauses, the first a mental clause and the second a material one. (See Section 3.3.)

Comment Process selections in this text are spread very evenly across the four major types: material, mental, verbal and relational, with two examples of behavioural:verbal clauses also. In general then, three quarters of the Processes are of the non-material type: the text is about symbolic activity (thinking, perceiving, saying) and description of qualities more than it is about action.

The opening Theme is *Women who form relationships with prisoners* and the first two paragraphs of the text are primarily about their beliefs (construed by six mental:cognition processes). Also touched on are the prisoners' attributes and behaviour (construed by relationals and one behavioural clause). This version of reality is almost entirely reported in verbal clauses with Sister Glass as Sayer, representing the viewpoint of mainstream churches.

With the third paragraph, the Theme switches to a particular organization, Prison Fellowship – a less mainstream organization – and the Sayer shifts to PF's director with the women volunteers now construed as Actor (and prisoners' letters as Goal) as Coleman uses seven material process choices to describe their work.

In addition to the small amount of text directly in the reporter's voice, several perspectives are presented in this piece, as is typical of media texts. However, on the few occasions where the women visitors or the prisoners are Sayer or verbal Behaver, these roles are presented 'at one remove' by Sister Glass or Coleman. Sister Glass is construed almost exclusively as Sayer (and never in a Receiver or Target role) and has this role more often than any other participant.

Text 5: Procedure
[Actor:] Blackbirds [Process:material:] take [Goal:] the heaviest toll of raspberries. [Carrier:] They [Process:attributive:] are [Attribute:] more troublesome [Location: place:] in gardens [[where there [Process:existential:] is [Existent:] plenty of cover [[to nest in]], and fewer plants [[to feed from]]], than {they are troublesome} [Location: place:] in large open raspberry fields. Unless [Actor:] you [Process:material:] can devise [Goal:] a really efficient way [[of [Process:mental: affect:] scaring [Senser:] them]],|| [Actor:] you [Process:material:] will have to net. [Process:material:] To support [Goal:] the net, || [Process:material:] make [Goal:] a framework of wires or canes [[fixed to posts over the row]]. [Process:material:] Cover [Goal:] the tops of the posts [Manner:means:] with polythene or jam jars || so that [Goal:] the net [Process:material:] can be pulled [Manner:quality:] smoothly [Location:place] over them || without [Process:material:] snagging. Alternatively, [Process:material:] buy [Goal:] more expensive supports [[[Actor:] which [Process: material:] slot [Manner:quality:] together || [Process:material:] to form [Goal:] a rigid frame]]. [Carrier:] The net [Process:attributive:] should be [Attribute:] high enough above the row [[[Process:mat-] to prevent [Actor:] birds [-erial:] sitting [Location:place:] on the top and [Process:material:] pecking [Location:place:] through; [Carrier:] it [Process:attributive:] must hang [Attribute:] well clear of the sides || as [Goal:] fruit [Process:material:] is carried [Location:place:] on side shoots [[[Process:material:] growing [Location:place:] out from the canes]].

Text 6 Biographical Recount
[Goal:] George Bernard Shaw [Process:material:] was born [Location:place:] in Dublin, Ireland, [Location:time:] on July 26, 1856. [Actor:] He [Process:material:]

attended [Range:] four different schools ‖ but [Actor:] his real education [Process:material:] came [Location:place:] from a thorough grounding in music and painting, [Range:] which [Actor:] he [Process:material:] obtained [Location:place:] at home. [Location:time:] In 1871, [Goal:] he [Process:material:] was apprenticed [Location:place:] to a Dublin estate agent, and later [Actor:] he [Process:material:] worked [Role:] as a cashier. [Location:time:] In 1876, [Actor:] Shaw [Process:material:] joined [Range:] his mother and sister [Location:place:] in London, [Location:place:] where [Actor:] he [Process:material:] spent [Range:] the next nine years [Manner:quality] in unrecognized struggle and genteel poverty.

[Location:time:] From 1885 to 1898, [Actor:] he [Process:material:] wrote [Client:] for newspapers and magazines [Role:] as critic of art, literature, music and drama. But [Value:] his main interest at this time [Process:identifying:] was [Token:] political propaganda, and, [Location:time:] in 1884, [Actor:] he [Process:material:] joined [Range:] the Fabian Society. [Location:time:] From 1893 to 1939, the most active period of his career, [Actor:] Shaw [Process:material:] wrote [Goal:] 47 plays. [Location:time:] By 1915, [Carrier:] his international fame [Process:attributive:] was [Attribute:] firmly established and [Range:] productions of Candida, Man and Superman, Arms and the Man, The Devil's Disciple [Process:material:] were being played [Location:place:] in many countries of the world, from Britain to Japan. [Location:time:] In 1925, [Recipient:] the playwright [Process:material:] was awarded [Goal:] the Nobel Prize for Literature. [Location:time:] Between the ages of fifty-seven and sixty-seven, [Actor:] Shaw [Process:material:] wrote [Goal:] such dramas as Heartbreak House, Back to Methuselah, Androcles and the Lion, St. Joan. [Location:time:] During his lifetime [Goal:] he [Process:material:] was besieged [Actor:] by offers to film his plays, but [Actor:] he Process:material:] accepted [Goal:] only a few, [Value:] the most notable [Process:identifying:] being [Token:] Pygmalion, [Goal:] which [Process:material:] was adapted [Location:time:] (after his death) [Role:] as the basis for the musical My Fair Lady. [Actor:] He [Process:material:] died [Location:time:] at the age of ninety-four [Location:place:] at Ayot St. Lawrence, England, [Location:time:] on November 2, 1950.

Phase III Key to exercises

Exercise 1

1. It   was   the best movie I'd ever seen.
   Token   Value   identifying

2. It   was   pretty good.
   Carrier   Attribute   attributive

3. Isn't he   just the cutest little thing!
         Carrier   Attribute   attributive

4. One good batsman is   Lara; (another's Tendulkar.)
   Value   Token   Value   Token   identifying

5. If Scully's   a babe,   is Mulder a fox?
       Carrier   Attribute   Carrier   Attribute   attributive

6. *A dance* is   a Range   in *Do a dance*.
   Token   Value   identifying

7. 'You   're   the greatest', (he exclaimed.)
   Carrier   Attribute   attributive

8. He   's   a good player.
   Carrier   Attribute   attributive

9. That   has to be   the slowest century ever scored.
   Token   Value   identifying

10. Dolphins are   toothed whales with a clear dorsal fin...
    Token   Value   identifying

(While 'Dolphins are whales' would be attributive, the additional information provided in the Qualifier makes the 2nd participant a definition rather than a classification. The clause is thus identifying and reversible.)

Exercise 2

1. *Ulan*   means 'rain'.
   Token   Value   identifying

2. The report   reflected   their intelligence.
   Token   Value   identifying

3. The last item on the programme   said Secondary School Choir – Carol.
   Sayer   verbal

4. Our protest   shows || we're against apartheid.
   Sayer   verbal

5. It   means   peace in our time.
   Token   Value   identifying

6. It   indicates the lack of consensus on the issue.
   Token   Value   identifying

7. The clouds   suggest rain.
   Token   Value   identifying

8. The report   revealed || they're intelligent
   Sayer   verbal

9. He   indicated || he'd be there at six.
   Sayer   verbal

Exercise 3

1. I wondered <u>if she was winning</u>.   projected
2. It struck me [[that she was late]].   embedded
3. She had been upset [[she hadn't won]].   embedded
4. She expected <u>him to leave</u>.   projected
5. He rejoiced [[that she'd arrived]].   embedded
6. He was angry [[that she'd arrived]].   embedded

7. It piqued him ⟦that she'd won⟧.   embedded
8. He is hopeful <u>that she'll pass</u>   projecting

Exercise 4

1. They   tried to convince   them   that resistance was futile.
    Sayer   Receiver   verbal

2. He   'd have liked   Data   to take charge.
    Senser   mental

3. He   satisfied   them   that victory was possible.
    Sayer   Receiver   verbal

4. She   had   them consider that Tokens were Subject in the active.
    Inducer   Senser   mental

5. She   implored   them   to leave.
    Sayer   Receiver   verbal

Exercise 5

1. I   'm keeping   my windows   shut.
    Attributor   Carrier   Attribute

2. Dad   had called   their cat   Sally. (see IFG 171)
    Assigner   Token   Value

3. It   would make   her   feel   better.
    Attributor   Carrier   Attribute

4. You   can consider   it   done.
    Attributor   Carrier   Attribute

5. They   elected   her   chairperson.
    Assigner   Token   Value

6. I   declare   the games   open.
    Attributor   Carrier   Attribute

7. I   want   it   well done.
    Attributor   Carrier   Attribute

8. I   pronounce   him   the winner and new champion.
    Assigner   Token   Value

Exercise 6

1. She left town <u>exhausted</u>.   Depictive Attribute
2. She planed the edge <u>straight</u>.   Resultative Attribute
3. He kissed the cut <u>all better</u>.   Resultative Attribute
4. He cooked the onions <u>brown</u>.   Resultative Attribute
5. He walked out <u>happy</u>.   Depictive Attribute

Exercise 7

1. On the table was a vase of flowers.   existential
2. Immediately there took place a fearful conflagration. existential
3. The phenomenon occurs every few minutes.   material
4. Few of the books were on the shelf.   attributive

5. There wasn't much rain last year.   existential
6. It happens all the time.   material
7. Along the stream ran a worn path.   existential
8. The Renaissance began in Italy.   material

Exercise 8

1. She demonstrated [[that that was the case]].
   Assigner   Token   Value   identifying

2. She asserted that it was obvious.
   Sayer   verbal

3. She   proved   her point.
   Assigner   Value   identifying

4. The map indicates that this is the way.
   Sayer   verbal

5. Her actions confirmed their suspicions.
   Assigner   Value   identifying

6. He confirmed he'd be there by six.
   Sayer   verbal

7. The report proves   that   the best solution.
   Assigner   Token   Value   identifying

8. Their reply shows that to be the point.
   Assigner   Token   Value   identifying

9. Their efforts ensured a quick result.
   Assigner   Value   identifying

Exercise 9

1. Night   follows   day.
   Token   Pro:identifying&locative:temporal   Value

2. These voting patterns   resulted in   a hung Parliament.
   Token   Pro:identifying&causal   Value

3. He   faced   tremendous opposition.
   Token   Pro:ident&locative:spatial   Value

4. Taking on a new job   is related to   increased stress.
   Value   Pro:ident&accompaniment   Token

5. Pressure   influences   rainfall.
   Token   Pro:identifying&causal   Value

6. A bronzed skin   is associated with   health and beauty   in their minds.
   Value   Pro:ident&accompaniment   Token   Location

7. Spines   cover   its back.
   Token   Pro:ident&locative:spatial   Value

8. The earlier figures   correlate with   our results.
   Token   Pro:ident&accompaniment   Value

9. This chapter | concerns | the rise of imperialism.
   Token | Pro:ident&matter | Value

10. Jo Chaney | resembles | a young Marlon Brando.
    Token | Pro:ident&manner:comparison | Value

Exercise 10

1. He | was shot | in the elevator.
   Goal | Pro:material | Location
   Medium | Process | Location

2. They | were looking at | the dancers.
   Behaver | Pro:behavioural | Range
   Medium | Process | Range

3. She'd | been waiting | every evening | for ten nights.
   Actor | Pro:material | Location:time | Extent:time
   Medium | Process | Location:time | Extent:time

4. The clothes | dried | quickly | on the line.
   Actor | Pro:material | Manner | Location:place
   Medium | Process | Manner | Location:place

5. The dog | chased | the bird | in a frenzy.
   Actor | Pro:material | Goal | Manner
   Agent | Process | Medium | Manner

6. We really | enjoyed | the concert.
   Senser | Pro:mental | Phenomenon
   Medium | Process | Range

7. She | was | very unhappy.
   Carrier | Pro:attributive | Attribute
   Medium | Process | Range

8. It | made | her | (be) | very unhappy.
   Attributor | Pro:att... | Carrier | ...ributive | Attribute
   Agent | Pro... | Medium | ...cess | Range

9. Don't give | Peter | any more money, | will you?
   Pro:material | Recipient | Goal
   Process | Beneficiary | Medium

10. The whole business | excited | her.
    Phenomenon | Pro:mental | Senser
    Agent | Process | Medium

Exercise 11

1. The rice | lasted | them | a couple of weeks.
   Carrier | Pro:attrib&extent | Beneficiary | Attribute
   Medium | Process | Beneficiary | Range

2. She | kept | it | fresh | with daily watering.
   Attributor | Pro:attributive | Carrier | Attribute | Manner:means
   Agent | Process | Medium | Range | Manner:means

3. According to critics,   his dancing   reflects   tremendous artistry.
    Angle   Token   Pro:identifying   Value
    Angle   Agent   Process   Medium

4. This time   he   asked   her   the time.
    Location   Sayer   Pro:verbal   Receiver   Verbiage
    Location   Medium   Process   Beneficiary   Range

5. The region   boasts   a number of attractions   for visitors of all ages.
    Carrier   Pro:attrib&possessive   Attribute   Cause
    Medium   Process   Range   Cause

6. She   thought over   their proposal   without any assistance.
    Behaver   Pro:behavioural   Range   Accompaniment
    Medium   Process   Range   Accompaniment

7. He   sang   them   a moving ballad.
    Behaver   Pro:behavioural   Client   Range
    Medium   Process   Beneficiary   Range

8. They   walked   the horses   round and round the paddock.
    Initiator   Pro:material   Actor   Location
    Agent   Process   Goal   Location

9. She   passed   them   the contract   in light of their request.
    Actor   Pro:material   Recipient   Goal   Condition
    Agent   Process   Beneficiary   Medium   Condition

10. My daughter   proved   my harshest critic.
    Token   Pro:identifying   Value
    Agent   Process   Medium

Phase III Key to text analysis

Text 1 Description

The trail of the meat

[Carrier:]The land [Pro:attributive:] was [Attribute:] cold and white and savage. [Location:] Across it there [Pro:existential:] ran [Existent:] a thread of frozen waterway, ‖ with [Actor:] dark spruce forest [Pro:material:] looming [Location:] on either side. [Location:] Along this waterway [Pro:existential:] toiled [Existent:] a string of wolfish dogs, ‖ [Pro:material:] hauling [Goal:] a sled of birch-bark. [Location:] On the sled, along with the camp-outfit, [Pro:existential:] was lashed [Existent:] a long and narrow oblong box. [Location:] In front of the dogs, on wide snowshoes, [Pro:existential:] toiled [Existent:] a man. [Location:] Behind the sled [Pro:existential:] came [Existent:] a second man. [Location:] On the sled in the box [Pro:existential:] lay [Existent:] a third man ‖ [Carrier:] whose life [Pro:attributive:] was [Attribute/Location] at an end – a man ⟦ [Goal:] whom [Actor:] the Wild [Pro:material:] had beaten down and conquered⟧. [Value:] The bodies of the live men [Process:identifying&locative] were covered with [Token:] soft fur and leather. [Carrier:] Their faces [Pro:attributive:] were [Attribute:]

blurred and shapeless [Location:] under a coating of crystals from their frozen breath. [Location:] All around them [Pro:existential:] was [Existent:] a silence [[Actor:] which [Pro:material:] seemed to press [Location:] upon them ‖ as [Actor:] water [Pro:material:] does [Location:] upon a diver.]]

Comment In this text, two choices are very prominent, namely those of Location: spatial circumstance and existential process. Every single clause contains a Location, sometimes as a meaning feature mapped onto process or participant (Attribute), constructing the location depicted as a major motif in the narrative. In terms of PROCESS TYPE, there are twice as many existential clauses as any other type, in many of which the Subject *there* is not present and a 'material' verb is deployed. By this means the components of the scene are introduced in turn, without a totally static picture resulting.

Text 2 Historical explanation Key: nouns construing meanings that are not concrete things underlined. Concrete participants without grammatical metaphor in braces { }.

Agent [abstraction]	**Process** [caused]	**Medium** [abstraction]
the Long March	contributed to	the eventual Communist victory
it [= the Long March]	established	the leadership of Mao Zedong.
the prestige Mao acquired...	assured	his dominance.
Mao's leadership	brought an end to	the dominance of the Soviet Union...
["] The Long March	["] forged	a tightly knit army
{that [= the army]}	drew	strength.
The survivors	formed	the tough nucleus of the...Red Army...
The policy of going north...	stimulated	high morale...
[" " " "]	inspired	{patriots throughout China}
{the Red Army}	brought	message of Communism

others:
[Medium:] Mao [Process:] was challenged [Agent:] by the leader ...Zhang Guotao
[Medium:] it [Process:] passed [Location:] through twelve provinces.
[Medium:] who [Process:] would otherwise have never heard of [Range:] Communism]

Comment This text is typical of explanations in school history textbooks in that processes and qualities of various kinds are construed in nominal form as (or as parts of) participants – an effect referred to by Halliday as 'grammatical metaphor'. One such abstract participant (e.g. *the march*, Mao's *leadership*) is then represented through the ergativity structure as causing another. This 'written language' form of reasoning does not therefore rely upon the conjunctive links of causality (such as *so*, *because*, *for*) that are typical of reasoning in spoken interaction. Historians thus expand the meaning potential of the language to create an indefinitely expandable resource for construing causality. It is this resource – created by grammatical metaphor and ergative clause structure – that enables the discourse that is 'history'.

Text 3 Narrative (excerpt)

(1) The bushes twitched again. (2) Lok steadied by the tree (3) and (Lok)
   Actor   Pro:material Extent:temp Actor Pro:material Location   Beh.
   Behaver   Pro:behav
   Medium   Extent:temp Medium   Medium

gazed. (4) A head and chest faced him, half-hidden. (5) There were
Pro:behav   Token/Loc   Pro:ident&loc. Value Manner   Pro:exis.
        Agent   Med. Manner   Medium

were white bone things behind the leaves and hair.
                      Location
                      Location

(6) The man had white bone things above his eyes and under the mouth,
Carrier/Poss'or Pro:att&poss. Attribute/Possessed Location
  Medium   Range   Location

(7) so his face was longer than a face should be. (8) The man turned
    Carrier Pro:attrib. Attribute   Actor   Pro:material
    Medium   Range   Medium

sideways in the bushes (9) and looked at Lok along his shoulder. (10) A stick
Manner   Location   Pro:behav'l Range Location   Actor
                                       Carrier
Manner   Location   Range Location   Medium

rose upright (11) and there was a lump of bone in the middle. (12) Lok
Pro:material Manner   Exis. Existent   Location   Behaver
Pro:attrib Attribute
                        Medium   Location   Medium

peered at the stick and the lump of bone and the small eyes in the bone thing over
Pro:beh.   Range   Range

the face. (13) Suddenly Lok understood (14) that the man was holding the stick
                          Sen. Pro:mental:cognition   Actor   Pro:material   Goal
                          Med.   Agent   Medium

out to him (15) but neither he nor Lok could reach across the river.
Man. Location   Actor   Pro:material Location
Man. Location   Medium   Location

(16) He would have laughed if it were not for the echo of the screaming in his
    Beh. Pro:behavioural   Condition
    Med.   Condition

head. (17) The stick began to grow shorter at both ends. (18) Then it
         Carrier   Pro:attributive   Attribute Location   Actor
         Medium   Range   Location   Medium

shot out to full length again.
Pro:mat. Manner Extent: spatial Extent: temp
       Manner Manner   Extent:temp

(19) The dead tree by Lok's ear acquired a voice.
    Actor   Pro:material Range
    Medium   Range

(21) 'Clop!' (21) His ears twitched (22) and he turned to the tree.
               Behaver   Pro:behav'l   Ac. Pro:material Location
               Medium   Med.   Location

(23) By his face there had grown a twig...
    Location   Pro:existential Existent
    Location   Medium

(24) He rushed   to the edge of the water (25) and came back.
      Ac. Pro:material Location   Pro:material
      Med.   Location

(26) On either side of the open bank the bushes grew   thickly in the flood;
      Location   Actor   Pro:mat. Manner Location
      Location

                                  Medium   Manner Location

(27) they waded out (28) until at their farthest some of the leaves were opening
      Ac.   Pro:material   Location   Actor   Pro:material
      Beh. Behavioural*
      Med   Location   Medium

under water; (29) and these bushes leaned over
Location   Actor   Pro:mat. Man.
Location   Medium   Man.

Notes *An analysis of *twitch* (1, 21) and *waded out* (27) as Behavioural rather than
Material process brings out the animate quality of the natural world in this passage.
Faced is a process incorporating a circumstantial feature. An attributive version is
'was opposite to' where the circumstance is conflated with the Attribute instead of
the Process. Clause (10) is susceptible of interpretation either as a Material process
(like 18) or as a Relational process (like 17).

Comment This passage is presented from Lok's perspective and depicts a meeting
between the pre-Neanderthal Lok and a member of a more technologically sophis-
ticated tribe, who fires an arrow into the tree beside Lok. (This incident is presented
in terms of Lok's perceptions 17–24). An ergative analysis reveals only two agentive
clauses (4 and 14) – both describing the unknown and uncomprehended other. Lok
himself, like the features of the natural world around him is always and only
Medium. In the transitive analysis he can be seen to behave or act in a Location
(or Manner) but his actions do not extend to have an effect on another participant.
Halliday[1] puts forward the argument that the consistent representation of Lok and
his people in this way symbolizes their relationship with and their construal of their
environment, as well as their vulnerability when in contact with the group presented
by the author as 'agentive'.

Text 4 Written exposition Note: analysis of interpersonal structures is repeated here
together with analysis of transitivity.

TV Violence

It is   essential for the well-being of the Youth of Australia that we adopt a less tolerant
C.. Pro:att Attribute... ...Carrier............................
Su. Fi   Complement... ...Subject............................
Mood..   Residue———————————————————————— ...Mood————

attitude to violence in television. It has been known for some time that young children
.... Ph Pro:mental   Extent   ..Phenomenon.....
.... S.. Fi Predicator Adjunct   ..Subject...............
———————————————— Mood.. Residue —————————— ...Mood————

[1]Halliday, M.A.K. 1971: Linguistic function and literary style: an inquiry into the language of William
Golding's 'The Inheritors'. In Chatman, S. (ed) *Literary style: a symposium*, New York: Oxford
University Press, pp. 362–400. Reprinted in Halliday, M.A.K. 1973: *Explorations in the functions of
language*, London: Arnold, pp. 103–40.

can be disturbed by the violent scenes presented by the television scene. No apparent
.... Range...............
.... Subject.............
————————————————————————————————————— Mood——— —

effort however has been made by either the producers of children's programmes or the
.... Pro:material Actor...
.... Fi Predicator Adjunct...
————— Mo. Resdiue—————————————————————————

programmers of children's programmes to take this into account: one only has to look at
....Range (cont)..................... Be.   Pro:behavioural
.... Subject (cont)................. Su Adj. Fi Pred   A..
————————————————————— ..Mood———————— Mood———— Residue—

the extraordinary popular cartoon 'Teenage Mutant Ninja Turtles'. At some schools it
Range... Location   C..
Adjunct.. Adjunct   S..
Residue——————————————————————————————— Residue———-- M.

was necessary to ban the accessories associated with the programme because children
Pro:att Attribute ...Carrier.. Actor
Fi   Comp.   ..Subject.. Subject
..o.. Resid   ..od——————————————————— Mood——

were engaging in fights in the playground, emulating their cartoon heroes; this sort of
Pro:material Range Location   Pro:material Range................................. Carrier........
Fi   Pred.   Adjunct Adjunct   Predicator Complement   Subject.........
— Residue—————————————— Residue——————————— Mood..........

situation is deplorable, this incident also highlights how impressionable young children are.
.... Pro Attribute   Token   Identifying   Value...............................
.... Fi Comp.   Subject   Fi/Pred.   Complement...............................
——— Residue   Mood——   —Residue ———————————

There is a definite danger that children, after years of exposure to violence on television,
       Ex. Existent...
Su   Fi   Complement..
Mood—   Residue——————————————————————————

come to accept that violence is an acceptable solution to conflict. It   is   of vital
.... C... Pro:att. Att/Matter
.... S.. Fi   Adjunct
————————————————————————————————— Mood...... Residue–

importance for the future of Australia that young people realize that violence is not to
.... Carrier................................
.... Subject................................
——————————————————————————— .. Mood——————————

be condoned, nor applauded. It is also essential that young people do not associate
.... C..Pro:att.Attribute ..Carrier...
.... S.. Fi   Comp.   ..Subject...
————————————————— Mood.. Residue   .. Mood———————————

violence with bravery and heroism, which is	an inevitable outcome	if	we persist in
Token	Pro:id.	Value	Init
Su	Fi	Complement	Su	Fi/Pred
Mood		Residue———	Mood	Residue

allowing	our children	to be influenced	by the garbage that fills our screens every
	Goal	Pro:material	Actor..
Pred...	Comp.	..Pred.............	Adjunct..

afternoon and evening, and succeeds in passing for entertainment.	It is possible	that
	C..	ProAttribute ..C
	S..	Fi Comp	..S
	Mood..	Res	Mo

children come to accept violence as an inevitable, but vaguely unpleasant part of the

..od ——

world. If	this unfortunate scenario	becomes	true,	we	will	never combat	violence.
....	Carrier.........................	Pro:attrib	Att.	Ac		Pro:mat.	Goal
....	Subject.......................	Fi/Pred	Comp	Su	Fi	Adj	Pred./	Comp.
——	Mood ———————		Residue	Mood_____		Residue._____

It	is	of utmost importance,	then,	that the television industry	assumes	a sense of
C..	Pro:at.	Attribute/Matter		..Carrier................................
S..	Fi	Adjunct		.. Subject................................
Mood..	Residue ———			..Mood————————————————

responsibility by carefully regulating the materials that appear in children's programmes.

——

Comment One of the striking features of the transitivity selections in this text is the use of attributive relational clauses to modalize facts: *it was necessary..., it is of vital importance..., it is also essential..., it is possible..., it is of utmost importance.* In these examples the Carrier is discontinuous, in order to render the modality as what Halliday refers to as explicitly objective. The discontinuity reflects the stress the grammar undergoes to place ideational resources (relational attributive processes) in the service of interpersonal ones (MODALITY); grammatical metaphor in other words engenders the structural tension.

Embedded clauses: transitivity analysis

that	we	adopt	a less tolerant attitude to violence in television.
	Ac	Pro:mat	Range

that	young children	can be disturbed	by the violent scenes presented by the TV scene.
	Senser	Pro:mental	Phenomenon———————————————

presented	by the television scene
Pro:material	Actor

to take	this	into account
Pro:men..	Ph	.. tal

to ban   the accessories associated with the programme
Pro:mat   Goal

associated with   the programme
Pro:identifying&accompaniment   Value

how impressionable   young children   are.
Attribute/Manner   Carrier   Pro:attributive

that   children   come to accept   that violence is an acceptable solution to conflict
      Senser   Pro:mental   Phenomenon:fact

violence   is   an acceptable solution to conflict.
Carrier   Pro:att   Attribute

that young people realize ‖ that violence is not to be condoned, ‖ nor applauded.
    Senser   Pro:mental   Phenom   Pro:mental   Pro:behavioural

that young people do not associate violence with bravery and heroism
    Assigner   Pro:identify...   Token   ...ing   Value

fills our screens every afternoon and evening‖and succeeds in passing for entertainment
Mat Range   Extent:temporal   Pro:attributive   Attribute

that the television industry assumes a sense of responsibility
   Actor   Pro:mat   Range

by carefully regulating the materials ⟦that   appear   in children's programmes⟧.
Manner   Pro:material   Goal   Carrier Pro:attrib Location/Attribute

Key to Chapter 5: The clause complex

Phase I Key to exercises

Exercise 1

1. Old Mother Hubbard
   Went to the cupboard ||
   To fetch her poor dog a bone |||
   When she got there ||
   The cupboard was bare ||
   And so the poor dog had none
2. The Randwick mayor said || the Council was very enthusiastic about the new bowling centre for the Randwick shopping centre. ||| He said || he hoped || the AMF company would have the same success as the Manhattan bowling centre at Mascot, || which opened last year.
3. His cheeks were ruddy, || and his red, moist mouth was noticeable || because he laughed so often.
4. The Thai do not kill animals, || so the meat butchering is left to the Muslims and Chinese.

Exercise 2

1. Mrs Morel was full of information || when she got home from Nottingham.
         α   β
2. If you want to learn it, || you must begin.
      β   α
3. Roger remained, || watching the littluns.
      α   β
4. Seeing Ralph under the palms, || he sat by him.
      β   α
5. It was a dismal affair, || which might have belonged to Maurice Barres in youth.
      α   β

6. Whenever I'm having a good time ‖ he wants to go home.
        β   α
7. I looked back at my cousin, ‖ who began to ask me questions in her low,
                                                    thrilling voice.
          α   β

Exercise 3

1. William had just gone away to London, ‖ and his mother missed his money.
              1   2
2. He sent ten shillings once or twice, ‖ but he had many things to pay for at first.
          1   2
3. If a quarrel took place, ‖ the whole play was spoilt.
          β   α
4. In a few minutes she put on her coat, ‖ to walk the two and a half miles to the
                                                    station.
              α   β
5. Mrs Morel talked again to Paul, ‖ who was helping her with her housework.
          α   β
6. He resented Mr Bojanus's negleejay, ‖ he was pained and wounded by the
                                                    aspersion.
          1   2
7. Folding him in her arms, ‖ she swayed slightly from side to side with love.
          β   α
8. Throw it away ‖ or give it to your sister.
          1   2
9. Whilst Morel was progressing favourably in the hospital,‖ the family was
                                                    extraordinarily
                                                    happy and peaceful.
              β   α
10. The Thai do not kill animals ‖ so the meat butchering is left to the Muslims
                                                    and Chinese.
              1   2

Exercise 4

1. She had already told him ‖ she could not dance.
              α   β
2. She knew ‖ that it was not everything.
      α   β
3. Tell me ‖ where it hurts you.
      α   β
4. It would all come to an end soon, ‖ she hoped.
          β   α
5. She never believed ‖ that her life belonged to Paul Morel.
          α   β
6. She thought ‖ they lived in his own house.
          α   β

Exercise 5

1. Sometimes Mrs Morel would say: ‖ "You ought to tell your father."
              1   2

2. But the Sister says ‖ that it's the pain.
          α   β

3. The three children realized ‖ that it was very bad for their father.
          α   β

4. "Now I'll die," ‖ he said, in a detached, dreamy voice.
        1   2

5. I wish ‖ this boiler was at the bottom of the sea!
      α   β

6. He felt ‖ his son did not want him.
        α   β

7. Ask him ‖ if the London train's come.
        α   β

8. Paul knew ‖ that this girl, Louise Travers, was now Dawes' woman.
       a   β

9. She wondered ‖ who had been talking to him.
        α   β

10. "Who has been talking to him?", ‖ she wondered.
        1   2

Exercise 6

1. He didn't offer to help, ‖ but just watched her struggling.
        1   +2

2. Mrs Morel talked again to Paul, ‖ who was helping her with her housework.
       α   =β

3. It was getting very late; ‖ it was past ten o'clock.
        1   =2

4. It matters more than her cleverness, ‖ which, after all, would never get her
                            to heaven.
       α   =β

5. Take it inside ‖ or put it over there.
        1   +2

6. As well as headlining a special meal, ‖ meat composes several Thai delicacies.
      +β   α

7. Now he would transform it; ‖ he would add to it its better half
        1   =2

8. He was accompanied by his wife, ‖ whose manner was quite hostile.
       α   =β

9. The incident had no serious consequences, ‖ apart from upsetting his cousin.
       α   +β

10. He was very clever, very artistic; ‖ he seemed to know all the new things,
                           all the interesting people.
        1   =2

Exercise 7

1. If a quarrel took place, ‖ the whole play was spoilt.
      ×β   α

2. In a few minutes she was gone, ‖ to walk the two and a half miles to
                           Keston Station.
       α   ×β

3. They drew apart; ‖ they spent less and less time together.
        1   =2

4. Whilst Morel was progressing favourably in the hospital, ‖ the family was extraordinarily happy and peaceful.
        ×β   α

5. She dared not look at him, ‖ but sat with her head bowed.
        1   +2

6. To Miriam he more or less condescended, ‖ because she seemed so humble.
        α   ×β

7. His face quivered ‖ as he looked at his mother.
        α   ×β

8. The clouds empty their watery load ‖ and are then dispelled by the sun.
        1   ×2

9. Mrs Morel was not anxious to move into the Bottoms, ‖which was already 12 years old.
        α   =β

10. The women did not spare her, at first; ‖ for she was superior.
        1   ×2

Exercise 8

1. Sometimes Mrs Morel would say: ‖ "You ought to tell your father."
        1   "2

2. But the Sister says ‖ that it's the pain.
        α   "β

3. The three children realized ‖ that it was very bad for their father.
        α   'β

4. "Now I'll die," ‖ he said, in a detached, dreamy voice.
        "1   2

Note that the numbering of paratactic clauses simply indicates the sequence in which they occur. If the locution comes first, this is indicated by placing the logico-semantic symbol (") against the 1, not by marking the projection as 2.

5. I wish ‖ this boiler was at the bottom of the sea!
        α   'β

6. He felt ‖ his son did not want him.
        α   'β

7. Ask him ‖ if the London train's come.
        α   "β

8. Paul knew ‖ that this girl, Louise Travers, was now Dawes' woman.
        α   'β

9. She wondered ‖ who had been talking to him.
        α   'β

10. "Who has been talking to him?", ‖ she wondered.
        '1   2

Phase I Key to text analysis

Text 1 Descriptive report

The numbat is an unmistakeable slender marsupial with a pointed muzzle and short erect ears. ||| The body is reddish brown || **but** the rump is much darker || **and** has about six white bars across it. ||| The eye has a black stripe through it || **and** the long bushy tail is yellowish. ||| The toes are strongly clawed and very effective in digging out termites. ||| The tongue is extremely long, as in all mammalian ant or termite eaters. ||| Unlike most marsupials, the numbat is active during the day. ||| It shelters in hollow logs. ||| It was once relatively common ||| **but*** now lives only in a small area of S.W. South Australia.

Comment Four clause complexes contain more than one clause. All links are paratactic extension, providing an accretion of information about the animal's appearance, and a contrast between former and present habitat.

Text 2 Taxonomizing report

There are many species of whales. ||| They are conveniently divided into toothed and baleen categories. ||| The toothed whales are found worldwide in great numbers. ||| The largest is the Sperm whale,|| =**which** grows to about the size of a boxcar. ||| Other species familiar to Canadians are the Beluga or white whale, the Narwhal with its unicorn-like tusk, the Killer whale or Orca, the Pilot or Pothead whale,<<= **which** is commonly stranded on beaches>>, the Spotted and Spinner Dolphins,<<= **that** create a problem for tuna seiners>>, and the Porpoises || =**which** we commonly see along our shores. |||
 There are fewer species of the larger baleen whales, || = **that** filter krill and small fish through their baleen plates. ||| The largest is the Blue whale || =**which** is seen frequently in the Gulf of St Lawrence. ||| It reaches a length of 100 feet and a weight of 200 tons. ||| The young are 25 feet long at birth || + **and** [they] put on about 200 lbs a day on their milk diet. ||| Other species are: the Fins <<=**which** at a length of 75 ft blow spouts of 20 ft,>> the fast swimming Seis, the Grays <<= **(which** are) so commonly seen on migrations along our Pacific coast between Baja California and the Bering Sea,>> the Bowheads of Alaskan waters, the Rights, <<=**(which** are) so seriously threatened,>> the Humpbacks <<= **(which** are) enjoyed by tourists in such places as Hawaii and Alaska>>, the smaller Bryde's whales, and the smallest Minke whales, || =**which** continue to be abundant worldwide.

Comment Apart from one instance (*and*), paratactic expansion is deployed in this text not to extend clauses but rather to extend groups into group complexes, as different kinds of whales are listed. All the other clause complex links are hypotactic elaborating ones, building information by specifying a key characteristic of the various types of whales listed.

Text 3 Dialogue in narrative Key: Expanding links in CAPS, all other relations are projecting. Type of interdependency between the clauses set out on each line is indicated on the right.

---

*but has been interpreted in each case as adversative: e.g. *whereas it was once common, it now lives...;* see Section 3.5.1.

	PROJECTION
"What's your interest?" ‖ she asked. ‖‖	parataxis
"Oh," <<I replied breezily,>>	parataxis
"I wondered ‖ if it had anything to do with the National Bank robbery." ‖‖	hypotaxis
She didn't think ‖ it did. ‖‖	hypotaxis
'You got anything ⟦to tell us on that score?⟧' ‖ she asked. ‖‖	parataxis
I didn't. ‖‖	
I cast my line again into the Chinatown killing. ‖‖	
She said ‖ as usual no-one had seen anything. ‖‖	hypotaxis
Even in reasonably broad daylight. ‖‖	
I said ‖ I might have. ‖‖	hypotaxis
She found ‖ that [to be] interesting. ‖‖	hypotaxis
I asked her ‖ if the victim had been wearing a tie. ‖‖	hypotaxis
She said ‖ no. ‖‖	parataxis
I asked her ‖ if he'd been wearing kung fu shoes. ‖‖	hypotaxis
She said ‖ what is this, twenty questions? ‖‖	parataxis
I said ‖ no. ‖‖	parataxis
I told her ‖ I'd seen ⟦a man acting suspiciously in the Ch... G...⟧ ‖‖	hypotaxis
She asked ‖ what I'd been doing there ‖‖	hypotaxis
BUT I said ‖ it was irrelevant. ‖‖	hypotaxis
I said ‖ I'd seen the same man later that afternoon in Cabramatta. ‖‖	hypotaxis
She asked ‖ what I was doing in Cabramatta. ‖‖	hypotaxis
I said ‖ it was irrelevant. ‖‖	hypotaxis
I said ‖ it was a long shot ‖‖	hypotaxis
AND probably had nothing to do with anything ‖‖	
BUT it might be worth asking a few discreet questions around the place. ‖‖	
Check out the snooker hall. ‖‖	
I asked her ‖ if she could tell me any more about the victim. ‖‖	hypotaxis

Text 4 Argument Key: hypotactic links in **bold**, paratactic in CAPS.

I think ‖ [β **idea:**] governments like the Federal Government are necessary ‖ **because** they help to keep our economic system in order ‖ AND <<**if** any problems occur>> the Federal Government will more or less straighten it out. ‖‖

I also think ‖ [β **idea:**] that the State Government isn't necessary ‖ **because** there is the local Government, ‖ **which** is known as a shire or municipality, ‖ AND there is hardly any use for the State government ‖ **because** the local governments do all the work. ‖‖

Comment There are five clauses in the first complex and six in the second. This average of 5.5 clauses per complex creates a text that is 'grammatically intricate'[1] in the way typical of spoken, rather than written, language. It therefore comes across as 'speech written down'.

[1]Halliday, M.A.K. 1985: *Spoken and written language*. Geelong, Vic: Deakin University Press. [republished by Oxford University Press, 1989.]

Seven out of nine relations are hypotactic, a proportion which makes the text more similar to Text 2 than Text 1. However it contrasts with both Texts 1 and 2 in the logico-semantic choices made. There is a greater variety, with projection as well as expansion deployed. Projection is of ideas and occurs because of the use of *I think* as a 'modality metaphor' (see Chapter 3). Within expansion the dominant choice is enhancement (*because, if, because, because*) rather than extension or elaboration. All these characteristics relate to the fact that the text is arguing a position rather than simply documenting information.

Phase II Key to exercises

Exercise 1

1. They lived , <<she thought,>> in his own house.
2. Mrs Blackmore's car, <<which can't be more than two years old,>> is already full of rust.
3. Meg and Paul, <<although they despised the others,>> remained with the group ‖ and took part in their schemes.
4. The older man, <<who had been sitting in the corner ‖ and seemed uninterested,>> suddenly got up ‖ and approached them.
5. Marco Polo << journeying through Yunnan in the thirteenth century, ‖ after it had been conquered by the Mongols,>> observed that the people ate their meat raw.

Exercise 2

1. So that the children could fetch the money,‖ school closed early on Friday afternoons.
   $^{\times}\beta$ α
2. Paul always examined the big grass bank, ‖ because in it grew tiny pansies.
   α $^{\times}\beta$
3. He knew the order of the names ‖ – they went according to stall number.
   1        $^{=}2$
4. If they got half a pound ‖ they felt exceedingly happy.
   $^{\times}\beta$ α
5. Well, there wasn't any blackberries, ‖ so we went over Misk Hills.
   1        $^{\times}2$

   Note that the structure here is paratactic even though it construes cause-effect. An effect need not be 'dependent' on the cause in terms of grammatical interdependency relations.

6. He nodded sympathetically to Miriam, ‖ and became gently sarcastic to Beatrice.
   1        $^{+}2$
7. "Well, you can't be stuck in the house for ever," ‖ Annie agreed.
   "1   2

   Note that the numbering of paratactic clauses simply indicates the sequence in which they occur. If the locution comes first, this is indicated by placing the logico-semantic symbol (") against the 1, not by marking the projection as 2.

8.   Agatha says ‖ you're as good as any teacher anywhere.

         α   "β

9.   He held her wrists ‖ while she wrestled with him.

         α   ˣβ

10. He bent forward to her ‖ to light his cigarette at hers.

         α   ˣβ

Exercise 3

1.   Hurriedly taking off her bodice, ‖ she crouched at the boiler.

          ˣβ   α

    (As she hurriedly took off her bodice, she crouched at the boiler.)

2.   The valley was full of corn, ‖ brightening in the sun.

          α   =β

    (The valley was full of corn, which was brightening in the sun.)

3.   Roger remained, ‖ watching the littluns.

         α   ⁺β

    (Roger remained and watched the littluns.)

4.   Mr Pappleworth arrived, <<chewing a chlorodyne gum,>> at about twenty to nine.

         α...   << ⁺β >>

    (Mr Pappleworth arrived and was chewing a cholorodyne gum.)

5.   The Thai << being Buddhist>> do not kill animals.

   α...   << ˣβ >>

    (The Thai, because they are Buddhist, do not kill animals.)

6.   On retiring to bed, ‖ the father would come into the sickroom.

       ˣβ   α

    (When he retired to bed, the father would come into the sickroom).

Exercise 4

1.   1   Paul cleared away,

     ⁺2   put on the kettle,

     ⁺3   and set the table.

2.   1   Add the pork

     ⁺2 α and stir fry

       ˣ β until it changes colour.

3.   ˣβ   If you're scared of someone

     α 1 you hate him

      ⁺ 2 and you can't stop thinking about him.

4.   α   They thought

  'β α anything might happen

     ˣ β if one came from London.

5.   1 1 Percival finished his whimper

     ⁺ 2 and went on playing,

   ˣ2   for the tears had washed the sand away.

6.   "1   "Now I'll die",

    2 α he said, in a detached, dreamy voice,

     ˣ β as though he were the dying motion of the swing.

7.   "1 α "You know

   ' β that you like them,"

    2   she said.

8. [×]β   Hurriedly taking off her bodice,
    α α she crouched at the boiler
      [×] β while the water ran slowly into her lading-can.
    The notation indicates the status of the first clause as Theme of the complex. See
    3.6 (iii)
9.   1 α She complained about the incident to my father
       [×] β when he returned from work
     ⁺2 α and was mortified
       [×] β when he laughed
       [×] γ until the tears rolled down his cheeks.
10. "1 α "I wish
      ' β this boiler was at the bottom of the sea!"
      2 α she exclaimed,
       [×] β wriggling the handle impatiently.
11. 1   The minister glanced several times at his watch,
    [×]2 1   so I took him aside
      ⁺ 2 α and asked him
       [×]β to wait for half an hour.
12. 1   He went to the station in a sort of dream,
    ⁺2 α   and was at home
      ⁺ β α without realizing
        ' β he had moved out of her street.

Exercise 5
1. Soon the larvae begin to hatch || and the queen must feed them.
2. He hopes to make this a particularly boring campaign.
3. She had decided, ineptly, || that everything was very very sad.
4. He tried frantically to escape || but it was no use.
5. Maybe he means || it's some sort of ghost.
6. Why couldn't you say || there wasn't a beast?
7. He wanted to crush her onto his breast || to ease the ache there.
8. "Why on earth don't you let him stop?" || he exclaimed.
9. The heat seemed to increase || until it became a threatening weight.
10. I had expected || that he would be a florid and corpulent person in his middle
    years.
11. He began to poke about in the water, || while the brilliant fish flicked away.
12. "You must make him come back", || he insisted.
13. She told him || not to hurry; || there was plenty of time.
14. "I didn't mean to interrupt your lunch," || I said.
15. He would dearly have liked || the children to talk to him, || but they could not.

Exercise 6
1. I was one of the few guests [[who had actually been invited]].
2. I'm the first man [[who ever made a stable out of a garage]].
3. Next year she will be issued with a school bus pass ||which will save us a lot of
    money.
4. We all looked in silence at Mrs Wilson, || who removed a strand of hair from
    over her eyes || and looked back at us with a brilliant smile.
5. I wanted somebody [[who wouldn't gossip]].

6. I glanced at Daisy, ‖ who was staring between Gatsby and her husband.
7. He was a photographer ‖ and had made the dim enlargement of Mrs Wilson's mother ⟦which hovered like an ectoplasm on the wall⟧.
8. Those littluns ⟦who had climbed back on the twister⟧ fell off again.
9. They spoke to the gardener, ‖ whose wheezy cough interrupted every question.
10. Japan had a major earthquake in Hokkaido a year ago ‖ which shook the island with a magnitude of 7.9 on the Richter scale.

Exercise 7
1. I could have sworn ‖ I heard ⟦the owl-eyed man break into ghostly laughter⟧.
2. When Mrs Morel entered, ‖ she saw ⟦him almost running through the door to the stairs⟧.
3. They heard ⟦their father throw down his boots ‖ and tramp upstairs in his stockinged feet⟧.
4. I can remember ⟦Tautina O'Brien coming there at least once⟧.
5. ⟦Playing the piano in the evening⟧ had always calmed her ‖ but now she could not play.
6. I thought ‖ that it was a fire ‖ and tried to get out.
7. Sometimes they watched ⟦the three or four lamps growing tinier and tinier ‖ swaying down the fields in the darkness⟧.

Exercise 8
1. extending
2. enhancing
3. enhancing
4. enhancing
5. enhancing
6. extending
7. enhancing
8. enhancing
9. extending
10. extending

Phase II Key to text analysis

Text 1 Parent-child conversation

C: How could birds die?
M: ...Like the one in the garden, are you thinking of?

1   α   Well, sometimes birds die
 × β   when they get very old,
+2 α   or maybe they get sick
 × β   because they got some disease,
+3   or maybe a cat got it.
1   α   Baby birds sometimes die
 × β   when they fall out the nest,
+2 α   or, in the winter – << >> – birds might die
 <<×β>> <<if you were in a cold place>>
 × γ   because they can't get enough food.

```
1  α   C:  Yeah, but what happens
  × β        if one bird falls out
×2  α         and then – and << >> it flies
  <<× β>>     <<when it's just about at the ground>>
  × β   M:  Yes, well if it's big enough to fly
    α         it'll be all right.
```

Comment Mother's speech is structured (through paratactic extension) as a series of alternative propositions in relation to the child's query. Many of these propositions are themselves modified, in terms of hypotactic temporal, causal or conditional relations. The relations between clauses therefore harmonize with the strong presence of modality within the clauses.

One of the alternatives put forward by M: *baby birds sometimes die* || *when they fall out the nest* is perhaps puzzling to the child, who does not realize that newly hatched birds cannot necessarily fly. He therefore creates a complex of four clauses to construct a hypothetical sequence of events to probe the issue further. The informal dialogic construal of knowledge thus provides contexts where children may have cause to deploy (and extend) their available clause complexing resources.

Text 2 Recount

```
  × β        If I would be too late in the morning
    α        the station owner would pour cold water over me.

1  α         Sometimes I would watch the cattle
  × β  1     while they had their lunch
     + 2     or got ready in the morning,
+2  1  α     and <<       >> he would yell out from the camp:
  <<× β>>    <<if a calf would walk away>>.
  " 2  1     "Hey, what do you think,
     = 2     don't you want that calf, eh?"

    α        I wouldn't know,
  ×  β       because I was looking in another direction.

1            He would come up
+ 2  1       and say:
    " 2       "You've got to start watching those cattle."

    α        I couldn't talk back to him
  ×  β       because I was too small.

1            That bloke always did that to me,
+ 2          and he would give me a good beating with a whip.

  × β        When I was working there
    α        I really had a terrible life with that man.

  × β        And if I didn't do my job,
    α  1     he would starve me for two days
      + 2    and just give me dry damper.

  × β        And if I didn't do my job well,
    α        he would next time just give me a piece of meat.
```

Comment An oral monologic text like this, which is reconstructing past experience, can be expected to be more grammatically intricate than a written text documenting or interpreting experience, partly because it does not involve nominalization. This text may well have been more intricate in its original spoken form than in the written version which was published. (For a transcription of an oral narrative, see Phase III, Text 1.) Note that both paratactic and hypotactic relations are in evidence, with enhancing relations to the fore as the speaker explains the reasons and conditions for the incidents related.

Text 3 Children's story (opening)

1	My name's Laura
+ 2	and this is my place.
	I turned ten last week.
	Our house is the one with the flag on the window.
1 α	Tony says
" β	it shows
" γ	we're on Aboriginal land,
+2 α	but I think
' β	it means the colour of the earth, back home.
1	Mum and Dad live here too,
+ 2	and Terry and Lorraine, and Aunty Bev, and Tony and Diane and their baby Dean [live here].
1	He's my nephew
+ 2	and he's so cute!
1	We come from Bourke,
×2 α	but Dad thought
' β	there'd be more jobs in the city.
	This [picture] is me and Gully.
α	I have to keep her on a lead
×β	because she chases cars.
	She comes from Bourke too.
α	I guess
' β	she thinks
' γ	they're sheep.
	This is a map of my place.
	We've got a McDonalds right on the corner!
1	In the McDonald's yard, there's this big tree,
+2 α	and << >> it always makes me feel good.
<<×β>>	<<whenever I sit in it>>
1	There's a canal down the bottom of the street,

```
+2  α      and Mum says
   "β      it must have been a creek once.
 1          It's too dirty [[to swim in]],
×2  1      but Tony made me a tin canoe
   +2      and now some of the other kids are making them too.

×β  1      If you tip over
   +2      and go in,
 α  1      the water tastes yucky
   +2      and your parents go wild.

 α          For my birthday, Mum said
 "β        we could have tea at McDonalds!

 1          We sat in the outside bit, under the tree,
+2         and it felt just like home!
```

Note on *buts*

Tony says it shows we're on Aboriginal land, but I think it means the colour of the earth, back home.

Taken as extending: adversative – 'Tony says ... **but in contrast** I think ...' (or if Tony is interpreted as an authority: enhancing: causal-conditional: concessive – 'Although Tony says, I nevertheless think ...').

We come from Bourke but Dad thought there'd be more jobs in the city

Taken as causal-conditional concessive –'**although** we come from Bourke (which might lead you to expect that we'd be living there) **nevertheless** Dad thought there'd be more jobs in the city (and so we're here).

It's too dirty to swim in, but Tony made me a tiny canoe

Taken as causal-conditional: concessive – '**although** it's too dirty to swim in, Tony **nevertheless** made me ... ' Alternatively it could be interpreted as extending: varying: replacive – 'It's too dirty, **and instead** Tony made me ... ' The example may be a blend of these two senses: 'It's too dirty to swim in, **so instead** Tony made me ... ' See Phase III for practice discriminating extending from enhancing *but* relations.

Comment The text is grammatically intricate in parts, successfully approximating the voice of a ten-year-old speaking. Most of the expanding relations are paratactic, this being the unmarked choice for extension – the principal choice for adding information here. There is no dialogue in the excerpt but through hypotactic projection various members of the family group are made known to the reader through their reported representations of experience.

Text 4 Written argument

```
 α              I think
'β  α          governments like the Federal Government are necessary
  ×β  1        because they help to keep our economic system in order
    +2  α      and <<  >> the Federal Govt will more or less straighten it out.
   <<×β>>      <<if any problems occur>>.

 α              I also think
'β  α          that the State Government isn't necessary
  ×β  1  α     because there is the local Government
      =β       which is known as a shire or municipality.
```

ᐩ2 α   and there is hardly any use for the State government
  ˣβ   because the local governments do all the work.

Comment The notation displays the grammatical intricacy of this text and the similar structuring of the two paragraphs. As analysed, the modality metaphor *I think* projects the whole paragraph in each case. Alternatively the *because* clause could be regarded as the justification for the opinion (modality) :

α α   I think
  ' β   governments like the Federal Government are necessary
  ˣβ   because...

Phase III Key to exercises

Exercise 1

1. It infuriated him ⟦that she could not give him an answer⟧.
2. It is instructive ⟦to recall the invitation for expressions of interest⟧.
3. ⟦That its likely market value had diminished⟧ had certainly occurred to him.
4. It is good ⟦to be seen as the great reformer⟧.
5. It wasn't true ⟦that he had seen her⟧.
6. ⟦To understand the natural order⟧ is a good thing.

Exercise 2

1. ⟦Whatever she sees⟧ she wants.
    Note the clause can be made passive: Whatever she sees is wanted by her. c.f. she wasn't wanted by anyone.

2. They didn't like ⟦what she was saying⟧.
    Note, mental processes of reaction do not project ideas. The wh- clause can be Theme predicated: 'it was what she was saying they didn't like' and can become Subject of the ranking clause. c.f. He wasn't much liked there by anyone.

3. Tell me ‖ what to do next.
    Note a quoted version is possible: Say to me "Do such-and-such next."

4. She asked ‖ if he was going by car.
    Note that this is a reported yes/no question: "Is he going by car?"

5. She asked ‖ where he was going.
    Note that this is a reported wh- interrogative: "Where is he going?"

6. *Note that Example 6 is ambiguous out of context.*
    I don't understand ⟦why you won't come out frankly ‖ and tell me.⟧
    This reading is equivalent to 'I don't understand the reason why you won't...'

    I don't understand ‖why you won't come out frankly ‖ and tell me.
    This reading is expecting an answer to the question "Why won't you come out frankly...?"

7. They didn't explain ‖ how to mix the colours.

Note that a quoted version is possible: They explained "You mix the colours like this."

8.   I hate ⟦how he always interrupts you with petty little queries and details.⟧
      Note the mental affection: reaction process here and possibility of Theme predication "It's how he interrupts you ... that I hate."

9.   *Note that Example 10 is ambiguous out of context*
      He doesn't know ‖ where they go on holiday.
      Perhaps the most likely reading – suggesting he has not been told the name of the place they spend their holidays.

      He doesn't know ⟦where they go on holiday⟧.
      This reading is equivalent to 'he isn't acquainted with that particular holiday place.'

Exercise 3

1.   The common factor is the belief ⟦that New Zealand has gone too far along the monetarist-free market path⟧.
2.   Our understanding was ⟦that they would accept the money as final payment⟧.
3.   Police believe ‖ the fire was lit on a pile of carpet in the stairwell.
4.   I see ‖ I have given the impression ⟦that the events of three nights several weeks apart were all that absorbed me⟧.
      Note that 'see' has a cognitive not perceptive meaning here.
5.   He noted (the fact) ⟦that civic leaders did not greet him ‖ wearing jacket and tie⟧.
6.   I read somewhere ⟦that the sun's getting hotter every year⟧.
7.   I would have accepted without question the information ⟦that Gatsby sprang from the swamps of Louisiana⟧.
8.   They were convinced ⟦that it was theirs for a few words in the right key⟧.
9.   She implied ‖ that a dozen chefs awaited her orders there.
10.   That's ⟦because your mother wanted to show you off⟧.
11.   You kid yourself ‖ he's all right really.
12.   One suspects ‖ they will have the same problem.
13.   NASA's satellite had discovered landmark evidence ⟦that the universe did in fact begin with the 'Big Bang'⟧.
14.   One prediction ⟦that comes out of the theory of inflation⟧ is ⟦that the mix of big and small spots in the early universe should follow a characteristic pattern⟧.

Exercise 4

1.   clause
2.   clause
3.   circumstance
4.   clause
5.   clause

Exercise 5

1.   hypotactic
2.   paratactic
3.   paratactic
4.   paratactic
5.   hypotactic
6.   hypotactic

Phase III Key to text analysis

Text 1 Conversational narrative

			There's lots of things that happen that you just take for granted really.
×β			When we first moved down here from Orange
α			we lost one of our bitches, the first day.
α 1			And we advertised
⁺2			and put little notes all around
×β			to try and get her back.
1			Anyway about a week later a man came down
⁺2 1			and asked
"2*			had we lost a dog.*
α			And he said
"β			he thought
'γ			he knew
'δ			where there was one in a yard.
1			So my husband went up
⁺2			and looked over the fence
⁺3			and there was our dog, only about a block away.
1			And they also had a male corgi there,
⁺2			and the two were running together.
1			So he brought ours home
⁺2 α			and he went back up later
×β α			to let the people know
'β 1			that we had her,
⁼2			that he'd brought her home,
⁺3			and offered to pay the food that she'd eaten for the week.
			Anyway, the people were very good.
α			I don't think
'β			they'd tried to steal her or anything like that.
α 1			But anyway, about two days after that, two big boys came down –
⁼2			they were about seventeen –
×β α			to let us know
'β α			that Mummy said
"β α α			not to be worried
'β			that the bitch would have puppies
×β α			because << >> she locked them up separately at night.
≪×β≫			<<even though they ran in her yard all day>>
1			Our bitch wasn't even in season
×2			so they obviously didn't take her for gain.
			They didn't know enough.

* Note on projection The sequence (*a man*) asked → *had we lost a dog* is an example of 'free indirect speech' in that the projected clause has the mood choice appropriate for a quote (interrogative here), making the structure paratactic, but the person and tense choice appropriate for a report (the hypotactic form of locution). See IFG discussion 260–61.

Note on layout A sequence of relations within the same logico-semantic type and the same taxis is normally displayed in a single line (1, 2, 3 or α, β, γ). However, because of the intricacy of the clause complex beginning *But anyway* it has been necessary to 'layer' the notation where the relation shifts from projection of locution (*Mummy said* → *not to be worried*) to projection of idea (*not to be worried* → *that the bitch would have puppies*). This allows the enhancement (*because...*) to be shown as linking to *not to be worried*.

Overall, the analysis shows the high level of grammatical intricacy that readily occurs in unselfconscious, unrehearsed speech when one speaker briefly holds the floor.

Text 2 Expository The text is analysed into ranking clauses showing embeddings, with clause complex analysis detailed below.

Advice such as this ⟦i.e. be wary of approaching children ‖ before they are 'ready' to learn mathematics⟧ has produced teachers ⟦who are likely to be wary about interference into children's play ‖ in case they are not 'ready' ‖ or they spoil something spontaneous ⟦which is going on⟧⟧

and when they do so interfere

they expect

that they will have to provide children with experiences ⟦which will lead them to make the appropriate discriminations⟧,

which they will not expect

the children already to have mastered.

1					Advice such as this ⟦i.e. be wary of...
+2	×β				and when they do so interfere
	α	α			they expect
		'β	α		that they will have to provide children...
			=β	α	which they will not expect
				'β	the children already to have mastered

This can be represented in a single line as follows:
1 +2(×β α(α 'β(α =β(α 'β))))

The framework for the interpretation of errors is therefore given by the pedagogy:

that is, that children will fail

because they are not 'ready' for that kind of learning,

which will in turn lead the teacher to feel implicitly at fault because (by implication) she was also not sensitive enough.

1			The framework for the interpretation of errors...
⁼2	α		that is, that children will fail
	×β	α	because they are not 'ready' for that kind of learning,
		⁼β α	which will in turn lead the teacher to feel...
		×β	because (by implication) she was also not...

Analysis displayed in a single line: 1   ⁼2(α ×β(α ⁼β(α ×β)))

This provides one aspect of a 'regime of meaning', a regime of 'truth' ⟦in which the teacher herself is positioned⟧.

This creates her insertion as subject into the practice

and provides both the basis of her readings and the aspect of the regulation ⟦to which she is subjected⟧.

1   This creates her insertion as subject into the practice

⁺2   and provides both the basis of her readings and the aspect of the regulation ⟦to which she is subjected⟧.

Analysis in a single line: 1   ⁺2

The regime is not one ⟦which is provided by the teacher⟧.

but which itself produces her consciousness of ⟦what teaching means⟧:

thus it produces not only her assessment of the children

but is bound up with her assessment of herself.

1 1   The regime is not one ⟦which is provided by the teacher⟧,

⁺2   but which itself produces her consciousness of ⟦what teaching means⟧:

×2 1   thus it produces not only her assessment of the children

⁺2   but is bound up with her assessment of herself.

Analysis in a single line: 1(1   ⁺2)   ×2(1 ⁺2)

The teacher can in no way be judged as ⟦standing outside the practices ⟦in which she as teacher is positioned ‖ and which delimit, define, and evaluate her work⟧⟧.

INDEX

ability 64 (*see* MODALITY)
Absolute 235
Accompaniment 104 (*see* circumstance)
act 180, 181, 200
Actor 101, 103
Adjunct 160 (*see* conjunctive Adjunct, modal
    Adjunct, circumstantial Adjunct)
    modal or conjunctive *yes* and *no* 72–73
    Mood or Residue 72
    vs Complement 73–74
AGENCY 158
Agent 110–113, 128–129, 154–155, 161–162
    Assigner 110–111, 124, 153
    Attributor 110–111, 124
    Inducer 110–111, 151–152
    Initiator 110–111
    vs Manner 128–129
agnation 10
Angle 104 (*see* circumstance)
Assigner 110–111 (*see* Agent)
Attribute 103, 106, 125, 128, 144
    conflated with attributive process 125
    depictive Attribute 118, 152
    in material process 118
    part of Process 125
    resultative Attribute 118, 119, 152
    vs Manner 128
attributive 106–107, 123–124, 140, 142–144
    Process/Attribute 125
    vs identifying 123–124
Attributor 110–111 (*see* Agent)

Behaver 103, 109, 142
behavioural 108–109 (*see* PROCESS TYPE)
    vs mental 120
    vs verbal 125–126
    with more than one participant 127

Beneficiary 103, 105, 113, 125, 128, 139, 161–162
    vs location 128
but 186–187, 200–201

Carrier 103, 106, 144
Cause 161 (*see* circumstance)
circumstance 100–102, 104, 127–130, 133,
    134–135, 139, 145–146, 157, 160
    vs dependent clause 129–130, 178–179
    vs non-finite process 179
    vs participant 127–129
    vs Qualifier 129
    vs textual conjunctive Adjunct 130
circumstantial Adjunct 66, 72, 73–74
    vs modal Adjunct 72
circumstantial (relational clause) 107, 144,
    153–154
clause complex 166–167, 197, 198–199,
    206–207
    boundaries 174–178, 190–191, 197, 204
    layering 187–188
    laying out analysis 173
    identifying logico-semantic relation 184–185
    implicit linking 188
    implicit Process in dependent 188
    linkers (both hypotactic and paratactic)
        184
    separate clause vs circumstance 178–179
    unit of analysis 174–177
    vs verbal group complex 116–117, 177–178
Client 105 (*see* Beneficiary)
cohesion 176
    cohesive elaboration vs parataxis 176
    cohesive extension or enhancemant vs
        parataxis 176–177
Complement 66–67, 73–74, 160
    vs Adjunct 73–74

complexing 17–18, 35, 116–117, 129, 165–167,
    177–178
    verbal group complex vs clause complex
        116–117, 199
conjunctive Adjunct 72–73, 130
    vs circumstance 130
congruent 58 (*see* grammatical metaphor)
constituency 7–10, 16–17
Contingency 104 (*see* circumstance)
continuative 68
class labels 2, 7–10

declarative 61 (*see* MOOD)
    vs imperative 76
    vs yes/no interrogative 75–76
depictive Attribute 118 (*see* Attribute)
dependent 168 (*see* TAXIS)
    vs circumstance 129
dominant 168 (*see* TAXIS)

effective 112, 158
elaboration 171–172 (*see* expansion)
    vs embedding 179
ellipsis 29, 70, 79
embedding 17, 35, 177, 179–184, 189–190,
        199–200, 203 (*see* act, fact, relative clause)
    embedded clauses 177
    'surfacing' from an embedding 189–190
    vs hypotactic elaboration 179
    vs ranking clauses 182–183
enhancement 172 (*see* expansion)
ergative 110–113, 154–155, 159
exclamative 61 (*see* MOOD)
Existent 103, 109–110
existential 34, 90, 140 (*see* PROCESS TYPE)
expansion 167, 171–172, 174, 194
    elaboration 171–172, 176
    extension 172, 176
    enhancement 172
experiential 100
    experiential, interpersonal and textual
        159–162
Expletive 67
extension 172 (*see* expansion)
Extent 104 (*see* circumstance)

fact 35, 151, 180, 181, 202–203
Finite 59, 62, 71–72, 80 160
    combined with Predicator 71–72
function labels 2, 7–10

Goal 103, 118–120, 143
    vs Range 118–120
grammatical metaphor
    interpersonal 58, 68–70, 91–92
    ideational 178
    metaphorical realisation of logical relation
        178

hypotaxis 36, 129, 168, 184, 191, 192, 204
    vs parataxis 184

idea 106, 145, 151, 172–173
    vs phenomenon 121–122
ideational 5, 100
identifying 106–107, 123–124, 140
    vs attributive 123–124
imperative 61 (*see* MOOD)
    vs declarative 76
    vs yes/no interrogative 75
inclination 64 (*see* MODALITY)
included classes 177
indicative 60 (*see* MOOD)
Inducer 110–111 (*see* Agent)
intensive 106, 144
interdependency 165–167, 207 (*see* TAXIS)
interrogative 61 (*see* MOOD)
    vs declarative 75–76
    vs imperative 75
INFORMATION 53–54
Initiator 110–111 (*see* Agent)
interpersonal 5
    interpersonal and textual 55, 98–99
    interpersonal, textual and experiential 159–162
intransitive 111–112

Location 100, 122–123, 128 (*see* circumstance)
    vs Beneficiary 128
locution 108, 145, 172–173, 181, 189
    without explicit projecting clause 189
    logical 100, 165–167
LOGICO-SEMANTIC TYPE 170–173, 184–187, 193, 208

macrophenomena 180 (*see* act)
Manner 128 (*see* circumstance)
    vs Agent 128–129
    vs Attribute 128
material 103–105 (*see* PROCESS TYPE)
    vs non-material 117–118
    vs relational 122–123
Matter 104 (*see* circumstance)
Medium 111–113, 161–162
mental 105–106 (*see* PROCESS TYPE)
    vs behavioural 120
    vs relational 120–121
    vs verbal 126
metafunction 54, 206 (*see* ideational,
        experiential, logical, interpersonal, textual)
metaphenomena 172 180 (*see* locution, idea,
        fact)
metaphor (*see* grammatical metaphor)
method of development 22
middle 112, 158
minor clause 71
modal Adjunct 62, 72–73, 85
    comment Adjunct 62–63
    mood Adjunct 62–63, 80, 91
    vs circumstantial Adjunct 72
modal responsibility 64–66, 161
MODALITY 63–64, 68–70, 76–77, 80, 91
    explicit objective 69
    explicit subjective 68–69
    vs TENSE with *will*

MODALIZATION 64
MODULATION 64, 65
Mood (grammatical function) 59, 61–66, 79–80
MOOD (system) 12–15, 55, 57–60, 75–76, 78–79,
   95–96
  declarative 61
  imperative 61
  indicative 60
  interrogative:yes/no 61
  interrogative:wh 61
  exclamative 61
  unit of analysis 70–71
Moodtag 61, 77–78

New 22, 53–54
non-finite clause 70–71, 86, 179, 198
  vs circumstance 179
non-finite verbal group 117

objective 69 (*see* MODALITY)
obligation 64 (*see* MODALITY)

paradigmatic 10–12
parataxis 168, 184
  vs cohesive elaboration 176
  vs cohesive extension or enhancement
   176–177
  vs hypotaxis 184
participant 100–102, 133, 139, 157, 160
  vs circumstance 127–129
Phenomenon 103, 105, 121–122, 127
  vs projected idea 121–122
phrasal verb 73, 85–86, 127–128
POLARITY 63–64, 76
Possession 106
possessive (relational clause) 107, 123, 144
Possessor 106
Post-Modifier 182
Predicator 66–67, 71–72, 160
  combined with Finite 71–72
  with phrasal verbs 73
prepositional phrase vs clause 179
probability 64 (*see* MODALITY)
Process 100–102, 133, 157, 160
  implicit in relational process 178, 188
PROCESS TYPE 100, 102–103, 114–115, 132–133,
   134, 158
  ASTROPOLOGY 114
  behavioural 108–109, 127, 141, 142
  existential 109–110, 152–153
  material 103–105, 117–118, 143, 152–153
  mental 105–106, 120–121, 122, 140, 141, 142
  one process or two? 116–117
  relational 106–107, 122–125, 149–150, 152–153,
   178
  verbal 108, 125–127, 140, 141, 150, 152, 153
projection 106, 108, 121–122, 132, 167, 174,
   188–189, 194
  locutions without explicit projecting clause 189
  notation 188–189
proposal 58, 173

proposition 58, 173

Qualifier 129
  vs circumstance 129

Range 103, 104, 108, 113, 118–120, 127, 142, 143
  vs Goal 118–120
rank-shift (*see* embedding)
readiness 64 (*see* MODALITY)
Receiver 108, 126
Recipient 105 (*see* Beneficiary)
relational 106–107 (*see* PROCESS TYPE)
  benefactive relational 125
  causative relationals 124–125
  with implicit Process 178
  vs material 122–123
  vs mental 120–121
  vs verbal 126–127
relative clause 179
Residue 59, 79–80, 84
resultative Attributive 118 (*see* Attribute)
Rheme 21–22, 53
Role 104 (*see* circumstance)

Sayer 103, 108
Senser 103, 105
SPEECH FUNCTION 58
Subject 59, 62, 64–66, 87, 160
  split Subject 74–75
  Subject *it* 31–34, 74–75, 90
  there 34, 110
subjective 68–69 (*see* MODALITY)
system 13
system networks 12–15

Target 126, 142
TAXIS 167–170, 191–193, 208
TENSE 76–77, 131
  or MODALITY with *will* 76–77
textual 6
  textual and interpersonal 55, 98–99
  textual, interpersonal and experiential 159–162
Theme 21–22, 53
  existential *there* Theme 34
  hypotactic clause as Theme 36
  ideational Theme (*see* topical Theme)
  interpersonal Theme 25, 29–30, 39–41, 54–55
  interpersonal or topical Theme 29–30
  longer Themes 34–36
  marked Theme 24–25, 46–47, 188
  predicated Theme 32, 34, 49, 159–160
  Subject *it* as Theme 31–32 (*see* Subject *it*)
  unmarked Theme 24–25, 46–47
  textual Theme 25, 29, 30–31, 38, 54–55
  textual or interpersonal Theme 29
  Theme/Rheme boundary 28
  Theme in elliptical clauses 29
  textual or topical Theme 30–31
  topical Theme 24, 29–31, 37, 54–55
  unit for analysis 28
THEME 21–22, 53

Token 103, 106, 124, 143–144
   vs Value 124
transitive 110–113
TRANSITIVITY 100–102
   one process or two? 116–117
   probes for analysis 115–116

usuality 64 (*see* MODALITY)

Value 103, 106, 124, 143–144
   vs Token 124

verbal 108 (*see* PROCESS TYPE)
   vs behavioural 125–126
   vs mental 126
   vs relational 126–127
verbal group complex 116–117, 177–178
Verbiage 108, 127
Vocative 59, 67, 83
VOICE 83, 161–162

Wh- 30, 35, 67, 84–85 (*see* MOOD)